D1560798

CLASSIC
CARMICHEL

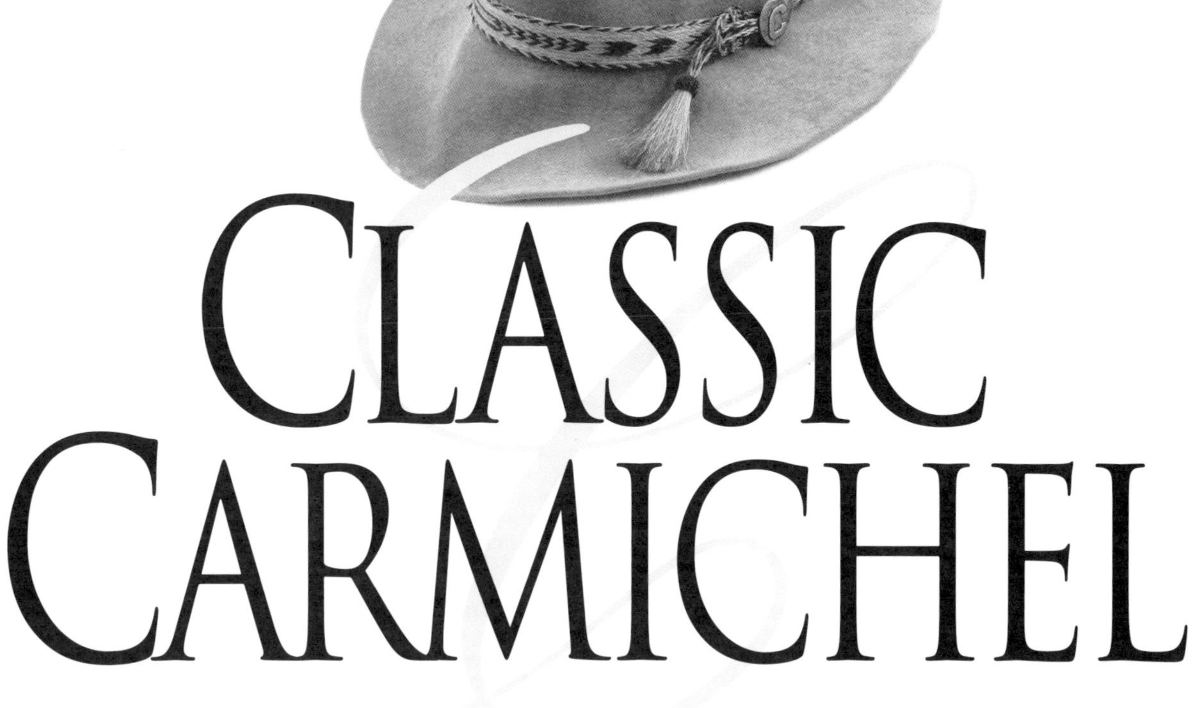

# Classic Carmichel

## Stories from the Field

Jim Carmichel

Sporting Classics

Published by Sporting Classics, 2015

All rights reserved. No part of this publication may be reproduced or used in any form or by any means – graphics, electronic or mechanical, including photocopying, recording, taping or information and retrieval system – without the express written permission of the publisher.

All field photographs and stories copyright © Jim Carmichel.

*The author has taken all reasonable precautions in the preparation of this book and believes the facts presented are accurate at the time of going to press. The author and the publisher do not assume any responsibility for errors or omissions. In addition, the author and publisher specifically disclaim any liability resulting from the use or application of the information within this book.*

Editor – Chuck Wechsler

Book Design and Still Photography by Michael Altizer

**Collector's Edition:** ISBN 978-1-935342-12-0

**Deluxe Edition:** Limited edition of 400, signed and numbered – ISBN 978-1-935342-10-6

Library of Congress Control Number: 2015950979

TO LINDA

*For reasons beyond counting.*

# PREFACE

— by Jack Atcheson —

The first time I ever met Jim Carmichel, I could tell he was a "good guy." I already knew that he was renowned as a wing- and benchrest shooter. *Unsurpassed.* But he also had a good sense of humor and exceptional knowledge of firearms and big game, which impressed me most. So we went hunting!

When you hunt often with someone, you get to know his other side, especially when they're wet, tired, and the animal has not been at all cooperative. Some alleged hunters can react badly. Sometimes the quarry seems to disappear, then reappears. A lot of sitting on cold, windy slopes is required. There is a mad dash to overtake the trophy, make a clean kill, and hopefully have enough light for pictures. Then a rush to hang the meat high enough to prevent wolves, bears, and hyenas from eating your steaks. Then you will likely walk miles back to camp. Hopefully, you brought a couple of flashlights.

You must have a companion who takes things as they come and not complain, which can destroy the whole scenario of sport hunting.

Jim is tough and determined, ready to shoot instantly and rarely misses. Having hunted together for many years, Jim and I are known as the Golden Boys, which means we're lucky or reaching what's better known as the Golden Years. We've hunted in Montana, Idaho, British Columbia, Northwest Territories, Alaska, and Africa. Overall, our luck has been exceptional but never easy.

Jim relived our adventures on the pages of *Outdoor Life*—the animals, their environment, the many fascinating people in many fascinating places—in his masterfully written stories.

My favorite was his story of an 1,800-pound crocodile that came actively to life in a sinking boat. The dexterity of natives leaping from one side of the boat to the other to avoid the thrashing tail, the barrel-sized head with its Tyrannosaurus teeth—the drama was amazing. Jim said I could leap the highest of all. He was most worried that his beautiful .338 Winchester would fall into the lake or be eaten by a vengeful crocodile. Which hurt my feelings!

Perhaps one of my favorite events was to photograph Jim manning a fishing pole in Canada. He actually caught a couple of three-pound grayling and a 20-pound pike, then pleaded with me to destroy the film as his image as a Cape buffalo hunter might be tarnished. I said I'd think about it.

Those were surely the good old days and they won't happen again. We had the best years.

While waiting to be flown into our mountain camp, we sat out a storm in a newly built log cabin. Jim decided we should have a cup of tea, so we headed over to the cook tent. Suddenly a tremendous gust caught the gabled roof and

sent it flapping away like the wings of a bat. Jim said this was a rich display of nature on the move. We rushed back into the cabin to cover our gear. Inside, one of the logs had blown down, smashed into Jim's chair and then stuck in the floor like a giant pencil. I'm sure I brought Jim that good luck. If we had not moved, he would be dead. A good cup of tea can make you feel better.

On the same hunt Jim shot a mountain goat, which started a landslide, and he came within inches of tumbling down a thousand-foot cliff. Jim escaped, but the goat was crushed. His luck held! Except a sow grizzly with cubs carried the billy's carcass into the brush, where they sounded most unfriendly. Jim wisely agreed to let the bears keep the goat.

If that wasn't scary enough, the very next day the light airplane that had carried us back to civilization crashed and burned, killing our guide and an incoming client.

Many of our hunts entailed different degrees of risk, but the rewards were high. Every evening we would rehash the events of the day and enjoy a couple of glasses of expensive box wine in the crystal glasses I always brought along. In fact, I'm holding one right now as I write. I'm 83, but I think I'll call Jim to get ready for another adventure.

— Jack Atcheson

# CONTENTS

## AFRICA AND AROUND THE WORLD

## NORTH AMERICA



## GUNS AND SHOOTING

# FOREWORD

— by Michael Altizer —

*"When a lion comes to kill you he does not bound or leap or make a great show of terrible rage. Such theatrics are for television lions and fatted cats trained to frighten children at the circus. A killing lion makes quick darting movements, running close to the ground and angling back and forth with deadly feints. His eyes are always on you and you know that he knows exactly how he's going to kill you. Sharp snarls hiss at you like high charged static, and at the moment he reaches for you the world switches into slow motion . . . "*

When I first read the above words, I was still an all-knowing youth who was way too cocky and over-confident. But this single passage stopped me dead in my tracks and made me realize just how far I still had to go if I wanted to be a writer. A *real* writer.

For this single passage introduced me to the ethereal realm of real writing—writing that transcends mere storytelling and ushers the reader into the ever elusive realm of *Literature.* It changed my life for good and set me on a new and invigorating track, along with the hope that someday I might possibly write something like this on my own, knowing full well I would likely never quite get there. *And oh, by the way,* I asked myself, almost as an afterthought, *who exactly is it that has written these words, who's had the temerity to go about upending my life like this?*

*Oh yeah, I see . . .*

*Some guy named Jim Carmichel.*

For the past several months, I have been priviledged to watch as this still-youthful gentleman whom I have now known for years re-visits some of the most sublime chapters of his life.

As I said, his name is Jim Carmichel— *yeah, that very same Jim Carmichel of my youthful aspiriations*—whose hunting, shooting, and writing exploits across North America and around the world have thrilled those of us who have read his words in the pages of *Outdoor Life*, and of course in his many books.

Jim is now enthusiastically exploring his 70s, much as he has explored many other equally challenging and fascinating experiences, from his original home in eastern Tennessee to the mountains and alder thickets of Alaska, to the jungles of South America and, of course, the wild African plains, vleis, and bush country.

It seems as the rest of us have grown older, Mr. Carmichel has somehow grown *younger,* until now his long and storied life is rich with memories—both those he has already lived and those he is still making.

As Shooting Editor for *Outdoor Life* for 38 years, Jim Carmichel was at the epicenter of what is arguably the Golden Age of international big game hunting and wingshooting—in fact, it could well be argued that he *WAS* the epicenter—when the breadth of the hunting and the quality of the firearms intersected with the inception of international air travel, along with hunting opportunities that had never been more far reaching, nor were nowhere near as restrictive as they are today. And Jim Carmichel was there—smack in the middle of it, to experience it all and record those memories for his readers with a craft and eloquence that is the equal of any writer who ever aspired to archive such memories with the written word. Much to the benefit of us all.

And now those memories have been collected and recorded here, in this very book you are holding in your hands—a book that beautifully chronicles a well-lived lifetime of classic exploits and adventures around the world, through the perspective of a true artist's perception. This is not only a faithful and factual record of what he has done, but of what he was thinking and feeling during those adventurous times, written with a grace and elegance that is rarely encountered.

JIM

These are *NOT* merely the random tales of a well-traveled adventurer, as interesting and compelling as those tales surely might be.

Instead, they are a captivating collection of beautifully written, beautifully crafted texts, presented with a style and elegance that deserves inclusion in anyone's collection of great outdoor writers, from John Hunter and Theodore Roosevelt, to Beryl Markham, Robert Ruark, Ernest Hemingway, and Nash Buckingham. Here is a work that is destined to become an integral component in any treasury of great outdoor literature.

No matter what he has done throughout his long and fruitful life, whether as a hunter, a shooter, a writer, or a friend, Jim Carmichel has bettered those who went before and set the standard for those of us who follow. And now as I finish these words, I realize that all those tracks still stretching out ahead of me in this trail I have trodden for so long are *HIS*.

— Michael Altizer
October, 2015

# INTRODUCTION

— by Jim Carmichel —

Rarely does a writer get a second shot at what he has written previously. So let me say at the beginning that this is not just a collection of my old articles and hunting stories that appeared in *Outdoor Life* during my nearly 40 years as the magazine's shooting editor.

Though I was always honored to work for *Outdoor Life* and was never in doubt that I had the best job in the world, what was printed under my name wasn't always what I would have wished. Not just because I later wished I had written it differently, which was often enough, but because what appeared on the newsstands sometimes turned out to be significantly different from what I had originally written.

To be fair, I must confess there were times when my articles exceeded the allotted space, putting the editorial staff in the uncomfortable position of slicing and dicing as best they could to make everything fit, even though I never quite understood how the paragraphs I considered the best were invariably those that got cut. Then there were times when blocks of text were bumped because of last-minute ad insertions, followed by tearful calls from otherwise innocent staff editors begging my forgiveness. Which I dutifully granted, provided I make the selection of what was to be sacrificed on the altar of advertising.

What rankled most however, were the two or three editorial hotshots who over the years, swept into our New York office like ill winds, declaring themselves literary wizards, and setting about rewriting and rephrasing my articles, and those of others, in their own contorted images. Happily, they didn't last long, as did a couple other self-described gun and hunting experts who felt it their calling to correct and repair my incomplete and inferior know-how by imposing their own opinions under my bylines.

For these and other reasons, when I announced my retirement from *Outdoor Life,* I vowed to never again set pen to paper. I also pledged to avoid all temptations to do anything in book form, despite what might have seemed a logical project for a semi-retired writer who might have a few more stories to tell.

For a long while I strongly resisted all suggestions about gathering my favorite adventures into a book, even risking my wife's formidable ire by refusing to discuss the possibility. After all, the reason I had retired was to have more time for shooting and messing with my guns. Besides which, my former experiences with book publishers had been neither pleasant nor profitable, so I hadn't the least desire to get into their clutches again.

Quite likely I would have remained steadfastly opposed to doing a book had it not been for a conspiracy between my wife Linda and my friend Mike Altizer, aided by some subtle psychological prodding from Steve Fjestad. The founder of Blue Book Publications, Steve is one of the smartest guys I know, so when he began hinting about getting some of my old articles together in a book, I was halfway inclined to pay attention. I also became suspicious of our neighbor Tony Treadway, a clever guy who runs an advertising agency, when he began spoiling otherwise pleasant conversations with sneaky phrases like, "Say, have you ever thought about . . . "

Meanwhile, Mike Altizer, who is enormously creative and usually worth listening to, was making a similar pitch to the *Usual Suspects:* Jerry, Marc, Ron, Tom, and Larry, a cabal of hard-core gun guys with whom we regularly have lunch and who are generally hard to convince of anything.

Normally, I could have counted on them being on my side against a book deal, but apparently they turned against me and joined Mike's campaign when he showed them a beautiful book of his own that he had written and designed,

and that had been published by *Sporting Classics.* I think Mike promised me that he would make my book look almost as good as his.

Realizing I was outnumbered and outmaneuvered, I surrendered—but only on the condition that my articles be published *as originally written:* Raw, unedited, and, at times, profoundly politically incorrect.

Getting it all together meant finding and retrieving faded, decades-old typewritten onionskin copies from musty, nearly forgotten files, and digging color slides from creaky cabinets. Pausing from time to time to read a paragraph, or to linger over the image of an old hunting partner, the long-buried adventures began coming to life. New again were the voices of forgotten characters, and the sights and smells of faraway places.

Once again I was with Fred on a snowy mountain in northern Iran, sitting out a hurricane with Jack, and high in the Andes with Sam. Whispering in my memories were beacons of lantern-lit tents on snowy nights, the smoky smell of shower water in African camps, and the sparkling embers of a New Zealand campfire swirling into the Southern Cross.

With these and so many other memories newly awakened came the realization that I had one of the rarest gifts a writer could wish for—not just the opportunity to rewrite, correct, and polish previous work, but the once-in-a-lifetime chance to add the details and reflections of people and events as they really happened.

For this opportunity I offer my eternal gratitude to many people, some of whom now live only in my sweetest memories; for those still around, I'll thank them when I next see them. And special thanks to the angels whose efforts brought this book to life . . . like Carly Altizer, Mike's beautiful daughter, for sorting through what were often unreadable manuscripts and bringing them to digital life. For the gracious cooperation of Greg Gatto, the current head of *Outdoor Life* magazine, and a long-time friend to whom I will forever owe a martini. To Chuck Wechsler, for bringing fresh light to theses stories.

And especially to Mike Altizer, for keeping his promise to the *Usual Suspects*—and here is the proof.

— Jim Carmichel

# Africa and Beyond

*"Although the lion meant to kill me,*
*I had not come to kill the lion.*
*I was hunting giant eland,*
*and the rifle I carried was not intended*
*to stop dangerous African game."*

# Chapter 1

# When a Lion Comes to Kill You

hen a lion comes to kill you, he does not bound or leap or make a great show of terrible rage. Such theatrics are for television lions and fatted cats trained to frighten children at the circus. A killing lion makes quick darting movements, running close to the ground, and angling back and forth with deadly feints. His eyes are always on you, and you know that he knows exactly how he's going to kill you. Loud snarls hiss at you like high-charged static, and at the moment he reaches for you, the world switches into slow motion. Clawing, ripping death becomes a slowly danced pantomime.

Only it isn't happening slowly at all; the charge is lighting quick. It only seems that way because your senses and reflexes are boosted to a keenness never felt before. Even as every nerve in your body focuses on the source of immediate destruction, there is also a soaring awareness of the world around you. The Trees, the Grass, the Sun, the Sky are seen in vibrating detail. A tiny wildflower or a shy wren are encompassed and minutely examined in your new world of awareness. I expect man experiences this sensation only when he is hunting—or being hunted.

Although the lion meant to kill me, I had not come to kill the lion. I was hunting giant eland, and the rifle I carried was not intended to stop dangerous African game. To stop a charging lion you need POWER—muscle-smashing, bone-shattering, nerve-shocking power.

But the little rifle was all I had and I had to save myself. I was hitting the lion; the first shot at roughly 40 yards had been aimed at his heart, and the second shot, a bit closer, had ripped into his chest again.

As I flicked the Mauser's bolt open and shut, I could feel the little cartridges ride out of the magazine and snake into the chamber. Slow motion, the cat came half the distance between us—then half again.

Unbelievably, as I worked the bolt, I took quick steps *toward* the lion! *You're not hurting him,* something told me. *Get closer so you can hurt him with your little rifle.*

We closed on each other and I fired again. Twenty yards—no effect. One shell left.

The lion ducked into a clump of yellow grass. I could see patches of him angling straight for me; his final lunge would be from ambush. He was an old lion, experienced, a precision killing machine; he had killed like this hundreds of times.

As the bolt locked on my last cartridge, another form moved in the brush from where the lion had come. *A second lion!* Not charging yet, but nervously flicking his tail and studying me with his cold, yellow eyes.

*"This,"* I said to myself, "is about to get interesting."

I was hunting in the Central African Empire, which in Colonial times was the French Equatorial Africa, but since independence had become a republic, then an empire. Bounded on the north by Chad and on the south by Zaire, the CAE has always been one of Africa's most intriguing hunting areas. It is still probably the best place to take really big ivory, but my number one objective was Lord Derby's eland. They are the largest of the world's antelope, weighing a ton or more, and one of the toughest to hunt.

I'd been taken with the notion to hunt the giant eland a couple of years before when I spotted one of their cow-sized tracks in the Sudan. My hunting pal, Fred Huntington, the founder of RCBS, the reloading tool firm, had a similar urge, so we talked each other into going after the big antelope. Fred's tireless wife, Barbara, had been miffed because we left her at home while we hunted the Sudan, so she signed on for this trip. I thought this was a good idea because it meant that she, rather than I, would be sharing a tent with Fred, and I'd be spared his crocodilian snoring and, too, it's always nice to have a pretty redhead around camp.

The first leg of our trip took us to Paris where we were joined by old pals Hugh Nichols and Bob Speegle. Hugh grows cotton in Mississippi and Bob is a doctor in Texas, but mainly they are hunters, with Speegle being an acknowledged contender for the Weatherby Award. (Which he won later.) Hugh and Bob had struck out on the big eland a year earlier in Cameroon, but weren't about to give up.

When we left Paris the next day, we must have looked like a pack of refugees as we shivered about the airport in short-sleeved tropical gear. In Paris it was cold and icy, but we figured that when we stepped off the jet a few hours later, the climate would be too hot and muggy for anything but the lightest clothes. And it was.

Bangui, the capital city of the CAE, sprawls along the banks of the legendary Ubangi River with the other shore belonging to the nation of Zaire. After checking into the famous old Rock Hotel, our first order of business was a cool swim, then an even cooler drink on the hotel's tree-canopied terrace. The terrace reaches almost to the river's edge and from where we sat we could see native fishermen tending their nets from dugout canoes. Overhead, brightly colored birds screeched and squawked as they fought for roosting space, and a never-ending swarm of native peddlers elbowed each other for room to show us butterfly-wing artwork and mounted beetles as big as boxing gloves. It was a good place to begin a safari.

Our outfitter, SACAF, held exclusive hunting license to a number of huge tracts in the CAE. Elephants were hunted in the rainforests, while plains game were pursued in the northern grasslands stretching toward the Sahara. Our hunting area was about two hours flying time north of Bangui.

The plan of action had Bob and Hugh hunting in an area called Galongoso while Barbara, Fred, and I encamped several miles to the east near the small native village of N'Joko. Our area was surrounded by national game refuges, which ensures a good supply of game, but can also mean considerable frustration when, after hours of tedious tracking, the spoor of your quarry leads into the sanctuary.

The official language of the CAE is French, which I managed well enough in Bangui, but like every other African country in which I've hunted, regional dialects prevail in the bush. The local lingo is called Sahra and the people are renowned for their weaving skills, living in woven grass huts surrounded by woven grass fences and carrying their goods in artistically woven baskets.

Even the ground in some places was paved with intricately woven grass mats.

Our camp was situated at the edge of the Aouk River, the International Boundary between the CAE and Chad. We were forbidden to cross into Chad, not that it would have mattered. The local youngsters endured the midday heat by splashing in the river and crossed the boundary continuously, probably not knowing—or caring—to which country they belonged.

As far as I could tell the main industry was fishing, with dried fish being sold to Arab and native traders who drifted downstream in barge-like dhows.

Carlos, our professional hunter, was a native of Portugal who, like many other professionals, had left Mozambique back during the Communist takeover.

Our first day in camp we took a sightseeing tour along the river and spotted several head of Kob-de-Buffon, the French name for kob, a deer-sized, marsh-dwelling antelope. One old ram carried a great set of horns and was promptly dropped by Fred with a neat shot from his .300 Magnum. The kob was doomed anyway because even as we stalked him from one side he was being stalked from the other direction by a lean lioness and two nearly grown cubs. They were plenty aggravated at having their meal snatched from under their noses and sulked away into the grass not more than 80 yards away, while we dressed the antelope.

Strangely, the lions seemed undisturbed by Fred's shot and our presence. That night I was awakened by a serenade of lions coming from both sides of the river.

With so many lions about, we decided to postpone our eland hunting for a day or two and try to find a full-maned trophy for Fred. I had taken a great lion a few years before in Botswana, and was not especially eager for another, though I agreed to go along as back-up gun. Lions are unpredictable and can abandon their territory with no apparent reason. That's why it's a good idea to hunt them when and where you find them.

The lions thereabouts fed mainly on the little kob antelope, because they were plentiful and easy to ambush from the tall grass covering the marshy river. The river's floodplain spreads for thousands of acres and finding lions was mainly a matter of combing out each patch of grass.

We saw nothing until late afternoon when Eloi, our Number Two tracker, spotted a lioness and two cubs lounging on a low knoll near the edge of a lily pad-covered lagoon. No male lion was visible at first, but as we drove closer we could see the grass part as a crouching form snaked toward the dense cover of mangrove bordering the lagoon. In a second it was out of sight, but we could clearly hear the mangrove branches breaking as the lion made off no more than 30 yards away.

"C'mon," Carlos whispered, urgently motioning for his rifle, a Winchester bolt gun in .375 H&H caliber. "We might catch him in there."

"You mean in that swamp?"

"Have you ever hunted lions before?"

"Sure, a few times," I answered

"Are you afraid of lions?"

"Of course I am, isn't everybody?"

"I am not afraid of lions," he almost shouted, his nose inches from mine.

"Well, good for you, you're made of better stuff than I am," I said, or something to that effect, trying to put a lighter touch on the conversation and get our safari started on a friendlier basis. After all, I'd be hunting with this character for the better part of three weeks.

I usually get along well with professional hunters, and several have become lifelong pals. A half-dozen routinely stay with me when visiting the States. But it was pretty clear that this guy and I weren't going to be friends. And to be honest, I didn't like his looks all that much either. Elephant hair bracelets went halfway up to the elbows of both arms, a string of lion claws hung from his neck, and his picture-book safari hat, complete with zebra band, looked all too new. I also didn't like the imperious way he treated the camp staff, and his rifle was an ill-kept piece of rusty junk.

"Are you afraid to hunt lions my way?" The way he said it was a challenge and by then I'd had enough of his attitude and got right back in his face.

"Mister, just as soon as I get my rifle, we'll hunt lions any damn way you want to."

By then I'd already stuffed .338 Magnum shells into the magazine of the rifle I'd had made by David Miller of Tucson and stocked by his partner Curt

Crum. The rig carried express sights as well as a 4X Leupold scope and my ammo was handloaded with 250-grain Nosler Partition bullets. I had specified a stubby, 23-inch barrel for fast handling in tight situations, just the sort of condition now presented by the choking mangrove thicket, but if the rifle had been intended for lions at dead-close range, it would have been at least a .458 Winchester Magnum.

*What the hell,* I thought, adopting the native philosophy, *if he charges, the chances are only one in four he'll come after me.*

Beside myself, there were Carlos and Ramadon, our Number One tracker, and his brother Eloi, who had first spotted the lions. And thus began one of the most bizarre experiences I've ever had in Africa or anywhere else.

I've read and heard scores of hair-raising exploits of tracking lions in dangerous situations, but for all-out recklessness, the half-hour we spent in the mangrove thicket has to be the hands-down winner. At times the lion was no more than short paces away, and we could hear him as clearly as one might hear someone in the next room. But even if he had been just ten arm-lengths away, we could not have seen him in the dense growth.

As we worked farther into the mangroves, the black water became deeper, sometimes waist deep, and I had to carry my rifle overhead to keep it dry.

*Who in God's name ever heard of this,* I kept telling myself, refusing to believe what I was doing. Sloshing after lion in a swamp of all places.

If he turned on us, there would have been only a split second to point and pull the trigger. Aiming was out of the question.

But the lion had other ideas.

After some minutes he pulled away and we could no longer hear him. We were on firmer ground now, trying to run to keep up, but we lost the race. When we burst out of the thicket, the lion was a hundred yards ahead and bounding through the six-foot grass like a fox jumping through a wheat field. I saw him three times, black-maned, huge—magnificent.

We hunted lions another day then went back to our original program and sought eland. Fred and I took only a few trophies but what we bagged were record-book class. One time I passed up a shot at what was surely a record roan antelope, but because we were on fresh eland tracks, I didn't want to risk spooking them.

Meanwhile, Carlos and I were getting along pretty well, or at least we had an unspoken truce, and I was impressed by his skills at getting us to the good trophies, including a record-book buffalo. But still it was hard to ignore what seemed to be his bizarre obsession with personal bravery, as declared the day we sloshed after lions in the swamp, and on the evening when he rendered us speechless with a description of how he saved a lion from drowning by giving it mouth-to-mouth resuscitation. By then we'd learned to shift such campfire conversations to more humorous subjects, such as the decayed state of his rifle.

On our 11th day we came across the remains of a fresh lion kill several miles from the river. Carlos said a French hunter had missed a terrific lion there a few weeks before and apparently the cat was still in the area. It was near a heavily traveled game trail leading to the river, and Carlos reasoned the lion was lying in wait for animals traveling to the river or one of the surrounding waterholes.

Fred had just about had his fill of eland hunting by then, but was still eager for a lion, so Carlos suggested we hang a bait and set up a blind Fred could shoot from.

We found a clump of trees growing out of a hummock, which was just high enough to allow good vision over the tall grass. Its perfection as a shooting blind was soon demonstrated when a hartebeest wandered by and was quickly converted to lion bait by Fred.

Our crew opened up the animal's body cavity, dragged it about for a while so as to leave a good scent, then tied it about five feet up in a tree with a piece of thick nylon rope. The purpose of tying it so high was to get it out of reach of the hyenas and also to prevent it from being dragged off by a lion who might want to eat it elsewhere. Shooting from a blind sounds simple enough, but if the effort is to be successful, the hide must be skillfully planned and prepared.

The bait looked good, and I guess we all shared a strong hunch that we would see lion the next day. That evening at dinner there was less conversation than usual, each of us with his own thoughts of lions, and everyone turned in before the normal time. About midnight a lion began roaring from across the river, and I did not sleep well. If I could have known what the next day held in store I would not have slept at all.

An hour before daybreak we left the Toyota a mile or so from the blind and cautiously made our way on foot along the moonlit game trail. It was still dark when we entered the blind, and though I tried to see into the darkness, I could only make out the upper branches of the baited tree outlined against the sky. My ears were no help either, because the African night is alive with sounds and any one of a thousand noises could have been teeth slashing into flesh. There was nothing to do but wait for the sun.

The sky had barely begun to change from black to inky blue when Eloi, our sharpest-eyed tracker, leaned forward and whispered something to Carlos.

"Damn," Carlos said. "The bait is gone, the lion came and stole the bait."

For a moment I was too surprised and shocked with disappointment to speak. Not disappointed for myself because it was not to be my lion, but disappointed for Fred who really wanted this trophy.

The evidence was all too clear: the frayed ends of the stout nylon rope told how it had been snapped by a great strength, and a rut in the sand showed the direction in which several hundred pounds of dead weight had been dragged. Along the way we found scraps of hair and bones and, finally, the cleanly gnawed backbone. The entire hartebeest had been devoured and its bones left in the dust.

"How many?" I asked Ramadon, who understands some French.

"Deux," he answered, pointing to where the tracks led into the high grass. There were two, probably a male and female.

"Let's take a little hike," Carlos said, "and see where the tracks lead. I'll send for the truck to be brought up for Fred and Barbara, and they can catch up with us in it."

"Fine," I replied, "I got cold and stiff sitting in the blind; a good walk will feel good."

The sun was now high over the treetops, casting the lions' pug marks in deep relief.

The terrain was almost dead flat with alternating stretches of bare, sandy soil and patches of tall grass burned yellow by the sun. Occasional clumps of trees dotted the plain, but even so it was a featureless land where distance has little meaning.

The three of us—Carlos, Ramadon, and I—had been moving fast for about an hour when suddenly Ramadon stopped and pointed through a break in the grass to a clump of trees about 60 yards ahead.

The lions had stopped and we had almost walked up on them. A huge male was standing broadside to us and nearby I could make out the back legs of another cat lying in heavy brush. I figured this one to be the lioness.

Quick thoughts raced through my brain. I hadn't come to kill the lion; it should be Fred's. But Fred wasn't here, and the lion would soon be gone. He was the biggest lion I'd ever seen in the wild, and I was sure I would never see his equal again. But my little rifle, *was it enough?* Sure, plenty of lions have been killed easily with even smaller calibers. But they were shot from the safety of blinds or from safari cars where even a wounded lion is of little threat. But we were less than 50 yards from the animal, on foot, and with no cover whatever—no tree to climb and the sun in our eyes.

Only four cartridges in my rifle, two more in my pocket.

Would the lioness run away?

Ramadon had the good sense to back away, as this was clearly going to be a shooting situation, and Carlos was saying something I didn't understand so I simply told him to stay calm and not get excited, as this was no time for another of his bravery lectures. To which he turned to me and started sputtering something about not being excited, looking at me and not the lions. But it was of little matter . . .

The lion was coming! Not fast at first but dead after us—me! He was looking straight at *me!*

*Ker-r-Whap*! The blast of my rifle seemed to come from far away. The bullet had to hit the beast's heart, too close to miss, but the effect seemed only to make him come faster. *Ker-r-Whap*, my second bullet was again aimed into his chest. Still coming, running low.

*Ker-Whang*. I heard Carlos' .375, and when I glanced his way I saw that the front sight of his rifle was no longer there, useless.

My third bullet, fired at about 20 yards, turned him into a patch of grass and for an instant I thought he meant to ambush us. With each shot I had been moving toward the lion and now for some reason I went into the grass after him. It wasn't bravery, just an overwhelming impulse to get close enough to kill him.

Until now, as trophy hunters are apt to do, I aimed only for the body, trying to miss the head so as to save the skull. But now with the lion still coming and only one shell left in my rifle, I meant to blow his brains out!

It wasn't necessary. When I found him in the grass, he was still on his feet but not moving so fast. The last bullet went high into his shoulder, shattering bones, and he was down.

But suddenly there was another lion, and I whirled around to see what it was going to do, cramming my two remaining rounds into the empty rifle.

The second lion was not a lioness at all but another male, nearly as big as the first. For a moment it stood watching, nervously twitching its tail the way lions do when they're about to charge. With two cartridges now in my rifle, I leveled the crosshairs between his eyes and waited for the charge.

It never came. The big cat turned and walked away a few steps, stopped and looked back for a long moment, then loped away, melting into the lion-colored grass.

# When a Lion Comes to Kill You

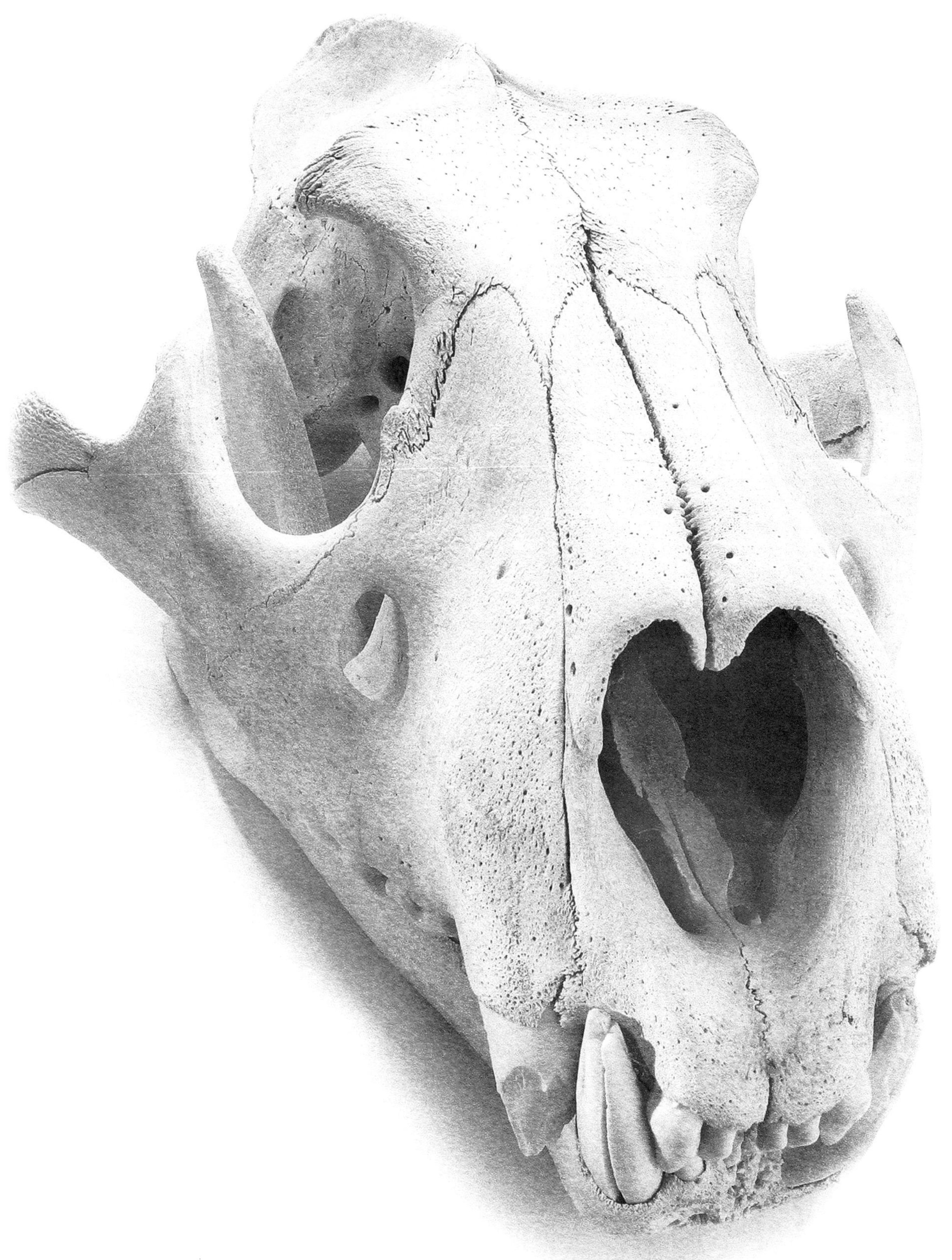

*Even grizzled old Malkopje joined in.*
*"Ah, look at those horns, the biggest buffalo*
*I've ever seen in my life."*

# CHAPTER 2

# THE GREAT BUFFALO CON JOB

“Hurry and shoot before he runs away” urged Totze. “Yes hurry,” added Bawlo. “He’s a wonderful trophy and if he gets away we’ll never find another half as big.” Even grizzled old Malkopje joined in. “Ah, look at those horns, the biggest buffalo I’ve ever seen in my life.”

I didn’t know it at the time, but I was the beneficiary of an African con job. It probably would have worked too, except the trio of African trackers crouched behind me were jabbering in a bush lingo as strange to me as my language was to them.

The object of their urgent encouragement was a big Cape buffalo standing in the midst of three smaller bulls some 80 yards away. All had their heads up and muzzles leveled at us like a quartet of heavy artillery.

The bull was big, no question, by far the biggest I’d seen in six days of on-and-off hunting. He was also very old, nearing the end of his years, so old that almost all the hair was gone from his grayish-black hide, leaving his shoulders like granite boulders. His horns were craggy and worn with age, but even so they out-spanned those of his companions by several inches. This, I figured, was the one I’d been looking for, but before pulling the trigger, I wanted an opinion from Lew Games, my professional hunter.

“What do you think?”

“He’s pretty good,” Lew answered, “but I think we might find something a bit better.”

Which was all I needed to hear, so I dropped the big .458 Magnum from my shoulder to the accompaniment of a chorus of groaning disappointment from the three trackers.

“What’s wrong with this fellow?” they lamented. “We find the biggest bull in the world and he doesn’t shoot!”

Back at the truck, a laughing Lew supplied me with a translation of the trackers' comments and also explained the reason for their disappointment.

Africans have a well-founded fear of the Cape buffalo, and their idea of a shootable buffalo is one that can be bagged with as little risk to life and limb as possible. The buffalo I'd just passed up had been situated on fine running ground and hadn't been too far from the truck. If anything had gone wrong, the trackers would have had a good chance of making it back to the safety of the vehicle. Plus, the fact that the surrounding vegetation was sparse enough meant that tracking a wounded animal would have been relatively safe and easy. Which, basically, is why they had been so much in favor of my shooting the bull.

Thinking it over, I was much inclined to share their point of view, because only a couple hours earlier we'd narrowly escaped what could have been a showdown with a vengeful buffalo cow.

To my notion, the Cape buffalo is the real nitty-gritty of African hunting. I've long been fascinated by the huge black beast with tremendous horns and terrible temper. Weighing close to a ton and born with a vengeful nature, the Cape buffalo has a well-earned reputation for being able to absorb a magazine full of thumb-sized bullets and still have enough meanness left to grind his adversary into the ground.

According to accounts I've read, and stories I've heard from survivors firsthand, a favorite tactic of wounded buffalo is to escape into dense cover, then circle back to ambush his pursuers. Memories of which had resurfaced throughout the morning when I found myself almost at the center of a buffalo herd, at moments so close that I could have hit them with a tossed stone. At one point I had even put the crosshairs of my heavy rifle on a bull and came within a whisker of pulling the trigger.

We had started out just after daybreak from our camp near the edge of Botswana's Chobe swamp and planned to hunt west along the Kwando River. It was my first African safari, and in less than a week I'd already seen more game and had more adventure than I'd ever dreamed of.

I'd been named shooting editor of *Outdoor Life* a couple years before and ever since signing on I'd been dropping hints to Bill Rae, my boss, that he needed to send me to Africa to do some "field testing" with a few rifles and some of the exotic-looking new generation bullets I'd hand-load for them.

Rae, who ruled the magazine like an Olympic deity, finally agreed that the African experience would probably do me some good, and seeing as how hunting adventure articles always sold well, sent me on my way with orders to find something interesting to write about and take lots of photos.

"Focus your camera and hold it still," had been his parting instructions. By the end of just this first week of a month-long safari, I'd already bagged enough game and taken enough pictures to fill the magazine for a year. And I still had a buffalo license to fill.

We'd been seeing buffalo every day, but they had either not measured up to what I was hoping for or had disappeared before we could get near enough for a close look. Which is why we were headed for the Kuando and a change of scenery. Lew had done some scouting there during the previous season and thought it would be a likely area to find bigger horns than we'd been seeing. There was a chance we'd see sable antelope, which I had a license for.

The road to the Kuando, as Lew remembered from his last trip there, was little more than an uneven, untraveled track, and it would probably take us better than an hour to get to the river. So we took along lunch and extra water, and I was looking forward to making a day of it, especially since no other hunters had been in the area since the year before, and I'd be having a first look at the game. As it turned out, we never made it to the river.

About a half-hour along the way, while skirting the edges of the swamp, we came to wide stretch in the road where the crust of its hard-baked dirt surface had been ground to powder by the hooves of passing buffalo. Judging by the width of their trail, and the numbers of overlapping tracks, it had been a good-sized herd, possibly 50 or more, and they had crossed only a short time before. So recently, in fact, that the pall of powdery dust still hung in the cool morning air. Obviously, they had watered at the swamp and had crossed the road on the way back to their home grounds.

We immediately abandoned our plans for the Kuando, because a herd of that size would very likely include some good bulls. So, with my .458 Magnum rifle in hand, we set off after them.

Their trail led away from the swamp's dense green foliage into a more open landscape of tawny-colored grass and Botswana's ubiquitous scrub of brushy mopane trees. Though shoulder high in some places, the brittle, winter-dried grass was easy to pass through, so we made good time and within a couple miles caught up with the herd, which had stopped and scattered out between patches of mopane. Most of them had bedded down and the high grass made it difficult to see, but here and there we could make out the outlines of their reclining hulks.

This was not exactly an ideal situation, but Lew figured that the tall grass and scattered trees would give us enough cover to tippy-toe around the herd and see if any big bulls were in residence. Performing a ritual I had witnessed dozens of times over the preceding days, Lew pointed at his foot and shuffled the toe of his shoe into the dry ground. A small cloud of dust rose and then lazily settled from where it had risen. There was no wind, meaning we might get even closer to the animals without being detected. But the prospect of getting close to a herd this size reminded me of something Lew had warned me about just the day before.

A herd of buffalo can be utterly unpredictable, he had said, and like most cattle they are quite curious. It is their curiosity that can be the undoing of an unsuspecting hunter.

When a herd spots an unfamiliar creature, such as a human, they have a natural tendency to stop and stare. The buffalo at the rear of the herd want to have a look too, so they begin to push and crowd toward the buffalo at the front. This shoving from behind pushes the front ranks toward whatever they are watching and can cause them to panic. And when they panic, they are liable to stampede and whatever or whoever happens to be in their way will probably be the worst for it.

This bit of information had made quite an impression on me, and I had resolved at the time to never get involved with any curious buffs. Yet now, here I was at the edge of a herd, and of my own free will, about to get very much involved.

When we'd slipped to within a hundred yards or so of the closest animals, Lew instructed Bawlo and Malkopje to stay behind, because the buffalo would be more likely to spot the five of us if we stayed together. The two Africans enthusiastically agreed, but Totze didn't appear the least bit happy about Lew's directive, and even less so when Lew handed him his rifle, indicating that as gunbearer, he would be in the thick of whatever ensued.

Totze was not one of our original crew and had simply appeared at our camp three days earlier, seemingly out of nowhere. Almost naked except for a string of crude ornaments hanging from his neck along with equally rough bands on each arm, he'd been squatting at the camp's perimeter when I spotted him on the first morning of our hunt. Apparently he was uncertain if he would be welcome in our camp and was waiting for some signal as to whether or not to come closer.

The odd-looking stranger was still there when we returned later that afternoon, looking like he had not moved from the same spot. When Lew drove close to him and stopped, I instantly recognized the man as a member of a fascinating race I'd read about, but never thought I'd see face to face. Standing scarcely five feet, crowned with peppercorn hair, and with almost oriental facial features, the man was unmistakably a Bushman, the distinctive race known for uncanny survival in the harshest environments such as their Kalahari homeland, and for their almost mystical tracking skills.

Speaking in a language punctuated by odd tongue-clicking, Lew and the Bushman had a short exchange, after which the newcomer followed us into camp. After hanging around for a couple days, the Bushman decided life there was pretty good, no doubt immensely better than wherever he'd come from, and the evening before had come to our campfire appealing to hire on as a tracker. After considerable discussion in the Bushman's peculiar language, then more in another language, Lew agreed to give him a try, explaining to me that good trackers are always valuable, especially one possessing the skills for which Bushmen are legendary.

His name was Totze, Lew said, and he thought he understood the local languages well enough to follow orders and get along peacefully with everyone. I had already noticed that several of the staff regarded him as something of a curiosity and had even provided him with some ragged clothes.

Which is how Totze came to be hunting with us on his first day after being hired, and why I was surprised when Lew handed him his rifle, a job usually reserved for the most reliable assistants. His purpose, I decided, was to test the little Bushman's skills and staying powers. There couldn't have been a more ideal circumstance in which to do so, as I would soon discover.

By snaking through the grass and taking advantage of the scattered clumps of mopane, we worked our way closer to the herd than I would ever have guessed possible. The buffs were divided into groups of threes and fours, and Lew's technique was to slip to within 50 yards or so of each lounging group and check for big bulls. Sometimes a head would be turned so we couldn't see the horns and we'd have to wait a few minutes for the buff to move its head. Then we'd sneak off and find another bunch.

There wasn't a breath of air stirring. If there had been, our quarry would have surely caught our scent and become too wary—and dangerous—for us to get as close as we were. Before sneaking from one brushy concealment to the next, Lew or I would test the air by sifting a handful of the powdery Botswana soil between our fingers, but there was never a hint of a current that might carry our scent to suspicious noses.

Gradually we worked our way so close to the center of the herd that dark shapes loomed all around us and I could even hear their bellies rumble as they belched up hunks of cud. Once, just as we had slipped through an opening in the brush, we found ourselves only a dozen feet from an old cow on her feet and looking straight at us. She studied our frozen forms for a few long moments and must have decided that we were part of the foliage because she went back to chewing her cud and flicking her ears at the flies. We had been standing so motionless that a bird landed no more than ten inches from Lew's face and gave him a good looking over.

Each time we stopped to check out a batch of heads, Totze would squat down close to my legs in a huddle of bare, trembling flesh so tiny that I could have almost cover him with my two hands. He was obviously terrified of the nearby buffalo, but stayed right with us, maintaining a death grip on Lew's rifle all the while. Every time we moved, he would be right on my heels, watching my every move, his eyes shifting from me to my rifle and back again. His behavior struck me as rather peculiar, and I made a mental note to ask Lew about it later.

On the first day of my safari, I had made it clear that no matter how many reliable gunbearers we had on hand, I would carry my own rifle at all times. The main reason being the stories I'd heard and read about hunters who had been left to face dangerous game empty-handed because their gunbearers had run away with their rifle. Now, with dozens of buffalo all around us, I was feeling doubly righteous for having pledged to do my own gun-toting. I also had a camera strapped around my neck, and probably could have taken some great shots of buffalo, but I was afraid the shutter click might spook them. We were that close!

Cautiously zigzagging through the mopane scrub, we had checked quite a few heads but had spotted nothing but cows and calves and a few smallish bulls. If there were bigger bulls in the herd, they had to be off by themselves where we couldn't see them. We were wasting our time, not to mention risking our necks pussyfooting around cows with calves, which can be every bit as dangerous as bulls.

Then, just as we were backtracking out of harm's way, a serious situation presented itself in the form of a little black calf. We had noticed it frisking about earlier, but it had been about 40 yards away and no particular cause for concern. But now, it had suddenly taken an interest in the clump of brush where we were and came trotting over for a closer look. When he spotted us, he skidded to a stop and stood there no more than 15 feet away, twitching his nose and trying to figure out what we were. After a few moments of this standoff, his momma, some distance behind, got curious too and heaved herself to her feet.

This, I figured, was it—the old gal was going to come over for a closer look and probably decide that we were picking on her kid. Remembering what Lew had told me the day before, I had visions of a buffalo stampede with us caught in the middle.

For the moment, our only defense was to remain absolutely motionless and hope the little bugger didn't bellow for his mom. After a few several breathless minutes the calf lost interest in us and scampered off to join his playmates. His mother took a final long look our way, then lay down again.

I breathed a long sigh of relief and I think Lew did too. Totze never took his eyes off me.

Doubling back the way we had come, we picked up Bawlo and Malkopje and made a wider circle around the herd to look for any isolated bulls.

While we were taking a short break, Totze gave his fellow trackers an animated account of his adventure among the buffalo, with special emphasis on his coolness in the face of imminent danger, with a chuckling Lew providing a translation of the narrative. Which reminded me to ask Lew why the little Bushman had followed so close and eyed me so strangely, which for several minutes he couldn't answer for being choked up with laughter.

"Damn, I guess I forgot to tell you, Jim, but I told Totze you would shoot him with your elephant gun if he ran away with my rifle. He must have been convinced you would do it."

The only bulls we found on our circuit around the main herd were the four with the bigger bull that our trackers had tried to con me into shooting. So after leaving the old guy to spend the rest of his days in peace, we went back to the truck and resumed our trip to the Kwando. It was past noon by then, and after the morning's hours of creeping among the buffalo, I was looking forward to a peaceful lunch along the river's cool banks.

Along the way the narrow road left the open grass plain and meandered into denser riverside growth. Rounding a copse of trees, we almost ran into a band of four bulls standing right in the road! They looked like big ones with good horns, but before we could get a better view, they charged into thick cover toward the river, snorting and wringing their tails over their backs.

Lew, thinking fast, hit the gas and we raced down the road, then stopped out of sight from where the bulls had been. Grabbing our rifles, we ran toward the thick woods, which would provide enough cover for us to get a closer look and possibly even a shot. But it didn't worked out that way, because when we spotted the bulls again, they were 80 yards away, headed back to where we'd first seen them. The animals were ambling across mostly open ground with scattered clumps of waist-high grass. To get closer we would have to cross part of the open area in full sight of the bulls.

"If we're lucky, they might let us get close enough for a good look," Lew whispered. "But even if they spook and run, we won't be any worse off than we are right now."

"Let's go take a look," I whispered back, trying to sound casual, even though my heart felt like it was banging its way out of my chest.

Motioning for the three trackers to stay back out of sight, Lew took his .458 and, with me close behind, we approached the bulls at an angle so as to appear to be headed somewhere other than in their direction. Walking fast and bent over with our heads down, the tactic worked, and when we'd shortened the distance to about 70 yards, we stopped and straightened up enough to see over the grass.

The buffalo knew we were there because they were looking straight at us, nervously flicking their tails as if undecided what to do. Standing before us were three trophy-sized heads, all bigger than the bull I'd refused earlier. One, however, made his companions look like a bunch of boys. His horns swept down to his jaw line, then curved out and upward in a tremendous arc, forming a symmetrical circle so nearly complete that the tips pointed back at his massive head. His wide boss spread over his head like a helmet of black armor. There was no need to ask Lew about this one; he was one for the record-books—the trophy of a lifetime.

My fantasy of 30 years was suddenly becoming reality. The flood of memories must have caused me to hesitate; I don't know how long I hesitated, an instant perhaps, but long enough for the bull to wheel and charge back into the denser river vegetation.

Gone.

My heart was sinking but there was still a chance for a fine trophy—and a great adventure story for the magazine—if any of the other bulls would stay for a moment. They thrashed around for a moment, acting like they were about to run but then settled down and resumed looking at us, their curiosity overcoming their natural instinct to escape. But I knew they wouldn't stay long, and if I was going to get a shot, I'd have to make a quick choice and shoot.

Scanning the bulls through the low-power scope on my rifle, I could see no difference between them and had settled the crosshairs on the closest bull when Lew grabbed my arm.

"Hold it! The big one's coming back . . . there he is."

Off to our left, the bull stepped through the trees to where I could see his head, then his shoulders, and finally nearly half of his body. And then he stopped, looking straight at us. Would he come out farther; I didn't care.

I'd hesitated too long before, but not this time. At the roar of my big rifle, all of the bulls spun and charged back toward the river, crashing out of sight through the wall of trees. My bull disappeared even before I could cycle the bolt of my rifle, so there was no way I could hit him again.

*Damn! Had I wounded a buffalo?* All I knew was that he wasn't where he was when I shot and was now lost somewhere in heavy cover.

"Lew, I called the shot good," was all I could think of to say, certain that the crosshairs had been on target before the rifle recoiled, hoping he'd seen the bullet hit and the animal react before disappearing. The answer I hoped for did not come.

Seeing what had happened, the trackers came on the run and gathered around Lew who, gesturing toward where the bull had disappeared, quietly gave them an analysis of the situation and a plan of action.

Though I couldn't understand the language, I clearly knew what he was explaining to the three serious-faced men, just as I also understood the meaning of solemn nods of understanding from each of them. They had a job to do and they knew it. I also understood the purpose of their standing quietly for long moments with hands cupped behind their ears and facing where they thought the buffalo might be. They were hoping to hear a clue—the groaning bellow of a dying buffalo perhaps. I cupped my ears too, desperately listening, but the only sounds were the distant cries of river birds.

Shaking their heads, the trackers indicated they heard nothing. The buffalo might be dead, but he might also be waiting for us, and there wasn't anything to do but go in after him.

I had heard about similar situations where the PHs have requested, even ordered, their hunters to stay behind and out of the way. Lew made no such suggestion, and even if he had, I would have refused. When I'd told him my shot looked good, he had seemed satisfied that it had been. But as the five us moved nearer the trees where a wounded buffalo might be waiting, my confidence plummeted. The shot had looked good, and I was confident it was. But had I shot too fast, before I could see all of the buffalo?

*Should I have waited for a better angle? Would it have been wiser to shoot one of the closer buffalo?* Either way, no point in second-guessing myself; I had done what I'd done and right or wrong I would live with it.

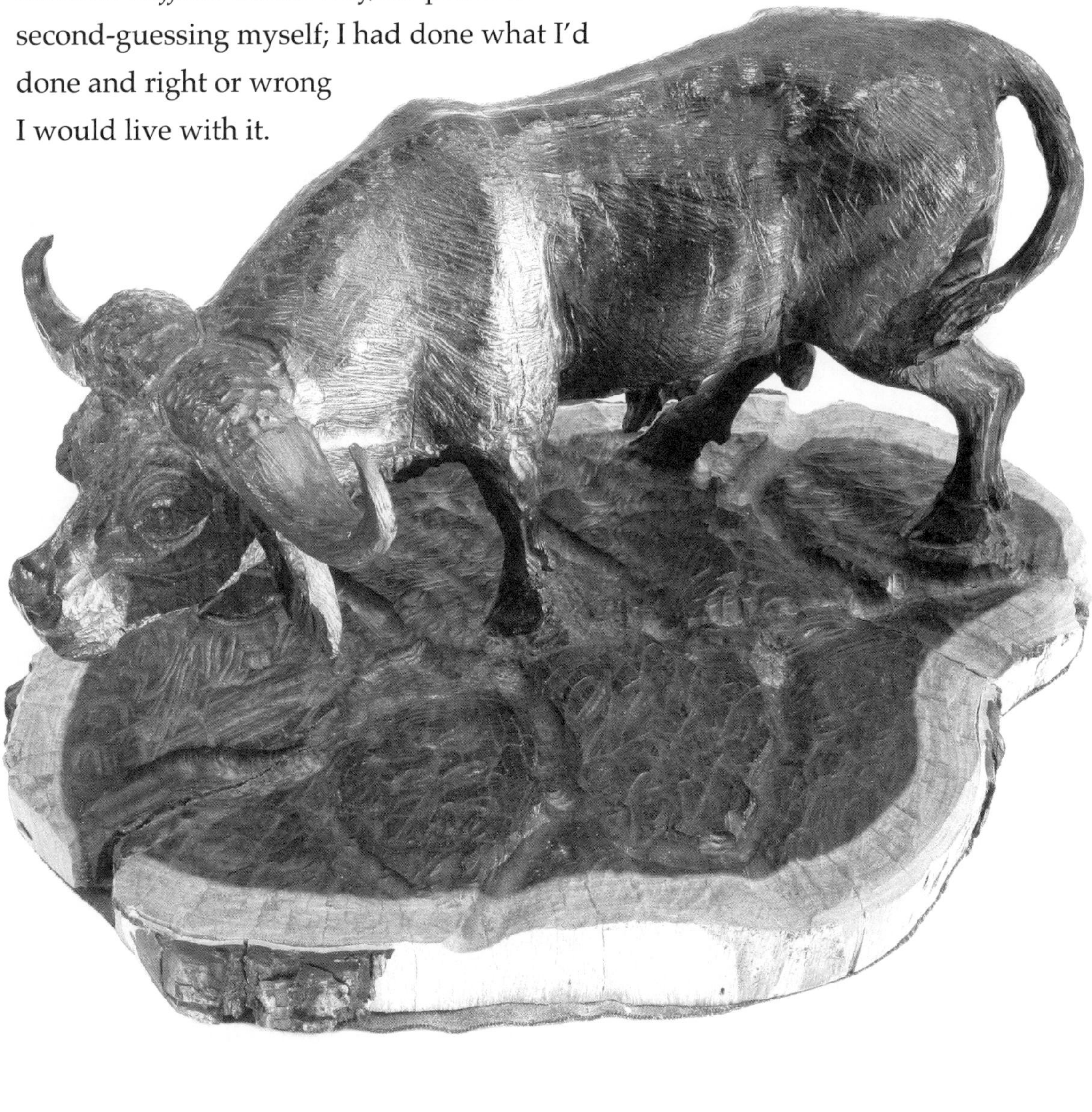

Such doubts were erased seconds later with a loud yelp from one of the trackers, followed by an even louder shout from another, and then all three of the men waving their arms. A grinning Malkopje pointed to blood splotches on the side of a tree and then another tree even more spattered with red. Beyond the trees lay a wide trail of blood-sprayed vegetation that ended at the unmoving form of my buffalo.

It looked very dead, but then, dead buffalo have been known to get up and charge. Lew and I made a wide circle around the animal and cautiously approached its head until we were close enough for Lew to touch its eye with the muzzle of his outreached rifle. Nothing, no reaction. It was truly dead.

The heavy solid bullet had gone completely through his chest and he had died in seconds, but enough time for the tough animal to spin around and run nearly 20 yards. Now there were black hands grabbing mine, rejoicing and laughter, joyous relief from the fears and tensions of only minutes before.

Then it was time to go about the other business I had come for, taking pictures for what would be my *Outdoor Life* story about this incredible day. My cameras were sent for, and as I was posing with the three trackers around the buffalo, a happily smiling old Malkopje made a brief comment to his companions that prompted their enthusiastic agreement. Whatever he said caused Lew to laugh, and I asked what was so funny, especially since I figured it was something about me.

"They are saying you should be happy they didn't let you kill that bull you wanted to shoot this morning, because they all knew it was much too small," he explained.

*"I've never really understood*
*'because that's where they want to go,'*
*but I've learned to respect it as the mark*
*of a hunter gifted with an almost*
*supernatural instinct."*

# CHAPTER 3

# THE MAKING OF A PROFESSIONAL HUNTER

It was June, the dry winter season in Tanzania, and a late-afternoon chill seeped up from the crusty African soil as Mike threaded the Land Cruiser between clumps of autumn-leaved mopane and long-tendriled thorn. With the cab windows rolled up, Linda and Mike were protected from the thorn, but in the open-sided rear of the safari truck, Ian and I were easy targets for the needle-sharp hooks that reached in to tear our clothes and flesh.

On the vehicle's roof, mainly above of the thorn's reach, Oomo and Jason attempted to help Mike navigate the sea of vegetation by waving a curved stick in front of the windshield, indicating passable passageways through the brush in what they believed, with no apparent conviction, to be the general direction of camp.

By my reckoning, our camp by the Rungwa River was an hour away, perhaps two, and uncertain in both distance and direction. There was no road to follow, not even a faint native trail, and every turn of the Toyota's steering wheel signaled a fresh exploration into the unknown.

Mike Rowbotham, the driver, is one of the last of a species of "Gentleman Adventurers" who came out from England at the close of WWII to seek riches and adventure, and found professional hunting to be just their cup of tea. After apprenticing with such legendary hunters as Tony Henley and Harry Selby in the hunting fields of Kenya, Rowbotham struck out on his own and soon earned a reputation as one of the best in the business.

During the making of the great African adventure movie *King Solomon's Mines*, young Rowbotham was one of the professional hunters hired to see to the safety of the film crew and, most particularly, the delicate person of flame-haired actress Deborah Kerr. (Remember that great elephant charge scene when a bullet from the hero's rifle knocks the big bull down? Rowbotham says that the bull went down like a stone—the part we saw in the movie—then got back on his feet and charged into the bush, never to be seen again despite the frantic searching of a whole posse of PHs.)

With the closing of big game hunting in Kenya (which freed the then-government to commence the wholesale slaughter of elephants and the sale of ivory without the intervention of concerned sportsmen's organizations), Rowbotham, like dozens of other Kenya PHs, packed his rifles and headed south, ending up in what was then called Rhodesia.

I met Mike in the mid-1980s when Jack Atcheson and I were on safari in Zimbabwe and spent a couple of weeks in Mike's camp on Lake Kariba. Our stay there turned out to be a fantastic adventure, and Mike and I became such great pals that he later used my home as a base on his trips to the U.S. During one of these visits he told me he'd made a deal with the Tanzanian government to open a hunting concession in the game-rich but seldom-visited western region of the country. And would I like to be on his very first safari there?

That's how my wife, Linda, and a couple of my long-time hunting pals came to be in a land that was as virtually undisturbed as when David Livingston passed that way over a century earlier. Which explains why Mike and his trackers had no idea as to where we were or how to get to camp. We weren't lost, getting back was a simple matter of following the sun to the river and tracing it home, but the immediate problem was escaping the seemingly endless maze of brush and thorn.

Ordinarily, finding your way out of the African bush is a simple matter of backtracking, but earlier in the day we'd spotted a small herd of topi and I had set out on what became a two-hour stalk. Then, after crossing and re-crossing our tracks, the original set of tire marks was lost, and we set off in a direction that led us into the increasingly higher and thicker vegetation that now engulfed us.

Now that you know the peculiar circumstances that led us to this particular spot on earth, this story really begins with a shout from the truck's rooftop and a rapid exchange of Swahili between Oomo and Ian Rowbotham, Mike's 19-year-old son.

"They see the way out . . . there's a grassy spot just beyond . . . now we'll make it to camp before nightfall."

Once out of reach of the thorns, I sat back and dreamily looked forward to a hot shower and clean clothes. Allen and Don, my pals from home, had gone off that morning with their PH to set up a leopard blind and shoot something for bait. This was their first safari, and they'd have adventures to tell as we sat around the campfire, mutually blessed by the distiller's magic.

I had bagged only a topi that day, a swift, cinnamon-colored antelope with rear-curving horns. As a trophy, they're not in the class with, say, a kudu or other glamorous members of the antelope family, but mine was a good one and would rank near the top of the record list if I were inclined to fret about such things. More important, the stalk had been a good one and the trophy well-earned.

We'd spotted the big topi among a group of six or seven grazing in burned-over plain about a mile across. Grass fires are common during the dry season and within a few days of the burn, new grass begins to sprout and game moves in to graze on the tender shoots. The burns also offer grazing animals the protection of virtually unlimited visibility for spotting predators. Which was the problem we faced when we spotted the topi contentedly grazing near the center of the blackened plain. Considering the distance, which was far too great to attempt a shot, plus the openness of the plain, the topi were in an impossible position. Impossible, that is, until one of the grazing bucks lifted his head and gave us a better look at his horns. Even in the shimmering distance his horns stood out bold and black, the longest and heaviest horns on a topi that I, or even Mike, had ever seen.

The only possible way to get within shooting range was simple: old-fashioned crawling. So after circling downwind of the topi, I bellied down on the black, ash-covered earth and commenced slithering toward them, sliding my rifle before me and taking advantage of slight depressions and the cover of a few charred tree snags, and also being damned careful not to venture to close to any ant mounds.

Earlier in the week Mike had almost stepped on a deadly gaboon viper, the memory of which contributed mightily to my caution. A couple of times when I was almost within shooting range, the animals moved off a distance, adding yards to my route and no doubt adding suspense to the drama for those watching my sooty progress.

At length, with the noonday sun bearing down, I slithered up behind a leg-sized log that offered a solid rest for taking the 250-yard shot. The big topi had grown suspicious and was looking directly toward me when I put crosshairs about halfway up his neck and pressed the trigger.

It was the kind of shot that makes hunters sleep peacefully, which was probably what I was daydreaming about a few hours later when we finally got clear of the thorn thickets and were speeding across the smooth, grassy *vlei* when suddenly our truck slugged to a halt with a sucking sound we'd come to know—and dread.

A *vlei* is a meadow-like plain, usually nestled between hills, and looks like an overgrown lawn. Even during the dry season vleis tend to be green because of under-layers of water near the surface. This is what causes trouble for unwary travelers like us, because you can be happily motoring along and suddenly the dry crust breaks and you're up to your axles in black, sucking muck. We were in it up to the truck's floorboards. Four-wheel drive is of no benefit—spinning tires just dig you deeper—and the only way out is to jack up the truck and lay a trail of tree branches under the wheels and creep along inch by inch until finding solid ground, a frustrating and time-consuming task we'd repeated almost daily during our explorations of this unknown territory.

Figuring that we'd be stuck for the better part of an hour, Mike filled a tea kettle (an essential utensil in any safari vehicle) while Ian started a fire. At least Linda could enjoy afternoon tea while Jason and Oomo chopped and carried saplings from a nearby knoll to make a roadbed under the truck. But even before the water was boiling, Oomo came galloping off the knoll and making the soft tongue sucking "tssks-tssks" sound African trackers make when they spot game, and pointing back to where he'd come.

*"Sapal, B'wana, Sapal."*

"What?" I asked, not yet understanding his attempt at English.

"Sable," Mike explained. "They saw sable on the other side of that knoll."

Instantly my adrenaline was pumping, because the magnificent sable antelope is one of Africa's greatest game animals.

"How many?" I asked. "Are there any good bulls?"

Mike was asking the same questions in Swahili, but there was no need to interpret because the way Oomo fluttered his fingers and swept his hands back over his head told me all I wanted to know.

It was a big herd and there were bulls!

The names taxonomists give creatures usually don't tell us much, but naming the sable *Hippotragus niger* says it all: Black Horse.

Almost the size of an elk and standing up to five feet at the shoulder, a mature bull sable is an impressive animal with its deep black coat, distinctive white facial markings, and its stiff ruff of hair bristling down his neck and spine. But his most striking feature is the matched pair of long, ridged horns that curve saber-like over his back. Sometimes nearing four feet in length (even larger for the rare giant, or royal sable), the magnificent horns end in sharp points, and a big bull can use them with deadly effect. Lions, among other predators, have come out second best in encounters with a mean-tempered bull sable.

I carried three rifles in the Toyota's gun rack: a heavy .458 Win. Mag., and a light 7x57 Al Bieson Mauser that I'd used to shoot the topi. Now, I reached for my medium rifle, a .338 Win. Mag. built on a Mauser action by David Miller. The rifle, and its hand-loaded, 250-grain Nosler Partition bullets, were about right for the tough sable, if there proved to be a shootable bull. But that hope was based on the vague assumption that we could find them again. So far my only assumption—as transmitted by Oomo's hand-waving—was that the sable were somewhere beyond a nearby hill and moving. They could be running and we'd never catch them on foot, but we'd soon find out.

"Ian, take Jason and go with Jim and see what there is," Mike ordered. "I'll keep Oomo here to help get us unstuck."

I didn't like the sound of this because it told me that Mike figured there was little chance of catching up with the sable. Ian was smart and hard-working and had great rapport with the trackers and camp staff, chatting with them in their diverse dialects as naturally as he spoke English, but he had little or no experience as a guide or hunter. He didn't even own a rifle or binoculars, the basic tools of any professional hunter.

"Here," I said, taking the .458 out of the rack and handing it to him, "there might be something mean and ugly on the other side of the hill."

Jason had already run ahead and when we neared the crest the hill, we heard his soft "tssk tssk" and found him crouching in some scrub brush. Beyond, in the direction of his hand-waving, was another vlei but no sign of the sable. Apparently we'd come on a wild goose hunt, as Mike must have suspected. Still, a sable is one of Africa's most beautiful trophies and worth every effort, even when there is slim hope of success.

I'd taken a sable years earlier on my first safari in Botswana. With its perfectly matched 44-inch horns, it is one of the crown jewels of my trophy room and I never expected to find another as good.

"Looks like they gave us the slip, Ian."

"Not yet, Jason saw two big bulls circle behind that next knoll over there. He says they weren't spooked, and I think we can head them off if you are up to a bit of walking."

"Then let's get after them," I said, handing my rifle to Jason and heading down the slope.

"Not that way, Mr. Carmichel, we'll go over here," Ian said politely but with solid conviction, pointing in a direction nearly 90 degrees from where Jason had last seen the sable. "They're going over there."

"How do you know?"

"Because that's where they want to go."

My question was one I've asked other good guides and hunters, and their answer has always been the same as Ian's. I've never really understood "because that's where they want to go," but I've learned to respect it as the mark of a hunter gifted with an almost supernatural instinct. Of the dozens of professional guides I've hunted with, no more than five or six have possessed this rare talent, plus perhaps another half dozen non-professionals I've known and hunted with. I know for certain that I do not have the gift and claim only to belong to the "work hard, hunt hard, and climb the steepest mountains and you'll be rewarded" school of hunting.

The late Ben Rogers Lee, the champion turkey caller and maker of turkey calls, had the gift. Of the several times we hunted together, he nearly always picked the right place to be and was as successful with deer as with turkey. He called the talent "woodsmanship"—having a special sense of how the woods and animals related, even in places he'd never before visited.

My son Scott is also so blessed, and although I've never understood his talent, I've been amazed at his ability to divide the landscape into its individual components and analyze what he sees—plus infinite patience and total belief that game is nearby.

Now I saw the same gift in young Ian Rowbotham. He neither boasted nor speculated. The sable were there! Now it was only a matter of going to the place where they wanted to be. So we went where Ian led and in fact we arrived there even before the sable. We took good cover on the side of a sloping knoll overlooking a burned-over flat, and from a solid sitting position I braced my rifle in the fork of a low tree. For long minutes and as the sun sank lower, there was no sign of the sable, but Ian's cool confidence was so powerful that I too was convinced. Now it was just a matter of patience.

Then they really were there! Circling from behind a brushy knoll, they came in twos and threes; reddish hued cows and frisky young bulls, all angling toward us and starting to cross less than 150 yards away.

Then a big bull came into view, walking slowly, his head held high and the tips of his horns reaching almost to his rump. He seemed to be totally aware of his magnificence, and even without using my binoculars I could see that he equaled the sable in my trophy room, possibly even better. Closer he came, giving me an almost ridiculously easy shot.

But wait . . . Jason had said there were two big bulls. Where was the other one? Could he possibly be as good as this one? Now the bull had passed by and the range was growing longer. Should I shoot now? More cows came, and more young bulls. And then HE came, the last in line, slower than the rest, on legs stiffened with age and battle. An oxpecker foraged in his thick ruff.

It was not a matter of comparison; this was the bull, his horns four inches longer than the other, perfectly matched, reaching high then sweeping gracefully over his back like the arches of a bridge. I put the crosshairs on his shoulder and kept them there as he came closer. A sable deserves a good shot and I gave him my best, pressing the trigger gently and applying the last ounce of pressure at the perfect moment.

The sable was there. Just as Ian had said it would be.

It was long after dark when we got to camp. Dinner was cold and the shower water had cooled, but no matter. Don and Allen had gone to bed, but I rousted them out to tell about Ian and the sable, and getting stuck in the vlei and about the topi and . . .

Before turning in for the night, I gave Ian my binoculars, a good set of Bausch & Lombs, and predicted he would be a great professional hunter because he has the gift. I will always remember the first words Ian spoke as a working guide: "Because that's where they want to go," but I'll never know how he knew.

*"Moving an inch at a time, I eased myself a bit higher and guided the rifle into a shallow crevice that would serve as a sort of rest. But just at that instant the rams spotted me."*

## Chapter 4

# The Littlest Sheep

The oil-producing nations of the Middle East are usually thought of as scorched stretches of shifting sands where the midday sun broils your brain and sizzles skin like spit on a hot griddle.

In truth, though, as my hunting pal Fred Huntington and I found out, Tehran, the capitol city of Iran, is on about the same latitude as Nashville, Tennessee, and come winter the noontime sun is liable to shine on a foot of snow. On the day Fred and I arrived in Tehran, in the first week of January 1974, it began to snow. Four days later, when we were scheduled to fly out to sheep country, the snow was still coming down, and therein lies a tale within a tale.

Iran Safaris, Lt. had booked us on a quick jet flight to Tabriz, a good-sized city in the northwestern panhandle of Iran, not far from the Turkish and Russian borders. There we were to meet our guides and drive into the rugged mountains of the Iranian-Russian frontier where we would hunt ibex and the sporty little Armenian sheep.

Unfortunately, four days of heavy snow proved too much for Mehrabad airport, and our plane was grounded until the following day. This was no real problem because we had a bit of extra time anyway, and besides, I'd grown rather fond of watching the traffic of Tehran perform in the snow. In the best of weather the average Iranian driver is an unguided missile who apparently never attempts a left-hand turn except from the outside right lane. When the streets get a little icy, it's a downtown demolition derby with two million contestants and lots of fun to watch—from a distance.

Our flight the following morning was again cancelled and with the snow still coming down, we thought it wise to forget the airplane and try a train. Which is why the afternoon found us not only comfortably encased in the brocaded and varnished mahogany elegance (if somewhat worn) of a 1914

French railway coach, but also sharing our tiny first class compartment with two very apprehensive young ladies. One was a mod-dressed gal who identified herself as a nurse and spoke just enough English to let us know that she wasn't at all keen on spending 18 hours boxed in with two American men. The other was dressed in the centuries-old fashion of full-length robes and the face-hiding veil of traditional Moslem womanhood. All we ever saw of her were flashing black eyes and hints of a lithe form under layers of exotic garments.

"Fred, do you think we ought to tell our wives about this?"

"I don't know about yours, but mine's not going to believe me anyway. What worries me even more is what we're supposed to do when it's bed time."

"I wish you hadn't said that. Now I'm worrying too."

Late in the evening the worst of our worries came true when a porter came by and converted our seats into four beds, two above and two below. The women claimed the upper and lower on one side and there was no curtain between. So with nothing left to sit on, it was all too clear that we would all have to hit the sack.

With a chorus of nervous (I suppose) giggling, the two ladies scrambled between the sheets and Fred, who can sleep anywhere, promptly claimed the lower berth on our side of the dimly lighted cubicle and was soon snoring like a hippo in heat.

This was all too much for my modest soul, so I slipped out the door and spent much of the night on the freezing cold observation platform in the company of a turbaned Mullah (I think that's what he was) who apparently didn't appreciate my company and expressed his displeasure with lots of shouting and hand-waving in my face. In addition to whatever it was about me that he found so aggravating, he also suffered from weak kidneys because periodically he would rush into the nearby restroom (a hole in the floor), only to return and continue his remonstrations.

The train never exceeded 20 miles-per-hour and stopped every 15 minutes, and thus did two American hunters chug across snow-swept Asian plains that in centuries past had been crossed by Alexander the Great, Genghis Khan, and the Abyssinian hordes.

Just after dawn we arrived in Tabriz and met our two guides, Manouchehr

Abdollohian and Hooshang Bakhtiar. After a brief but verbal Iranian-style baggage hassle, we were on our way north toward the Russian border. Our home for the next week was to be only a dozen miles or so from what was then the USSR.

Our hunt was arranged to include ibex, a goat-like creature with high, sweeping horns, and three varieties of Iranian sheep: the red, urial, and Armenian. The urial sheep is probably the best known and most popular of the Iranian sheep, at least among American hunters, because the curl of its horns is fairly similar to that of North American wild sheep. The Armenian sheep, on the other hand, is probably the least known and, in fact, has been taken by relatively few American hunters. Among the very smallest of the world's wild sheep, the Armenian stands no more than three feet at the shoulder and sports horns that curve back over the neck and shoulders, as opposed to curving around the jaw like the horns of North American sheep.

Armenian sheep range over parts of Turkey, the northern mountains of Iran and the southern tip of Russia eastward from the Caspian Sea. They roam in herds numbering from only a few members up to several dozen, and as the seasons change they wander over a large area, seeking the high country during the summer and dropping to lower elevations during the cold months. When they come down to the lower pastures, they come in contact with domestic sheep and shepherds often enough to become extremely spooky. This wildness, plus their small size, makes them a challenging trophy to stalk and shoot.

Our game plan for the first day was for Fred, guided by Manouchehr, whom we quickly nick-named Manny, to go after the little sheep while Hooshang and I went into the high country for ibex.

After a lung-busting climb and a cliff-hanging stalk (literally), I took a fine ibex ram. Fred and his porter located a herd of sheep, but unfortunately, found out firsthand how wild and hard to hit they can be.

According to Fred's account that night, a herd of the little sheep had spooked at the sound of someone's coat brushing against a boulder some 200 yards away. Later in the day they had gotten reasonably close to another ram, but Fred overestimated the range and shot a little too high. The small size of the

Armenian tends to make them look farther away than they actually are, a hint I made a point to remember.

After my good luck with ibex I thought the sheep would be a snap, but I figured wrong because the herd we finally spotted wasn't down low at all, but high up on the snow-covered face of a steep mountain. A three-hour climb got us to within about 500 yards of the herd, but beyond that we were stymied. There were no trees, boulders, or gullies to hide behind, nothing but a steeply slanting expanse of landscape covered by a foot of snow.

The herd was bedded down when we first spotted them, but as we came closer, they stood up and began nervously milling about. Clearly, there was no way we could get closer without spooking them all the way to Russia, so my only choice was to try a long shot. At that distance I needed a solid rest, or at least to shoot from the prone position, but there wasn't anything around that could be used for a rest. After I had floundered around in the snow for a moment, trying to get some sort of steady position, it became clear that the only way I would get anything near a solid rest would be to support my rifle over the supine torso of Hooshang or one of the others. But asking someone to plop down and stick his face in the snow while you use his back for a shooting bench takes a bit of diplomacy, and I wasn't all that confident I could persuade anyone to do it. Hooshang, though, must have been reading my thoughts.

"Jeem," he said, "I have a plan. I will get down into the snow and you can fire your rifle over me."

"Now why didn't I think of that?" was my answer. "Okay, but put your fingers in your ears. I'll be very careful."

"Ah Jeem," he smiled back with charm and a soft pat on my shoulder, "it is a pleasure and honor to be of service to so great a hunter."

*Oh oh,* I said to myself, *the price of tips to guides just went out of sight.*

A few moments later Hooshang had wriggled himself face down into a fairly stable position, and I was aiming my .280 rifle across his back, trying to time my trigger pull to the up and down of his breathing.

It was a pretty hopeless shot, I guess, and by the time the echo of report stopped bouncing from mountain to mountain, the sheep, including the one

I'd shot at, were long gone.

Besides Hooshang and me, our party included the local game guard, a young fellow who carried our lunches and tea-making gear and a grizzled old sport who helped me with my rifle and cameras. They all had seen me shoot and the unanimous option was that I'd missed the sheep.

Yet, something was puzzling me and I told Hooshang to ask them if anyone saw the bullet kick up a puff of snow.

After a flurry of conversation in Iranian and Turkish, the report was in; "No one saw where your bullet hit. It was a very long shot and too far to see."

"Then tell them I want to go up to where the sheep were and see where my bullet hit."

"But Jeem," he stammered, bewildered at my crazy notion, "the sheep is gone, we must go to another mountain to find other rams."

"We'll do that later," I insisted. "When I miss, I want to know why and how far."

The truth was that I had a pretty good feeling that my bullet had not missed, but I didn't want to insult them by saying that I thought they were mistaken. At the same time I didn't want to sound too boastful either.

"If it is your desire, we will find the place where your bullet made a hole in the snow."

"You are most kind," I answered. "That will make me very happy."

The others just stared in amazement at the crazy American who would climb a mountain to see a hole in the snow.

When we climbed to where the sheep had been, they were treated to an even greater dose of amazement. Near where the ram had stood, like sprinkles of rose petals, was a crimson-splotched trail leading around the mountain.

"Jeem, Jeem, I do not believe what I see," whooped Hooshang. "I have never seen such a shot."

"Just luck," I replied, trying to sound modest but feeling smug and wholly satisfied at having insisted on a closer look.

My self-satisfaction was short-lived, however, because it soon became apparent that the ram wasn't badly hurt after all. After some three hours of hard trailing through knee-deep snow, we got only one final look at him. He was running along the rocky side of an almost vertical mountain face and except for a somewhat stiff rear leg, looked to be in good health. Somewhere in the mountains of northern Iran I believe there still lives a very fine, but extra wary, Armenian ram that walks with a slight limp.

By Iranian hunting rules, a hit is the same as a kill and you pay the full price. This is the reason the game guards accompany hunters, not just to see that no one cheats, as I was happy to learn, but also to assist the guide and make every effort to find wounded animals so the hunter can claim his trophy. Though I'd now lost one sheep, my license was for two Armenian rams and time-wise, thanks to my first-day luck on ibex, I was still ahead of the game.

The next day we headed west along a river that snaked through a broad, red-soiled valley. Mostly, the land was used for grazing, but here and there one could see where a cotton crop has been coaxed out of the rocky ground. Once, generations ago, there were trees but they were used up and never replaced. Now the landscape was so barren that a tree is a treasure and dried sheep manure fuels even the stoves used for cooking as well as heating homes. Actually, the land looks very much like certain areas of the American west—washed and gullied with tough grass and cactus growing through pavement-hard ground of basalt gravel.

Hooshang had the foresight to rent a couple of scrawny horses that proved especially useful when we came to the river. Fed by melting snow in the mountains, the river was about 150 yards wide, belly-deep to a horse, and treacherously swift. It was all our horses could do to fight the current and at any instant I expected to be swept away by the icy torrent. The nags were tougher than they looked though, and we made several crossings without so much as a wet sock.

Toward mid-afternoon we topped a low range of hills and descended toward a mud-walled village. So far as I could see there were no roads leading to the village, no motor vehicles and no electric lines. Nothing at all, in fact, to suggest that the date was 1974, or 200 or even 500 years earlier. As we came closer we were met by a trio of horsemen who turned out to be an official welcoming party. One of the three was the mayor, or at least so I judged by his official air and pinstripe suit, who displayed his wealth and position in the form of several gold teeth. He bid me welcome in the formal way by bowing stiffly while patting his chest with his hand. This gesture means, "I make myself humble before you," and when I returned the centuries-old salutation, he beamed in 24-karat delight and surprise.

The local lingo turned out to be a Turkish dialect not understood by Hooshang, so for a while we only stood around, politely grinning at each other. His Honor, I noticed, kept eyeing my rifle, so I unloaded the magazine and handed it to him for a closer look. He was especially fascinated by the scope, a 6X Leupold, and after squinting through it at the surrounding mountains, commented in Turkish to the game guard, who translated in Iranian to Hooshang, who passed on in English, "The sheep must now be very careful because they do not know about such a wonderful rifle as this."

"I think they already know," I answered, "and they all ran away."

This must have been precisely the right thing to say because everyone cackled in delight at my fine wit, and we had a parting round of handshaking and chest-patting.

Taking our leave, we crossed the river again and coaxed the horses to the top of another range of hills where we rested and boiled tea over a sagebrush fire. As I sipped my tea Iranian fashion, with a lump of sugar held behind the teeth, and nibbled a chunk of crumbly cheese, I studied the valley and its village and wondered how many caravans, invading armies, and bands of raiding bandits had followed the river's winding route into this heart of the ancient Persian Empire.

We didn't see a single sheep all day, but Fred and Manny had located a good-sized herd. When they found them it was too late for a stalk, but they had high hopes for the next day. Despite the lack of game, it had been a fascinating day, and that evening, appropriate apologies to Allah, a bottle of Iran's famous eye-watering vodka appeared on the table.

The next day dawned cold and still with a high gauze of clouds hinting at a weather change. To the west of camp was a low range of hills, which looked like fairly easy going. Hooshang said that there were lots of sheep there but that the climbing was extremely difficult. An hour later I knew what he meant.

They were not only a lot steeper than they looked from a distance, but also covered with a layer of loose, baseball-sized rocks that made climbing treacherous. Even more bothersome was the free-standing nature of the hills: There were no ridges to follow; instead, each hill had to be climbed, investigated and descended, one at a time. Thus the day was a muscle-knotting exercise of up and down frustration. Occasionally we would spot a band of sheep, but there was never enough cover for a stalk, and the sheep would scamper off as we tried to slip within rifle range.

Twice we completely circled around the mountains, trying to find a safe approach to the wary sheep, but each time they disappeared. There was nothing to do but keep climbing and hoping.

About mid-afternoon, dead tired and weary of chasing sheep that vanish like wisps of fog, we had just topped an especially grueling mountain and were heading down when the game guard stiffened and pointed into the rocky ravine below. My first thought was that we'd blundered into a bunch of sheep, but instead, I saw only three reddish brown forms streaking out of the gulch and up the side of the next hill. Wolves!

I wasn't clear on what the law said about shooting wolves and lost too many seconds questioning Hooshang and the game guard. By the time I got an explanation that wolves were a despised predator and I could shoot all I saw, they had rounded the hill and were out of sight. But as it turned out my few seconds of hesitation proved to be a stroke of luck.

Five minutes later we spotted three good rams taking their leisure on the crest of one of the closer hills. If I had shot at the wolves (who might have been stalking the sheep too), the rams would surely have spooked without our even having seen them. As we studied their position it became apparent they were bedded down where they could watch all approaches to their hill. Any attempt to get closer over such open ground would obviously be foolish and fruitless. Clearly, there was but one option, and Hooshang knew it better than I

"We can get no closer than 400 meters, do you want to try a shot?"

I'd already checked the wind direction and other factors that might affect the flight of my bullet and calculated there would be a fishtailing breeze whipping around the hills. I was also aware that one more wounded sheep and my license would be filled.

"Let's give it a try," I said.

A half-hour later Hooshang and I had climbed to within a few feet of the pinnacle of a hill closest to the sheep and, flat on our bellies, were inching toward the crest. I slid my rifle ahead of me so it would be very nearly in position as soon as we saw the sheep.

When we peeked over the top the sheep were still bedded down but were alertly scanning the countryside. I've never liked shooting at an animal lying down because the angle can fool you and at a distance of some 400 yards, it made the diminutive targets even smaller. One of them took a long, hard look our way, causing us to freeze where we were, but after a tense moment or two he looked away.

Hooshang whispered, "The one in the middle is the best one."

Moving an inch at a time, I eased myself a bit higher and guided the rifle into a shallow crevice that would serve as a sort of rest. But just at that instant the rams spotted me. In a flash the big ram was on his feet and in another instant he could have been out of sight, but he hesitated for another look in my direction. That was just enough time for me to get the crosshairs above his shoulder and send a 140-grain Nosler on its way before he disappeared.

At the sound of the shot, the game guard scrambled up beside us, and a moment later he was pointing at three rams darting among the boulders at the bottom of the hill and angling toward us.

"Shoot! Shoot!" he yelled.

I had already swung ahead of the lead ram and was about to press the trigger when Hooshang grabbed my arm. "Don't shoot! Don't shoot! Your ram is dead."

For an instant I thought that he meant one of the rams was hit and didn't want to risk me hitting the wrong one. But all three looked very much alive as they disappeared from sight.

I suppose I looked like I was about to argue the point, but Hooshang was laughing and explaining what had happened. When I fired, he was the only one who had seen my ram turn a flip and fall dead. The extra ram running away was actually a fourth sheep that had been bedded out of sight.

It took nearly an hour to get down the mountain and scale the hill where the dead ram lay, cleanly hit in the chest and much bigger than we had estimated. Armenian sheep horns that measure 80 centimeters are very, very, large indeed. My ram officially measured over 83 centimeters on both sides. *(See postscript.)*

Fred had his own run of luck that day and had connected on a long shot at a big ram. The sheep didn't drop in its tracks, and for a while it looked like the ram had gotten away. Fred's luck held though, and the trackers found the ram that evening and brought it into camp.

We were both luckier than we knew, because that night the weather went bad and piled in several more inches of snow, making any further hunting impossible for several days. Predictably, the plane to Tehran was grounded again, and we forsook another train trip and opted for a long but peaceful drive back to the capitol with Hooshang and Manny. One ibex, two Armenian sheep, and one Iranian train ride had been adventure enough.

— *Postscript* —

I was later to learn that my Armenian sheep created some problems in the Iranian Game Department. It seems that the Shah's brother, an internationally known trophy hunter, had issued standing orders for record-class game to be reported to him and kept under surveillance, presumably so he could add it to his personal collection. Somehow my sheep had gone undetected until the day I collected it myself, which resulted in some bureaucrat back in Tehran having a lot of explaining to do. I was not concerned.

*"Death on high mountains can take several forms. Falls will kill you, so will freezing and being crushed by avalanches or rock slides. Mountains can also kill you silently with a condition known as pulmonary edema."*

CHAPTER 5

# A HUNTING STORY

It was worse at night.

Sunlight seemed to add wisps of oxygen to the faint atmosphere, at least breathing seemed less painful, but when darkness fell, our tent became a claustrophobic tomb. We were exhausted, but that too was a terrifying specter because breathing required a conscious mind to order the body to gasp for one more breath, then another, and another. If we dared to sleep, would the body cease to labor for life? Rest came only in brief moments, tormented by dream fantasies of sleeping in a grassy meadow and breathing sweet oxygen. Then a voice from somewhere would shout, "Wake up, save yourself," and I'd bolt upright in the airless tomb, gasping for air, my throat seared raw by the heaving in and out of barren atmosphere.

Somewhere outside the tent in a jumble of equipment was a small bottle of oxygen. I longed to inhale its sweetness as a man dying of thirst craves water, but the bottle was old and scarred, and probably empty. Better to leave the bottle untouched, serving as a symbol of survival, than to discover it empty and lose the handful of hope it represented.

In our meager medicine kit were sleeping pills and tranquilizers. The sleeping pills could be deadly, a one-way ticket to everlasting sleep, but the tranquilizers were tempting because they might ease the claustrophobic panic. But would tranquilizer-induced relaxation bring with it a reduced will to survive? Like the oxygen bottle, it was best not to know.

I reached through the blackness to the silent forms of Sam and Bobby, listening for their breathing, feeling for movement. "Are you okay?" I whispered, the words burning my raw throat.

"Yeah, I'm okay," came a raspy whisper from the darkness.

"Tell me how much is four and a half plus nine and a quarter." Talking eased the panic of suffocation and, more importantly, helped us judge our respective mental conditions. Confusion and loss of memory are warning signs that oxygen starvation is taking a dangerous toll, so by asking each other tricky questions, we tested our ability to make rational decisions. "Who wrote War And Peace?" one might ask the others, or "How many hours did it take us to fly from Miami to Peru?" Mostly though, we only asked, "Are you okay?"

"Yeah, sure, I'm okay . . ."

Death on high mountains can take several forms. Falls will kill you, so will freezing and being crushed by avalanches or rock slides. Mountains can also kill you silently with a condition known as pulmonary edema. The irritated lungs begin filling with fluid, breathing becomes difficult and, finally, impossible. There was no doubt that we were suffering from the breath-robbing edema because three days earlier (or was it four?) when we came to this high place, we could breathe and move with less effort. But now with the efficiency of our lungs cut short, how much longer could we endure? A day? Two? Like a deep-sea diver suffering from the deadly illusions known as raptures of the deep and convinced he can endure underwater forever, would we become unable to make life-saving decisions? Already our simple pop questions were getting harder to answer and, worse, we were beginning to not care.

Earlier that evening we had pledged to stay on the mountain one more day, then get off no matter what. We had planned and worked hard to make this hunt a success and failure would be bitter. But how could we have prepared ourselves for the unknown? We were at altitudes seldom breached by hunters/explorers and our quarry was proving to be only a myth.

*What had made us come here? Through what gateways had we passed to arrive at this airless hell?* These questions had haunted me with increasing frequency during recent days.

Had it begun when I met Jose Poco Rada a few months earlier; or did it really begin nearly a century before when a titled Englishman wrote a few mysterious words in his diary? His name was Arbuthnot; he was rich and his passions were hunting and cricket. He loved the game of cricket so much that he owned his own team and sponsored his players on worldwide odysseys in search of teams willing to meet them on the green. When he traveled he also hunted, and as was the habit of gentlemen of his era, he kept a diary that he eventually published. Like most such diaries, the pages were filled with self-serving remembrances, the records of long-forgotten and little-cared-for cricket matches and bleak descriptions of the sundry game that fell to his guns. It was dull stuff, and like other dreary diaries of its type, Arbuthnot's literary endeavor would have long since been forgotten had there not been a brief passage that has captivated generations of hunters.

While visiting Peru he heard of a mysterious deer that lived high in the Andes—a deer that had two sets of antlers! The journal makes no mention that he hunted such a deer, or that he saw any evidence that such a creature existed, only that the Indians who dwelt high in the Andean mountains called it the Tyruka. Since then it has been known by hunters who quest for adventure simply as the Mystery Deer of the Andes.

I'd met Rada at a gathering of international hunters and when he told me he lived in Lima, I asked if he knew anything about Arbuthnot's journal.

"Oh yes, Señor Carmichel," he answered, "and I know what your next question will be, because everyone here wants to know about our legendary four-antlered deer."

"Well, do they exist?"

"Of course they do, señor. I have seen them with my own eyes."

The revelation caused my heart to skip a beat because Rada apparently held the key to a mystery that had kept hunters in suspense for decades, but I felt it best not to let my excitement show.

"Can they be hunted?" I asked, trying to sound casual. "Why don't I come on down to Peru in a week or two and collect one?"

"Oh Señor Carmichel, I myself can arrange for such a hunt but it will be difficult. Hunting the Tyruka will require an expedition of many men and that will be very expensive."

Rada's accent underlined the words *expedition* and *expensive*, and to make sure I knew where I stood in the scheme of such a hunt, he rolled his eyes upward and spread his hands in the classic Latin expression of dismay. My heart sank; he was telling me that the long-sought prize would be claimed by someone who could buy such an expedition, probably an oil-soaked millionaire hunter or one of the inheritance-keeping playboys, both of which were present in abundance at the gathering.

At that moment one of those coincidences occurred that make us wonder if indeed we are guided through life by a prearranged plot like characters in a poorly written novel. I was shaking Rada's hand and thanking him for the scoop on the Tyruka when out of nowhere appeared my longtime friend and hunting companion Sam Arnett III. Introductions were made, and I filled in Sam on Arbuthnot's diary and what Rada had just told me about the four-antlered deer, including the part about an expensive expedition. Sam seldom blinks when sizeable sums of money are mentioned, and when Rada offered an estimate of what hunting the Tyruka would cost, his only reaction was to ask what time of year would be best for a hunt.

"Señor Arnett, the best time will be in July . . . I can arrange a hunt for you by that time."

"Sounds good to me. What about you, Carmichel . . . want to go hunt those funny deer?"

The beginning had been as simple as that.

July was the best time to hunt Tyruka, because their four antlers would be at their prime and the always-hazardous Andean weather would be at its most forgiving. That would give us three months to get in top condition for hunting the Andean peaks. I don't smoke and unlike many hunters who suffer altitude sickness, I'd never had any difficulty when climbing the mountains of Alaska and our western states. A couple of years before, I'd hunted sheep in the high elevations of Iran, and even a tough hunt in the Karakoram Range of Kashmir had not caused me any particular breathing problems. Yet, one thing I'd learned about high-altitude climbing is that the air gets thin fast and only a few hundred feet can make a tremendous difference. Not only does this thin oxygen cause a swift reduction of physical stamina, but effects brain function as well. Oxygen-starved climbers have done strange and deadly things.

Hunting the Tyruka would be my greatest challenge yet, because Peru's Andean peaks soar to well over 20,000 feet. Rada was uncertain about the elevation at which we'd be running, because being a longtime smoker himself, he'd never climbed that high. However, he reckoned we might camp as high as 15,000 feet and possibly hunt even higher. Ancient Cuzco, one of the world's highest cities at some 12,000 feet, would be the starting point of our expedition, and we'd be going a lot higher from there!

My daily conditioning included running as fast as I could before completely losing my wind. As my conditioning improved, I added a backpack and gradually carried more weight as my legs and lungs gained strength and capacity. Running on the stadium track at a nearby university with a backpack filled with bricks, I'd run myself to staggering exhaustion, and then, when my body said it could take no more, I'd charge up the stadium steps to the topmost row of seats. The key to hunting success at extreme altitude—often even survival itself—is not just a matter of pushing yourself to exhaustion, but how hard you can keep going after you're exhausted. We're a lot tougher than we think.

To round out my conditioning I swam almost daily, especially underwater. I don't know if it helped, but I had the idea that swimming as hard and fast as I could without breathing would condition my muscles to working hard on a lean diet of oxygen. My initial goal was to swim the length of the pool, underwater, without coming up for air. Eventually I could swim three laps without coming up to breathe. This exercise may have saved my life.

At his home in Texas, Sam Arnett was also putting in his miles with a heavily loaded backpack. Sam had invited his nephew Bobby Fleiger to join our expedition. Bobby, a 21-year-old medical student, was a lean and tough daily runner who should have no problems with the mountains.

Rada had advised us that getting import licenses for our rifles would mean a long and uncertain hassle with the Peruvian bureaucracy. He said he had good rifles and plenty of ammo for us to use and that we'd be smart to leave our own rifles at home. At the time, the decision to take him up on his offer seemed like an easy solution to the firearms problem, but one that we were to later regret. *Profoundly.*

Our first stop in Peru was Lima, where we spent two days taking in the museums and other historic sights. We'd expected to go immediately from there to the hunting area, but discovered instead that South Americans have a rather relaxed way of being in a hurry. Rada assured us that all was on schedule and that we were to fly on to Cuzco and he'd catch up in a day or two with his men and equipment. "Everything is arranged," he assured us.

Four days later in Cuzco we were still awaiting Rada's arrival but the time wasn't wasted. The atmosphere there is so thin that it is not uncommon for tourists to step off the plane, take a deep breath of the pure sparkling air and faint dead in their tracks. Hotels routinely offer newly arrived guests a cup of coca leaf tea (the same stuff cocaine is made from), which improved the blood's oxygen-carrying capacity. In that rare atmosphere we spent our days running on a nearby playing field surrounded by giant walls made of boulders weighing many tons yet fitted together with such incredible precision by the ancient Incas that a knife blade will not fit between the joints. We also ran up

and down the steep, staircase sidewalks of Cuzco, always tossing and chasing a Frisbee Bobby had brought along. By the end of these twice-daily workouts we'd be accompanied by a dozen or more of Cuzco's children, all shouting and amazed by our wondrous toy. One day we made a trip to the unbelievable ruins of Machu Picchu and another day the owner of our hotel took us fishing on the Urubamba River. He'd never seen a spinning reel before and was amazed at the distance and accuracy of Sam's casts.

Jose Rada's arrival in Cuzco was nothing short of spectacular. In addition to trucks loaded with equipment, his entourage included three beautiful young women. In addition to their stunning looks, each spoke perfect English and could have passed for coeds at any American university. After introductions, Rada, grinning like an evil cat, explained that beautiful ladies were part of South American hospitality and that nothing was too good for his honored guests. In other words, Sam, Bobby and me. This, I realized instantly, was a situation that would require delicate handling, and the sooner the better.

After considerable negotiation on the matter, punctuated by howls of anguish from Rada and weeping by the girls, it was decided that the ladies would enjoy the scenic drive with us to our final staging area, then return to Cuzco before nightfall. It was a safe and sane plan, but by then we should have learned that any plans made by the always-charming Poco Rada will probably not develop as intended.

This particular interruption of our plans was a big truck blocking the only road through a small town about midway along what was to have been a five-hour journey. When we went to search for the truck's driver, we discovered that the truck had delivered some scraggly bulls for a bullfight that was the featured attraction of a day-long festival. It was the day of the city's mayoral election and to secure his popularity and reelection, the existing major had arranged to have a few puny bulls trucked in. The town had no bullring so the bulls were simply released, one by one, in the main plaza and everyone was welcome to try being a toreador, an enterprise that seemed to be directly related to the amount of whatever it was the aspiring bullfighters were drinking.

After a fruitless hour-long search for the truck driver, we took a lunch break at a tiny café on the square, whose proprietor apparently considered a rich coating of flyspecks sufficient decoration for the otherwise bare walls, ceiling, and tables. While we slurped surprisingly delicious soup in the company of our beautiful companions, a bull would occasionally stick his head in the doorway and render a lusty bellow. Further entrance was blocked by a barrel that the cautious proprietor had placed in the entrance.

Hours later the owner of the truck had been found and we were again on the dusty one-lane road, arriving at a sagging two-story shack at twilight. A sign proclaimed the building to be a hotel and restaurant, but mainly it was a trading station dealing mostly in beer and coca leaves. The hotel portion of what we soon dubbed the Tiltin' Hilton was in fact the home of the owner, and because the owner had not expected guests, he and his family were already occupying the only beds. This seemed to be a matter of little concern because he simply roused his family, smoothed the sheets, and announced with a smiling flourish that we would enjoy the comforts of "pre-warmed" beds.

Since it was too late to drive the three girls back to Cuzco, we had no choice but for them to spend the night at the Tiltin' Hilton and depart the following morning. Thus Sam and Bobby and I surrendered our warm beds and spread our sleeping bags in the hallway.

*What next?* I wondered, as I closed my eyes and contemplated the adventure that lay ahead.

Breakfast at the Tiltin' Hilton wasn't at all bad so long as we ignored the kitchen's dish-washing facility, which we discovered—too late—was an open sewer running past the kitchen door. The eggs were fresh and no doubt provided that very morning by a scrawny quintet of hens who now pecked at bugs scurrying across the dining room floor and occasionally hopped on our table, quizzically eyeing our plates as if inquiring about our satisfaction with their products.

While we ate, a steady stream of customers of all ages marched through the room to a narrow counter at the rear and departed with laundry-size bags stuffed with crinkly green leaves. These strange bundles, we would learn, were coca leaves, a staple in lives of the Andean Indians. Days later we were to discover just how important the powerful coca drug is to the existence of life in that region and how it would affect the progress—even success—of our hunt.

During the night Rada's ragtag crew of guides and packers had arrived, bringing with them a half-dozen of the most sad-faced and forsaken examples of horseflesh I'd ever laid eyes on. While we ate, we gazed with increasing apprehension out the dining room window at the packers who were displaying their utter ignorance of horse-packing by piling woefully unbalanced loads on the hapless beasts. When a load became so high or unstable as to cause the animals to wobble and totter, the men simply pulled the ropes tighter, as if strapping a refrigerator to an ATV with bungee cords.

Finally, Sam and I could stand it no longer and, ordering the stricken beasts unloaded, gave a quick demonstration of how to divide the gear into well-balanced, low-profile loads. Despite these efforts to better their lot, the horses looked as baleful as before, and the erstwhile packers simply shrugged and stuffed their cheeks with coca leaves.

Meanwhile, the three lovely señoritas had emerged, nun-like, from the rooms where they had been cloistered for the night and were sipping the tar-like coffee that only South Americans can tolerate. Our plan was to ship them back to Cuzco in one of our two vehicles, leaving us with only one (a situation that was to prove near disastrous during our retreat from the mountain several days later—but that's another story).

Waving the girls out of sight, we at last turned our eyes to the mountain but saw only a low-hanging roof of clouds. Somewhere in those clouds—or above them—we hoped, were the Tyruka, the mysterious four-antlered deer of the Andes that we'd come to find. We would be hunting at higher—much higher—altitudes than any of us had ever hunted before and even as we took our first step to the mountain, a forecast of doom settled itself about us. During the packing I'd noticed only two rifle cases. Rada had told us there was no need to bring our own rifles because he could supply excellent, scoped rifles for all. But now we were beginning the most important hunt of our lives with only two rifles between the three of us.

Though horses and saddles were provided for our journey up the mountain, our final conditioning strategy was to make the three-day trek to base camp on foot. We figured this would better acclimatize us to the increasingly thin atmosphere and make our final assault easier. After months of running with a backpack loaded with bricks and daily stints of underwater swimming, I felt as tough and springy as a grasshopper, and as it turned out, the trail up to the mountain was not the rough, unmarked trail we'd expected.

Within a century of Columbus' discovery of the New World, Spanish conquistadors had penetrated to the tops of the Andean peaks in their relentless quests for gold, enslaved the Indians and laid surprisingly good roads. The path we followed into the mountains, though steep and winding, was paved in places with closely fitted flat rocks that centuries before had borne donkeys carrying gold to the Spanish coffers. The bridges across the rushing mountain

streams were another matter, though, and for the most part seemed to be made of rotted sticks and straw. We usually opted to wade the cold streams rather than risk walking across the flimsy structures.

About noon of the first day we broke out above the fog and found ourselves surrounded by steep, green hillsides dotted here and there with clumps of trees and low brush. The clouds, which were now below us, rolled to the horizon with mountain peaks poking through like islands in a sea of white foam. In the distance a wall of granite soared to the heavens with such majesty that the surrounding mountains seemed to kneel before it. That's where we were going . . .

During a mid-afternoon break, Rada let it be known that we were in spectacled bear country and that we might get a shot at one. A variety of black bear that gets its name from the lighter colored hair around its eyes, the spectacled species hardly rates as one of the world's great trophies, but it was certainly worth getting our rifles ready in case a shot presented itself. But when we uncased the two rifles we were stunned to discover that one of the two "fine" rifles Rada had promised was an European model of humble origin fitted with a scope widely known for its tendency to fail under tedious circumstances. The other rifle had no sights at all!

"No problem," smiled Rada with his easy Latin charm. "I have brought for you a very fine scope." Sure enough, after digging through the packs Rada produced a scope still new in its box.

"That's great," allowed Sam, "so how in the world do we get the damn thing on the rifle?"

"Ah Señor Arnett, I myself know about such things, and I brought for you a set of rings and mounts for the rifle." And with a flourish produced a small box.

Sam read the label on the box, looked at the rifle, then at me, and tossed the box back to Rada. "Wrong damn mounts Paco, these won't fit the rifle."

"But Señor, how can that be?" shrugged Rada, his grin fading, "I bought them at a *mucho famoso* gun store in Lima where I buy all my fine guns; they were very expensive."

By then I'd taken the box from Rada and inspected its contents. The bases were indeed for another model of rifle but there was a chance they might be made to work.

"Look," I explained, "the front base fits but the rear is too high. If we can cut it down, some of it might work."

Sam looked doubtful but Rada's high spirits returned instantly. "No problem, no problem, I myself know it is very easy to fix."

Our campground that night was a more or less flat area beside a thatch-roofed church. It appeared to be abandoned but inside were signs of occasional use so our best guess was that a circuit-riding priest held services there once or twice a year. Also in the church were some distinctly non-Catholic ornaments that

caused us to speculate that the locals hedged their bets by resorting to the sun worship of their Inca ancestors when the priest wasn't around.

While the packers unloaded the weary horses and set up camp, Sam and I set about cutting the scope base down to a workable size. A broken file in Rada's skimpy tool kit proved useless, so we literally ground the base down to a workable height by rubbing it on the coarse stone of the church steps. Perhaps this provided a special blessing because by sundown the scope was fitted and both rifles sighted in.

The second day of our trek to the mountain was good and bad. The Indians in one of the valleys had sent word to Rada beforehand that if we were to hunt in their land, we would have to pay. The price set was enough soccer shirts to outfit two teams. When the villagers saw us coming, they came running and tried on the red, green, and yellow shirts as Rada passed them out.

"What kind of humans are these," I wondered as they posed for my camera, "that run after a soccer ball at fifteen thousand feet?"

The bad news that day was the foretaste of a weather phenomenon that could very likely doom our hunt. Like clockwork, about noon each day, moisture-laden warm air is blown in from the Pacific lowlands. When it collides with the cold mountain air, heavy fog develops, usually lasting until after dark, and the higher the elevation, the denser the fog. During the afternoon the fog billowed so thick we could scarcely see the trail and was still covering us like a tent when we made camp.

That night in the tent I got my first unpleasant taste of what I call the "tomb effect," a claustrophobic sense of being trapped in an airless tomb, brought on by a combination of thin air and the tight confinement of a small tent. Bobby suffered it, too, but Sam snored peacefully.

We arrived at our base camp, a squat, stone-walled village of thatch-roofed huts with a few dozen people, around mid-afternoon on the third day. We found the villagers engaged in a bacchanalia known as the festival of the animals. As it turned out, we were unwelcome guests at one of the most important ceremonies of the year, in which they honor their beloved llamas that provide them with warm clothing, food, and transportation. During the festival their custom is to get drunk on a local brew, herd a bunch of the better-looking llamas into a stone corral, and decorate them with bright ribbons. Then they get into the corrals with the llamas and dance a strange jig. Which pretty much explains why they weren't too happy to have us witness their ritual.

This unfriendly situation was made worse when the batteries of their boom box gave out, rendering them without dance music. Their appeals to Rada for fresh batteries were refused with the reasoning that without music, the festival would end sooner and the village men would sober up and be able to guide us the next day. This proved a bad call because even without batteries there was still plenty of the mean stuff to drink, and as the afternoon drifted into evening, the glares of the normally friendly villagers sliced at us with hostility. Their only friendly concession was to allow us to pitch our tents inside the protective stone walls of a corral that was deeply layered with llama manure. I'd been in favor of making camp a distance from the village but that could be dangerous, even deadly, Rada informed me, because in the night, sub-freezing winds roar down from the peaks at over 50 miles per hour. Without the protection of the stone corral walls, our tents would likely be swept away.

The first day of actual hunting began with more than the normal amount of first day confusion. Rada had planned on hiring the local Indians as guides but they were hung over and only a couple showed, which meant that we mainly depended on Rada's regular crew, who had no more idea of where to look for Tyruka than we three *Yankis*. But by then we were pretty much accustomed to Rada's plans going awry and faced the day's inevitable disasters with cheerful resignation and even subdued optimism. At last, we were going hunting.

Rada had to call it quits at the base camp because he smokes and was already having trouble breathing. Sam's pocket altimeter read slightly over 15,000 feet and we anticipated climbing another 3,000 to 5,000. Maps of the area showed peaks well over 20,000 feet. Now it was time to ride the tough little horses.

The mountain that rose almost perpendicular behind the village more or less leveled out on top and that's where we hoped to find the four-antlered deer. We were told the back side of the mountain was easier to climb than the steep face before us, but getting there was a half-day's hike. That left us no choice but to take the faster but steeper frontal route. Amazingly, the little short-legged horses were as steady and sure-footed as any mule I've ever ridden. Mine, which I nicknamed Pegasus after the winged steed of Greek mythology, considered each step with care and wisely avoided loose gravel.

Even more amazing were our Indian guides and packers. Bred for survival at high altitude, the men were seldom much over five feet tall, with short, thick climber's legs and disproportionately huge chests for lungs that gleaned every available atom of oxygen from the thin air. Not once did I see them breathe hard, even when I was gasping for breath, and they seemed to have no interest whatsoever in resting, a condition no doubt brought on by their ever-present cud of coca leaf.

When the going got especially tough, they'd take a softball-size lump of some chalky looking stuff from the folds of their llama wool ponchos and slice off a nibble. This unappealing substance turned out to be made of ashes mixed with water and kneaded into a solid chunk for easy carrying. As explained to me later, the ashes react with the coca drug to give an extra-powerful energy boost. Whenever I saw the guides fortifying themselves with the supercharger ash ball, I knew the climbing was going to be extra tough.

At about 18,000 feet the mountain rounded off into a relatively flat plain where dry, stubby grass squeezed up between dark-tinted rocks. The scenery was a spectacular as any on earth, with snow-covered peaks rising beyond more peaks in every direction like an endless ocean of mountains seen from outer space. From some of the ledges I peeked over, the earth plunged so steeply that one false step would have meant a free-fall of thousands of feet. Seen from almost directly above, our blue tent glittered in the maze of stone walls like a tiny sapphire caught in a spider's web.

The first hour or so on top of the mountain was spent enjoying the view and getting the lay of the territory. Once, when I'd dismounted Pegasus to glass some distant territory, one of the guides touched my arm and pointed into the far distance where his companions were intently gazing. I saw nothing and when I indicated that I didn't comprehend, he spread his arms gracefully and turned in a slow circle. Thus instructed, I realized they were seeing the Andean condor, but even with binoculars I could never get a sighting of the great soaring bird. The mountain to which the guide pointed was easily 50 miles away and I've often wondered since if the condor was large enough, the air was clear enough, and their eyes sharp enough for them to have seen it so far away.

Though the mountain seemed as unlivable as the moon, I spotted enough small animal droppings to convince me that something lived there, but the lack of cover and deer sign told me that this was the wrong place to hunt Tyruka.

If they behaved like other deer, they'd be in mountain pockets offering more cover and protection and we'd have to dig them out. Like hunting mule deer in the Rockies, this would be a matter of riding the rims and searching out each ravine and cul-de-sac, a not unpleasant prospect because at every turn there was a dazzling panorama of mountains and clouds.

Clouds! The day had begun bright and clear but at midday, as we lunched on cold, half-baked potatoes, a fog gathered around us and within minutes was so thick that the sun disappeared and with it all sense of direction. If we got lost in the fog, we'd have to spend the night on the freezing mountain and the alarm on the faces of the two guides showed they knew it as well as I did. Luckily, we were able to find the way we'd come up the mountain and the sure-footed Pegasus carried me back to camp, with Sam and Bobby getting there at the same time. We'd all had a scare trying to get off the mountain in the thick, disorienting fog and agreed that on following days we'd stay closer. At least we'd be lost together.

That evening as we sat around a stinking fire (llama manure was the only fuel, but there was plenty in the corral), a tiny woman brought us a basket of potatoes scarcely bigger than marbles. She was dressed in her finest, including a derby-shaped Indian hat with llama wool ear-flaps dangling about her face. Apparently the potatoes were a peace offering. Spanish was no more known to her than English but one of Rada's guides knew some of the Indian dialect, and through a two-way interpretation, punctuated by sign language from all, we learned that she had two sons who would go with us on the morrow. During the discourse she couldn't take her eyes off Bobby, who was probably the tallest human she'd even seen, and constantly shoved the basket of potatoes in his direction and batted her eyes at him with a shy, coca-leaf-stained smile. The potatoes had apparently been baked in llama manure and after cracking away the filthy shell, there was scarcely a bite left, but the gift was well intended and so for the next day we held high hopes. But as I crawled into my sleeping bag, the "tomb effect" overcame me and I noticed that rather than becoming more acclimated to the sparse atmosphere, breathing was becoming more difficult.

The next day was not what we'd hoped for. The two Indian guides seemed to have no interest in hunting the four-antlered deer, and instead led us to a valley where there was an enormous rockslide. Hopping about the rocks were marmot-sized animals that looked like rabbits with stubby ears and long, fuzzy tails. The Indians indicated they wanted us to shoot the animals and when we'd shot a couple they were eagerly retrieved. Closer inspection showed the critters to have a dense, chinchilla-like fur, which we learned was prized for its warmth and used to insulate shoes. The Indians indicated they wanted us to shoot more of the little fur-bearers, but after bagging one or two more we indicated that we'd come to shoot deer, not foot-warmers. This led to an impasse, but it didn't matter because by then fog was thickening and it was time to get off the mountain.

Breathing was harder now and increasingly painful; sucking in the dry air had made my throat raw. During the day I'd walked too fast for only a brief minute and had become so breathless that I had to lie down until I could get my wind back. Sam and Bobby were having similar experiences but more alarming was the change in our mental attitude. One symptom was an increasing feeling of disinterest in what we were doing. Another was a loss of appetite. On our trek into the mountains, we'd had hearty appetites, but now eating seemed such a chore that we devised an easy-to-drink, energy-rich cocktail of condensed milk and chocolate.

The third day of our hunt for the Tyruka began in disappointment, then teased us with a glimmer of hope only to end in despair. Our Andean guides didn't return, leaving us to make do with Rada's guides—who were convinced there were no deer to be found and sucked their coca leaves with glassy-eyed indifference. By now, though, Sam and Bobby and I pretty well knew the local geography and began searching out likely looking spots the same way we hunted deer back in the states. This resulted in our first positive deer sign and it was fresh! It was in a grassy basin on the sunny, lee side of a steep crest and the signs indicated that several deer had been feeding there. If we stayed below the crest on the high side of the basin, we could get within easy rifle range without being spotted. But would the deer return the next day? Time was running out.

Despite my exhaustion, I was terrified of sleep. The act of breathing required such conscious effort that I feared an unguarded sleep would be never-ending. I tried to tell myself that it was a foolish fear, but simple reasoning was also a labor. That day we'd begun checking our decision-making ability with simple riddles and memory tests. We realized that edema was robbing our lungs of their efficiency and making breathing increasingly difficult. It would kill us unless we got off the mountain. How much longer could we endure? And when our lives became critically imperiled, would we know it—or care? One more day we decided, then Tyruka or not, we'd go.

On that last day, we were on the mountain just after dawn and left our horses on the offside of the crest that rimmed the basin where we'd seen deer sign the day before. On previous days we'd taken turns with the two rifles and it was my turn to be without, meaning that there was probably no chance I'd get a shot, even if the deer were there. But I had my camera with telephoto lens and even a picture of the fabled deer would be a rare trophy.

The higher side of the rim offered a better view of the basin and better prospects for a clear shot, so it was quickly decided that Bobby and Sam would get the best shooting positions while I kept a lookout on the lower side where the basin curved out of their sight. If I spotted anything, I'd send one of the guides for them and they'd do the same for me.

With my breath coming in gasps, I crawled the last few yards up to the crest and peered into the basin. Nothing! "But they have to be here," I told myself, searching every rock and blade of grass with my binoculars. "They've got to be here."

The sun climbed higher and went about its business of warming the earth, but no deer came. *Was there such a thing as a four-antlered deer or was it only a hoax? Had we been chasing a myth?* The fog came again, sweeping by me in wisps and filling the basin like dingy water. Soon it would be time to leave and I had begun to pack my camera when a small stone came rolling from above. It had been thrown by one of the guides, who was standing about 50 yards above me, waving frantically, and pointing toward a part of the basin I could not see. They were there!

I tried to run but couldn't; it was too far and too steep. I would run a few steps and fall to my knees, desperately sucking air into my lungs, then rise and fall again. The fog, the damn fog, it was getting thicker, blotting out the man who was now only a few steps away. Would I ever see the deer? Damn the fog, damn it all to hell!

As I lay there panting for air and cursing our luck, the fog suddenly brightened and for a wisp of a moment, I could see into the basin. They were there! *Tyruka,* the mysterious four-antlered deer of the Andes really existed!! Frantically, I grabbed my camera and focused on their outlines, but even as I pressed the shutter button the fog was closing again, cloaking the forms in dense gray mist.

From somewhere higher on the crest, two rifle shots echoed, too close together to have come from one rifle. Then there was the long, high pitched *"WHOOEEEEEE"* of a Texas yell, like a cowboy herding longhorns, followed by an answering exultation from farther away. They had done it!

How the legend of the four-antlered deer began is shrouded in time, but is no doubt due to their peculiar antler formation of two long points forking from the base.

Seen even from fairly close, the deer do indeed appear to wear two sets of antlers. Would I go to that high place and hunt them again? Probably, for what is life without adventure—what is success without risk?

*— Postscript —*

Not long after our return to the U.S., young Bobby Fleiger died from sudden heart failure. In his diary of our hunt, read posthumously, he describes heart attack-like symptoms he suffered in the high camp. There was much suffering there, and he never mentioned his added pain.

He was a wonderful hunting companion.

*" . . . the vast form became motionless, and then it was very quiet. I heard no bird sounds or whispers in the trees, as if all of nature was made breathless at what it had witnessed. "*

# Chapter 6

# It's Elephants

herever I go, someone always asks me to name my favorite type of hunting. It's a fair question and deserves an honest answer. But usually I'm forthcoming with only a noncommittal, "Whatever I happen to be hunting at the time" and let it go at that. The reason I'm evasive is because even a hint of my true hunting passion invariably provokes shocked outrage or a cascade of questions.

That's because my true hunting love is elephants!

*African* elephants.

People who don't know anything about elephants can't understand why I'd want to hunt them, because the only elephants they've ever seen are the trained pachyderms that munch peanuts and trot around circus rings with pretty girls astride their necks. Those are *Asian,* or Indian, elephants. They can be recognized by their small size, stubby ivory, and stunted ears that dangle from their heads like limp rags.

The African elephant is another beast entirely, half again or even twice as big as the Indian variety. They weigh up to five tons, or even more, and may stand over ten feet at the shoulder. They have giant ears that extend like barn doors when they want to exhibit an awesome temper or merely to announce their magnificent presence. No wild creature that walks the earth is as fascinating, or as intelligent—or as dangerous.

No one who has hunted elephants is ever the same again; it changes their lives, and for many it becomes a passion. Legendary ivory hunters like Selous and Bell lived that passion. Taking the ivory, however, was only how they made their living; like a compulsive gambler, good—or lucky—enough to make a living in the casino, winning isn't what matters. Their passion was doing it.

If this were the age when herds of elephant freely roamed the African continent, I would chuck it all and go there forever. Hunting elephants is in my blood, and they are in my dreams.

Unlike the ivory hunters of legend, I cannot count my elephants by the hundreds or weigh my ivory by the hundredweight. But for adventure I'll match anyone—beginning with a cow that tried to grind my bones into the red dust of Africa on my very first safari.

We'd picked up the tracks of a good-sized herd that appeared to be meandering through the broken forest bordering the vast Okavango swamp. My guide, the late Pat Hepburn, and I, following a pair of his trackers, had made our way close enough to hear them ripping the branches of trees when suddenly all hell broke loose. There was a great thundering of earth, crashing of brush, and the shrill trumpeting of an elephant stampede, but we knew we weren't close enough to have spooked them.

Running hard to keep up, we heard more trumpeting and back and forth crashing as if the herd was running in circles, then they were suddenly quiet and we slowed our pace, hoping to sneak close enough for a look. I scrambled up a towering termite mound, hoping to see over the brush, and just as I got on top, a smallish elephant broke through the trees and came charging directly at us!

My first reaction was that it was only a young bull like those I'd seen on previous days, showing off with adolescent threats before turning and scurrying away. If I'd been more experienced, I'd have known that this beast meant deadly business, because instead of flaring its ears in the typical threatening pose, this one's ears were laid back flat. Any lingering misconceptions I may have had vanished when the onrushing animal crashed through a rotted tree trunk and exploded it into flying fragments. The damn thing meant to destroy us, just as it had the tree.

Though I'd had a better view of the charging elephant than Hepburn, he was quicker to figure out what was happening, and when I jumped from the termite mound, he was yelling and waving his arms at the animal, trying to make it understand what we were. In a final desperate attempt he fired a shot over its head, but to no avail. The second bullet from Pat's rifle hit high in the elephant's forehead, smacking a puff of dust and rocking its head back like a battering ram. The elephant hesitated and for an instant I thought it would turn, but then it regained momentum and there was no doubt it would kill us or die.

The world switched to slow motion then, and when I raised my rifle, the crosshairs seemed to casually wander across the elephant's wide forehead, probing for a route to its brain. It seems so uncomplicated, I later remembered thinking, the power of a trigger finger challenging the might of the elephant, as if I were only a bystander watching the duel from a safe sideline.

Then the vast form became motionless, and then it was very quiet. I heard no bird sounds or whispers in the trees, as if all of nature was made breathless at what it had witnessed. Neither Pat nor I spoke for a long while. What does one say an arm's length from crushing death?

*But why did it happen?*

This was answered minutes later when our trackers discovered the remains of a stillborn calf the cow had been guarding. The crashing stampede we'd heard earlier was the cow chasing other elephants away from the dead calf. We'd come between her and the calf, and her rage was the most powerful protective instinct in all of nature.

That episode was a turning point in my hunting career. Or perhaps it was the real beginning. Like hundreds of African hunters before me, I was entranced by elephants and wanted to learn everything about them, including 20th century ivory hunters such as the legendary John Hunter, Bror Blixen, the husband of *Out Of Africa* author Karen Blixen, and her doomed lover Denys Finch-Hatton.

I even found an elephant's skull and sawed it in half, so I'd know for sure the brain's location. Later, I would follow herds of elephants using the crosshairs of my rifle scope like a surveyor's transit to determine the straightest route to their brain from any position. I read books and found diagrams about where to hit an elephant, but most were not very helpful because they showed only a frontal shot.

The fact of the matter is that today, relatively few elephants are killed by frontal shots. Aside from my first experience, the others I've taken were with side shots to the brain, aiming at a crease just below the ear opening.

Despite romantic lore, frontal shots usually aren't a practical proposition in normal hunting circumstances, because the last place you want to be is in front of a wild elephant. Except when they shade up during the day, elephants are usually moving and the trick is to move up behind them and find a shootable position from the side. Every elephant I've taken with a shot to the side of the brain fell toward the bullet. Other hunters tell me they've had the same experience.

Most elephants bagged by sport hunters are killed by heart-lung shots. Many professional hunters encourage their clients to take heart shots, for a number of reasons, beginning with the obvious fact that the heart is a much bigger target than the brain. Also, in situations where the herd is milling around, a heart shot may be a wise choice because the stricken elephant almost invariably takes off in a dead run, followed by its companions. Shot in the brain, the elephant typically thunders to the ground, sending its buddies running off in screaming, panicky circles. Truth is, you're just as dead when trampled by accident as when they do it on purpose. More about this later.

Elephant rifles and cartridges are the stuff of books and legend. In few endeavors have gunmakers labored more magnificently than in the building of huge-bore double rifles for the elephant trade. Heft one to your shoulder and your imagination takes the fast lane. You see yourself firing a right and then a left, levering open the barrels, hearing the pinging ejection of jigger-sized brass cases and inhaling the exotic incense of cordite corkscrewing up from the twin chambers.

Back in the 1950s a Holland & Holland Modele DeLuxe, then their Best grade rifle, sold for about $1,350 and a Best quality Rigby went for a bit less. That was pretty pricey in those days, but still a sound investment for someone wanting to get into the elephant-hunting business. Today, a Best British double will set you back upwards of $75,000, which means they've become the playthings of tycoons and nabobs and explains why many of the old African professional hunters have long since cashed in their doubles and opted for relatively inexpensive bolt rifles. Four out of every five PHs I've hunted with carry only bolt rifles, and the few I've hunted with who own doubles uncase them only for special occasions.

The only time I've hunted with a double rifle was with a Grant & Lang that belonged to my PH. I accidentally lost one of the hard to find .500/465 Nitro Express cartridges and we spent half a day backtracking. After that, I decided it wasn't worth the bother and went back to using my bolt rifle.

The magical term "Nitro Express" applies to cartridges developed for smokeless or "nitro" powder. Earlier cartridges made for elephants were loaded with black powder, many of which are now known as BP Express calibers. Since black powder produced only moderate velocities, usually in the 1500-1800 feet-per-second range, energy was developed by using heavy, large diameter bullets. This practice continued even after the advent of nitro powders that generated velocities over 2000 feet-per-second and striking energies measured in the tons.

Until recently, the most powerful cartridge for double-barreled rifles was the fabled .600 Nitro Express, which delivered a thumb-sized 900 grain slug at nearly four tons of muzzle energy. Then H&H brought forth a .700 Nitro of even greater power. I fired one of these at their London test sites and the best way I can explain the experience is that one shot definitely gets you out of the mood for a fast follow-up shot, especially at over $100 per pop. Yet I'm told that several rifles in this caliber have been ordered, and there's even rumor of an .800 Nitro. I'll give that one a pass.

Before the invention of breech-loading rifles, the typical elephant gun was a massive muzzleloading affair, hurling hunks of lead nearing the size of golf balls. Back in the 1970s I went on an all black powder safari with Turner Kirkland, the founder of Dixie Gun Works, which was the world center of black-powder firearms and accessories.

Turner had a huge double-barreled muzzleloader that had been made in Capetown, South Africa, for a 19th century elephant hunter. The round, cast-lead balls weighed upwards of a quarter-pound apiece, and when he test-fired it at our safari camp, the bullet felled a good-sized tree, a sight that caused considerable wide-eyed admiration among the native onlookers, who then pronounced the gun to possess great magic.

Samuel Baker, the famed Nile explorer, fancied guns of gigantic caliber, and in his journals he describes steadying the barrels of his rifle on the shoulder of a porter for a long shot. The muzzle jump was so severe that it ripped off the porter's ear.

When Winchester announced their .458 Magnum in early 1956, it effectively ended the reign of the great British Nitro calibers. Though the .375 H&H had done good service for generations past, it had never gained real acceptance as a serious elephant round. The .458 however, loaded with a 500-grain full patch .45 caliber bullet and having over 5,000 pounds of muzzle energy, equaled or bettered the power and penetration of many of the traditional elephant cartridges. Better yet, it was inexpensive and easily available.

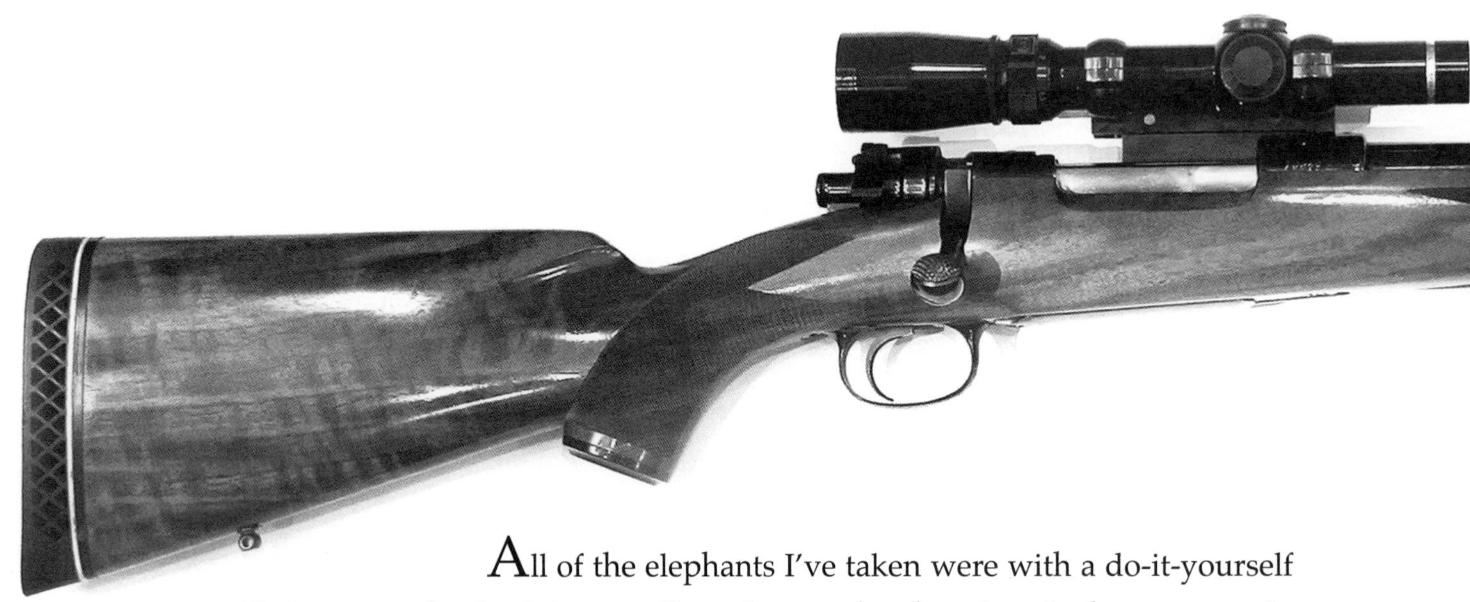

All of the elephants I've taken were with a do-it-yourself rifle I put together back in my college days—when hunting elephants was only a dream—and .458 Win. Mag. ammo I handloaded with 500-grain Hornady steel-jacketed bullets. The reason for using steel jacket solids is so the bullet will penetrate several inches of an elephant's thick, honeycombed skull without deforming or coming apart.

African lore is filled with stories of hunters being trampled to death because their bullets failed. Most of the old hunters also have stories of elephants they thought were down for good, but then got up and ran away. That's why I've always followed the rule of putting a safety shot into the back of the head after the animal is down. I also pay the skinners and ivory choppers a bonus if they recover the bullet. Usually the steel-jacketed bullets are bent or flattened, which gives you some idea of how tough an elephant's skull is, but one recovered bullet was so perfect that I've reloaded it for another elephant! Imagine that.

The only time I've thought a .458 wasn't enough gun was when I was in the rainforests of what was then the Central African Empire. We were hunting bongo in brush so dense that it looked like a green wall when one of the trackers stopped suddenly and pointed ahead. At first I couldn't see what he was pointing at, then I made out an incredibly long, curving form and a dull gleaming eye. It was ivory, the biggest tusk I've ever seen on foot! Well over a hundred pounds and beautifully curved.

The vegetation was so dense that I couldn't see the other tusk (one-tusked

elephants are not uncommon) or any other part of the body. Since we weren't hunting elephants, I didn't have a license, but right then I vowed I'd be back the following year to hunt that giant tusker. Because of the density of the vegetation, I figured I'd better be prepared to shoot from any angle so when I got home I began plans for building a short-barreled .460 Wby. Mag., which I had loaded with a 600-grain bullet that would drive through an elephant from any angle.

While the rifle was in the works, I learned that a woman had bagged a fantastic 150-pounder in the CAE, not far from where I had been a few months earlier. Figuring it was probably the one I'd seen, I never went back.

People who have never seen an elephant in the wild believe that since they're so big, hunting them is like shooting billboards along a highway. Truth is, they can be as elusive as a whitetail deer when they want to be and ten times as canny.

Once, when I was following a trio of old bulls through miles of scrub mopane, they ambled into a patch of taller trees that couldn't have been more than 50 acres in size. Thinking this was a chance to get close enough for a better look at their ivory and possibly a shot, we pussyfooted into the trees after them. But we couldn't find them! It's still a mystery how three elephants could elude two sharp-eyed African trackers, a professional hunter, and me in a patch of trees no bigger than a woodlot, but we never laid eyes on them again.

Another time I was hidden in some heavy cover along a dusty game trail when a herd of elephants came marching by almost within arm's reach. Despite their size, the only sound I heard was the soft puff-puff-puff of their feet on the trail as they glided by like ghostly galleons.

My favorite hunting technique is moving with a herd of elephants as they browse through scattered trees and scrub. They move a lot faster than you think and you have to hurry to keep up. My best memories are of the times when the wind and terrain were such that I was able to get inside the herd and single out good bulls. This can be a chancy proposition, because once you get inside a big herd of elephants, you also have to figure how to get out without being detected. One false move and a peacefully grazing herd can instantly become an earth-shaking stampede. They don't run in any particular direction, and as I said earlier, you're just as flat when they run over you by accident.

On a hunt in northern Botswana, my partner and I took a couple of pretty nice bulls but couldn't get rid of the rest of the herd, which numbered about 20 animals. The huge beasts were in a screaming panic and running in circles. When they'd run our way we'd fire a few shots over their heads to make them turn and run in another direction. Then they would turn and charge our way, and we'd fire another barrage, a tense situation that repeated itself three or four times before they finally got the idea and disappeared.

One question always raised by non-hunters is what happens to all that meat? Does it go to waste?

That morning we had driven past a ragtag army detachment on field maneuvers, so after extracting the ivory, we drove back by their camp to invite them to help themselves to the meat, which was less than a half-mile away. The campfires were burning and food was bubbling in the pots but nowhere was a soldier to be found. My guess was that they had heard all our shooting and figured there had been a revolution or invasion, a situation they apparently wanted no part of.

The fact is that even when you think you're a thousand miles from the nearest soul, there are always some protein-starved natives nearby. When an elephant goes down, they seem to appear from nowhere, coming by the dozens and with baskets to carry away the rich meat. So much free food puts them in a festive mood, and I've seen them slice an elephant's belly open and crawl inside to carve away the much-treasured fat, yelling to those outside to be careful where they plunge their long knives.Usually, by the time ivory has been removed from the skull, which generally takes about two hours, the rest of the carcass, including the trunk (a delicacy) will be stripped and the natives on their way back to the villages for a night of celebration and feasting.

Will I hunt elephants again? *Sure.* Despite a ban on hunting them in most African countries, elephants can be their own worst enemy and gradually overpopulate their range. When I was on return safari to Botswana in 1993, I hunted plains game in areas where I'd pursued elephants in the 1970s. There had been no elephant hunting for a dozen years, and I saw bigger herds than ever. The population had grown so that endless miles of vegetation were stripped of every edible leaf, and the few passable roads had been destroyed by thousands of pounding feet. I also saw some great ivory, some going over a hundred

pounds, and learned that the game department had realized that controlled sport-hunting was the only way the magnificent animals could be saved from themselves. Everyone benefits, especially the human population, because the price of an elephant license will now pay for a desperately needed schoolroom, or a teacher's salary for a year.

Yes, I'll go back for elephant.

It's in my blood, and they won't leave my dreams.

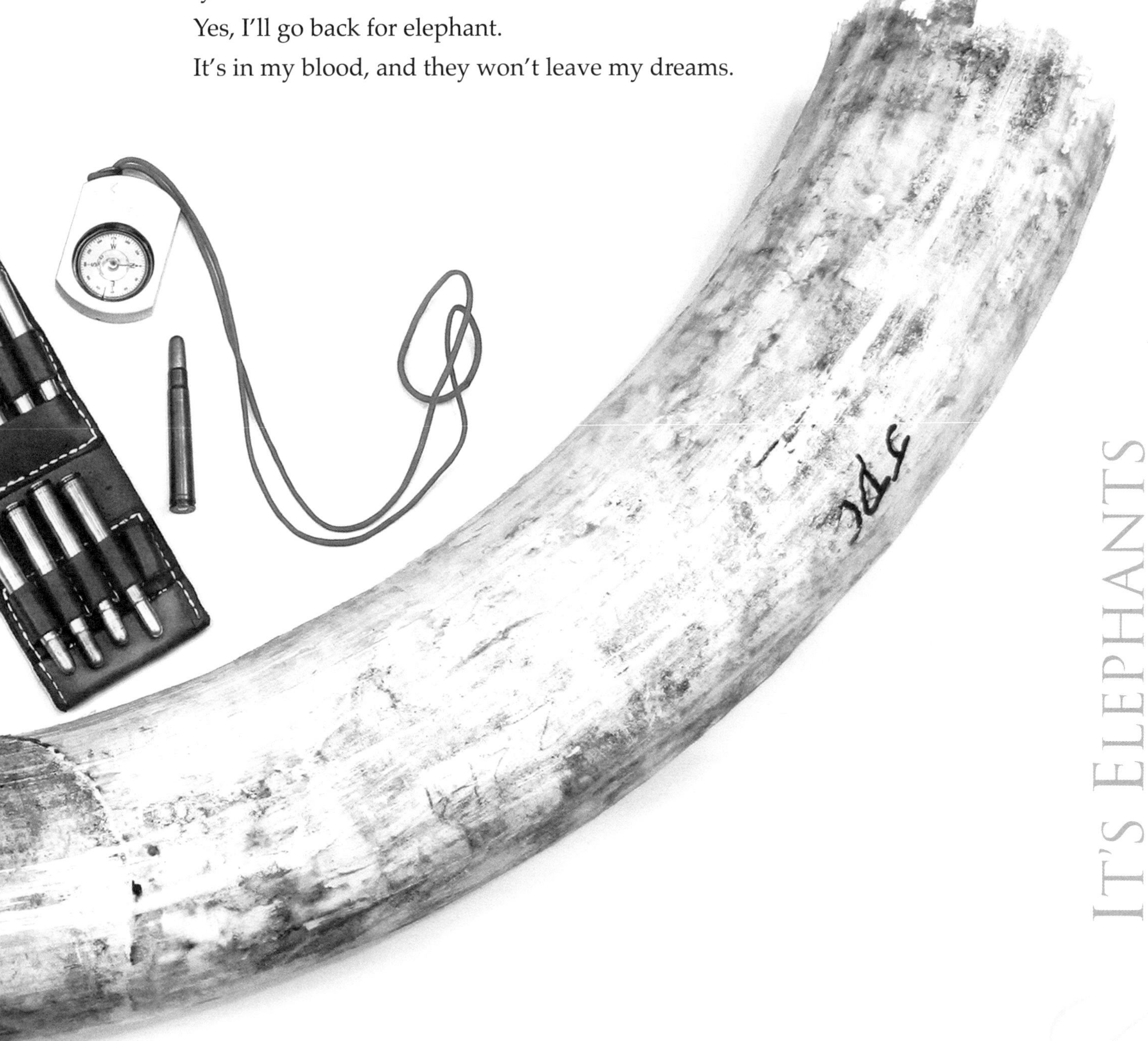

*"The whole problem, of course, was the huge crocodile, but there was no possibility of getting it out of the boat in the time we had left, so even in death it was taking a terrible toll."*

# CHAPTER 7

# THE EYES OF DEATH

ooking back, it's hard to remember just when we realized we might have a problem—probably when the creature opened its eye. But there's no question about when concern became panic, because that's when it opened its horrible mouth and lunged at me.

I'll never get over that mouth, with its row of flesh-tearing spikes, dripping blood, and the smell of rotted death when it roared. And another thing is for sure: If I had known the monster wasn't dead, I'd never have put my hand on its slime-caked hide or put my foot in its mouth.

It was June of 1984, wintertime south of the Equator, and I was on safari in Zimbabwe, the game-rich African nation once known as Rhodesia. My hunting pal was Jack Atcheson, the famed North American outfitter who books most of my hunts, and our professional hunter was the legendary Mike Rowbotham, now moved from Kenya to Zimbabwe and operating Hunter's Tracks PVT, one of the country's leading safari outfitters.

Our quest was bigger-than-average trophies, and during the preceding few weeks Atcheson and I had been hunting in South Africa where we'd bagged a half-dozen contenders for the Rowland Ward Record Book, including the shy, bush-dwelling nyala antelope.

Now we were after leopard, kudu, and reedbuck, which tend to grow especially big in northern Zimbabwe. Already I'd killed a better-than-good Cape buffalo, which had been quartered and hung for leopard bait. It sometimes takes a few days for meat to get ripe enough to appeal to leopards, so we were passing the days looking for the odd trophy or cruising Lake Kariba's shores, watching herds of elephant that came to drink and socialize.

The horror story had begun a week earlier when we headed our 16-foot fiberglass inboard-outboard runabout into the mouth of the Senkwi River and quietly cruised upstream. The Senkwi has another name, a long African name that I can neither spell nor pronounce, but when translated it tells a story of the fearsome god that dwells in a land where there is no sun and whose slobber is filled with such deadly creatures that everything it touches is killed and devoured. The legend goes on to explain how the god's deadly drool gushes out of the earth and flows from a mountain, spreading death across the land, until it meets and is conquered by the benevolent god of the Zambezi.

The river of death no longer flows into the mighty Zambezi, but into Lake Kariba, but the putrid waters that spill into the manmade sea are still filled with the devil's own creatures.

Beyond the first bend in the river of death, the world transforms itself from the present into the prehistoric. Trees do not bloom or bear leaves, having been raped by a blight that twisted them into pedestals for sulking vultures and carrion-eating water birds. Great shaggy nests of dead grass, as large as a native hut, sag from the gnarled tree limbs, and long-beaked birds cry out with cackling wails, lamenting the drabness of their plumage.

Little vegetation grew along the river; mostly the banks were bare earth and mud, dotted with shapeless stones and rimmed with a rock wall, all blending into a brown landscape. There was no game to be seen, but at one time or another wild animals had been there, for scattered along the shoreline we found skulls and other bones, as if a recent flood had cleansed the river's depths of its dead.

Such a place demands silence and little was said as we slowly cruised upstream. Oomo and Jason, the two black Africans who normally smiled and talked to each other continuously, were silent and watchful, clearly apprehensive but without knowing why—yet. Neither of them lived in the area and had not heard the legend of the river. Soon though, each would have his own story of the river to tell his grandchildren, and before the safari ended, both would tell me they would never travel up the river again.

As we rounded each bend, there would be a splash a few hundred yards ahead and a quiet ripple would radiate from the shoreline.

"Crocs," Rowbotham would say, his voice tight, "murderous bastards."

I'd seen crocs before, in Sudan's Nile swamps, in French Equatorial Africa, and once in Botswana where I'd witnessed an ear-shattering battle between a croc and a baboon. The baboon's troop-mates had viciously attacked the crocodile, but the hard-scaled reptile never loosened its jaw-lock on the unfortunate primate. It simply slid beneath the water and that was the end.

The crocodiles I'd seen before had never impressed me as being especially wild, but these crocs were so wary that there was little chance of getting a good look at one before it slid into the water and disappeared.

"Are they always this wild?" I asked Rowbotham.

"Oh yes," he answered, "they're bloody spooky buggers . . . tough to get a shot at one. They're more wary than any game animal."

That did it; until then I had never had any overwhelming desire to hunt crocodiles, but learning now that they were hard to bag presented an irresistible challenge.

"Mike, I've got to get a croc," I announced.

Rowbotham raised his eyebrow for a long moment, then gazed into the deathly green as if silently struggling with an unseen evil. Then the cloud passed from his face and he grinned with his characteristic good humor.

"Okay Jim, we'll get one."

Upstream a silent form stirred the water's surface for an instant and then disappeared, radiating an arc of ripples across the slowly moving current.

The next day the weather turned cool and remained so for several days, spoiling our chances of finding a crocodile in a shootable position. More at home in the water than on land, they mainly come ashore to bask in the sun. But now with the sun hidden by clouds and the air cooler than normal, they cradled themselves in the warmth of the sluggish African water.

Several times that week we saw crocs in the water, as many as a dozen at a time, their snouts and eyes barely breaking the surface, looking like floating slabs of rotten wood. A few times I was only a few feet from the creatures, and a killing shot through the eye and into the brain would have been simple. But shooting a croc in the water is usually a waste, because it will sink immediately,

Jim Carmichel with two of the world's most desirable game animals, the elusive bongo and the great African lion.

The moment of impact. Dust flies from the top of the old elephant's head as the big .458 solid bullet connects. The author (foreground, in shadow) had handed his camera to his professional hunter with instructions to snap the shutter as soon as he heard the report of the rifle.

Carmichel has hunted a wide array of game in Africa, including eland (above left), and on the opposite page (clockwise from top), greater kudu, Cape buffalo, red Cape hartebeest, waterbuck, sable, and gemsbok.

Outdoor Life

High in the Andes, where the author faced one of his most perilous challenges to survive while hunting the Tyruka, Peru's fabled four-antlered deer.

Carmichel's legendary passion for guns and hunting has led him to some of the most spectacular places on earth, from Persia for ibex and Armenian sheep, to New Zealand for tahr and chamois, and the Andes for the mythic Tyruka.

Carmichel's affinity for wingshooting has led him from the Himalayas for snipe in the wetlands of Kashmir, to the classic dove and bobwhite quail fields of the American South, to the pigeons roosting along the eaves of the Jonesboro Courthouse.

COURT HOUSE

Regardless of where his travels may take him, the author is always a fine dinner companion.

Glassing the Persian high country for ibex.

Ever the firearms connoisseur, Carmichel was fascinated by this 18th Century cannon from the time of Katherine the Great, just outside the Kremlin in Moscow.

and who wants to go diving for a crocodile in their watery haunts.

Once while we were watching a group of crocs, an unsuspecting coot landed in their midst and swam toward one of the motionless snouts. What happened next is as difficult to describe as the speed with which darkness fills a room when the light is switched off. The coot was there, the water exploded and boiled for an instant, and then there was nothing but a gentle whirlpool to mark the transformation of life into death.

Despite their twin rows of sharp, interlocking teeth, each as long and as thick as a man's thumb, crocodiles do not kill by biting or chewing their victims. The teeth are only a means of holding the victim while they kill it with quick, snapping rotations, breaking bones, and ripping flesh before chunking the dead or near-dead creature down its gullet. They don't chew their food and don't need to, relying on powerful gastric juices to finish the meal.

A more efficient and remorseless killing machine does not exist in all of nature. So precisely honed are their killing equipment, techniques, and instincts that millions of years have wrought no evolutionary improvements to *Crocodilia*. They are as they were at the dawn of creation, as patient, as watchful, as swift and as utterly incapable of remorse or pity.

By comparison, even such a killer of legend as the great white shark is a second-class performer. Both the crocodile and the great white kill without thinking, but the croc is infinitely more efficient because it *thinks* about killing, using practiced stealth to catch its victims. And it can do it on land as well as in the water, sprinting fast enough to grab even antelope.

The days following our trip up the Senkwi River remained cool and overcast, so there was little use in hunting crocs. Morning and evening we'd check our leopard baits, but our only trophy was a tremendous kudu bull Atcheson shot after a long and determined stalk.

After nearly a week of slow hunting, dawn broke clear with a promise of a warm day. While checking a leopard bait near the top of a rock ledge, we spotted a huge kudu bull on the thickly brushed plain below and after a nerve-rasping game of hide and seek, I finally got a shot. It was my biggest kudu ever, putting not only myself but the whole camp in a festive mood.

By noon the unclouded sun had shoved the temperature into the 70s, making the day right for crocodile hunting.

"How about it, Mike," I asked over lunch, "today's my lucky day. Let's go back up that weird river and try to bust one of those crocs."

For a moment Mike considered the possibilities, serious-faced, the way he looked the day we were on the river. Then with a grin, he shrugged off whatever was bothering him and said it was a great day to kill a croc.

Knowing from past experience that it was useless to try approaching a sunning crocodile by boat, we worked out a simple plan. Leaving Jason downstream with the boat, the rest of us would skirt the river on foot. By staying hidden behind the standing snags and logs that lay along the river's bank, we hoped to stalk within shooting distance.

The plan worked perfectly. After a mile or so of skirting the river, we topped a low hill and found ourselves looking down on a marshy floodplain. At first the area seemed to be void of life, but after a quick look Mike crouched behind the rotted shell of a tree and motioned all of us to do likewise. Cautiously peering from behind a stump and surveying the area with binoculars, I spotted a sleeping croc, then another and another. Lying along the opposite bank, there must have been a dozen or more. They were hard to see because their sun-dried hides blended perfectly with the black river mud. Their hides were not rich and glossy like a crocodile handbag, but dull and caked with mud and slimy moss. Hideously ugly yet possessing a hypnotic quality that made it difficult not to look at them. One can easily become transfixed by their evil majesty.

Some professional hunters become so obsessed by hunting crocodiles that they abandon their families, friends, and businesses for months at a time. If a man must fight his inner demons, no symbol is more fitting than the crocodile.

Crawling to the stump where I was hiding, Mike whispered his assessment of the situation. "If we all try to get closer, one of the bloody bastards will spot us and spook the whole lot. Jack and I will stay here while you try to make your way close enough for a shot. Take your time and stay low. And remember, you've got to bust the bugger's brain with the first shot or it will be in the water in a flash."

The usual advice for bullet placement on a crocodile is "hit 'em behind the smile." A croc's mouth ends in a crook that does in fact tend to look like a cruel smile and is more or less on a vertical line with the eye. Somewhere along this line between the eye and the smile is what passes for a brain, a target not much bigger than a walnut. If you study a croc's head, you'll discover there isn't even a place for a brain; indeed, the entire skull is designed for killing, not for thinking.

Hitting a big crocodile anywhere except the brain is pretty much a wasted effort. Unless you can blow one apart with a howitzer, their reaction to a body shot is almost no reaction at all. It takes death a long time to catch up with a reptile, so despite a crocodile's considerable size, its only vulnerable spot is a tiny target that has to be hit just right or the trophy will be lost, to die later at the bottom of the water where it can never be found.

I had brought just one rifle, a custom-made .338 Winchester Magnum built on a '98 Mauser action by the David Miller Company of Tucson, Arizona. This masterpiece had become my favorite big game rifle because it never changes zero, and the first shot is always dead on target.

My handload was a 250-grain Nosler partition bullet over 69 grains of 4350 and a CCI Magnum primer. This combination churns up about 2750 fps at the muzzle, more than enough horsepower to punch the Nosler all the way through a Cape buffalo, the way it had done earlier on the safari.

Crawling on the hard-baked earth, I zigzagged from stump to stump until I was within about 200 yards of the sleeping crocodiles. There, I found a tree stump big enough to hide behind. Getting into a sitting position, I slipped the rifle's sling behind my elbow and pulled it tight into a solid position. Then, by resting the rifle alongside the tree, the crosshairs jiggled as they settled on the nearest crocodile's head.

*Hold on . . . take your time and get a real trophy,* I told myself.

Until then, I hadn't given much thought to what a trophy crocodile should look like. The only difference I could see was size, so I resolved to shoot the biggest one. That turned out to be a simple choice, because the one that lay at the river's edge with its tail still in the water was easily twice as big as any of the others. Luckily, the biggest croc was also the closest, lying broadside so that I had a clear view of its grim smile.

For a moment the crosshairs vibrated on the crocodile's head, then for another instant they were still and the bullet crossed the river, crashing into the creature's skull. Its tail violently lashed the water a time or two and then was dead still. The only motion I could see was a growing spot of thin red—behind the smile.

"Well done, Jim, that's a really good croc." Rowbotham was beside me, studying the beast through his binoculars, making doubly sure it was dead.

"Oomo, run back and fetch Jason and the boat. Let's see if we can get that bugger back to camp."

A half-hour later, during which time the croc had not twitched, we crossed the river and I had my first close-up look at my trophy. It was absolutely incredible; no animal I've ever bagged or even seen was as awesome.

"My God," said Rowbotham, "it's one of the biggest crocs I've ever seen."

That's when I realized I hadn't just shot a big croc, but a monster croc.

"This is unbelievable," I said. "I think it's the best trophy I've ever bagged, better even than an elephant with hundred-pound tusks."

With Jack's videocamera recording the scene, I walked around the beast, pacing off its length, lifting and flexing its prehistoric feet, not believing, even with the evidence before me, that such a creature could exist, now or at any time. There was no bullet hole in the skull, only an inch-long crack where the .338 slug had busted its way toward the brain. Incredibly, there was no exit hole. The same load that could drill completely through a Cape buffalo was stopped by the crocodile's head.

"Open its mouth so I can get a shot of the teeth," Jack requested, aiming his camera at the creature's blunt snout. Slipping my fingers between the teeth, I got a grip on the jagged upper jaw and heaved it wide. Teeth rimmed the mouth, like spikes of broken glass imbedded in the rim of a harem wall. The mouth's lining was white and fleshy, like that of a snake, the whiteness spotted by watery reptile blood. Inside the throat was a clotting puddle of blood, dripping from where its brain had been. Even in death the crocodile exuded an aura of evil, as if it still possessed a will to kill.

"Now that you've got the beast in hand, what do you plan to do with it?" Mike asked.

"I want it . . . every bit of it. I want the hide tanned with the head on. If

I can't get it inside my house, I'll leave it outside to scare away stray dogs and peddlers."

"Well, the thing must weigh three-quarters of a ton. We'll have to tow it back to camp."

"Too risky, Mike. I don't want to lose it," I said. "We've got to figure out a way to get it in the boat, even if we have to skin it here."

"I think we can get the whole thing in the boat," advised Jack Atcheson. "I've been manhandling elk and moose for years and know a couple of tricks that might help us get the croc into the boat."

With Jack directing, we cut stout poles, and with two men to the pole, we levered the croc out of its slimy bed, and with considerable grunting and cussing in a variety of languages, heaved its head and forelegs over the bow. The massive head was too slippery to grip, so Mike rigged a rope bridle around the head and snout that offered a more secure handhold. As it turned out, this was about the only smart thing we did all afternoon.

When the crocodile was about halfway in the boat, we relaxed our grip for a moment to take a breather before the final heave. At that moment the massive body expanded as if it were taking a deep breath and the rear legs reached out with a jerky spasm of power. For a moment its feet ripped at the air, then the claws caught the edge of the boat and with incredible strength it pulled its mass into the boat, leaving only the six-foot tail dangling outside. Then it was still again.

I was the first to speak. "Reptiles will often do that. Their nervous system doesn't get the message that it's dead for hours after the fact."

Jack and Mike agreed with my assessment of the situation, but the two Africans didn't seem at all convinced.

"Well, anyway, it was nice of the bugger to help out, saved us a lot of sweat," Mike said. "Let's get the tail in somehow and shove off for camp."

The crocodile's 16-foot bulk almost completely filled the bow section, with its head jammed into the two-foot wide opening in the forward bulkhead. There wasn't room to tuck the croc's tail in the bow, so we secured it with a rope and pulled it more or less aboard. Then a new problem presented itself; the mass of weight in the bow was nearly dipping it underwater. A few more inches lower and the boat would sink!

This problem was eased to some extent when the five of us climbed into the rear of the vessel, leveling it to some degree. Still, the boat floated nose down until we gained enough speed to lift the bow. Thus, with the craft more or less level, we cruised down the river of death into the vastness of Lake Kariba.

Even with the added weight slowing the boat, I figured we'd make it to camp before dark. Nothing to worry about now; there were plenty of camp workers to unload the crocodile, and after sundowners and a warm shower to wash away the stinking river slime, we'd have a hell of a time at dinner telling crocodile stories. There was no way I could know it then, but the crocodile story we would live to tell about would be one of pure horror.

The first sign of serious trouble was a small but steady stream of water that rippled across the fiberglass deck from bow to stern. My guess was that the trickle was only water flowing out of the crocodile and would eventually stop. However, a few minutes later the trickle became a tide, causing me to go forward, crawling over the crocodile, to where the water was coming from. What I discovered was that both of the bow storage wells were flooded and overflowing, apparently by water washing under the gunwale cowling.

Jason was running the boat and when I announced what was happening, his reaction was to slow the engine. Deprived of its planing lift, the bow dived beneath the waves and we would have sunk right there had it not been for Mike Rowbotham's quick action.

Grabbing the throttle from the terrified Jason, he punched the engine to full power, causing the bow to lift just an inch or two above the lake's surface. But even then we still had one hell of a problem. We were a half-mile from shore in a rapidly sinking boat. *Could we make it?* I didn't think we could and began a mental inventory of the situation and our survival options.

The whole problem, of course, was the huge crocodile, but there was no possibility of getting it out of the boat in the time we had left, so even in death it was taking a terrible toll. The two Africans were in utter panic and probably couldn't swim. *Are there life jackets aboard?* I wondered.

Clearly, Jack would lose his expensive video equipment and the depths would also claim my David Miller rifle, worth at least $5,000. Mike's double-barreled William Evans, worth more thousands, would go down too. But still, what bothered me most, more than the boat, the rifles, and the equipment, was losing the crocodile. I really wanted that damn crocodile.

I didn't look at the shore, only at the waterline as it crept up over the gunwales and splashed inside, and at Mike's hand on the throttle, urging the last ounce of speed from the overloaded engine. *We can't make it,* I thought . . . but then I could see the bottom of the lake . . . five feet deep, then three feet. *We could make it! We made it!* The boat crunched to a stop on the gravel shore, the engine still screaming.

A half-hour later, with the boat bailed dry, we nervously eased back into the lake's main channel and resumed our course for camp. Not much was said about what had happened. We all knew how close we'd been to disaster, possibly even tragedy, and when you come that close, there isn't much to say. I sat on the engine cowling, holding my rifle and studying the hideous design of the crocodile's head.

And then its eye opened.

Considering the scare we'd just had, the idea of a live crocodile in the boat struck me as a hilarious possibility. The situation was made even more ridiculous by Jason's proximity to the croc, no more than ten inches separated the monster's teeth from his bare feet and legs.

"Look Jason," I said, pointing at the open eye, already laughing at what I anticipated the African's reaction would be.

For a long moment Jason didn't react at all; he just stood there regarding the red glowing orb with all the solemn detachment of a cow pondering a flower. Then the crocodile's other eye opened and Jason levitated to the gunwale and monkey-walked to the farthest corner of the boat, leaving the controls untended and the throttle wide open.

I groped for the wheel, brushing by the croc's snout and apparently it was my motion that brought the creature fully back to life. It lunged at me and would surely have had my leg had it not been for the rope looped around its mouth. But even so the rope was slack enough for the croc to open its mouth about four inches, showing its ugly teeth and making a gurgling roar.

There was no doubt that it was coming after me. Its feet scratched at the deck as it struggled to squeeze through the bulkhead walk-though. Luckily, as it wriggled and scratched through the opening, it wedged itself tighter. How long the bulkhead would have held against the croc's overwhelming strength I can't say, but with a final roar the beast's head slumped to the deck and was still, its eyes closed. Dead at last?

Stepping cautiously, fearful of arousing the croc again, Jason returned to the boat's controls and we raced on toward camp. The crocodile's return from the dead had given us all a bad turn and had there been a bottle of whiskey on board, it wouldn't have lasted much longer than a butterfly in a blast furnace. What would have happened if the croc had crashed through the bulkhead opening was plain enough. Even with its mouth tied shut, its thrashing would surely have capsized the boat. There were many ways it could kill, but now perhaps it was at peace and the rest of the trip would be safe.

And then the boat's engine quit. Out of gas.

There we were in the middle of Lake Kariba, our boat stalled, the sun sinking fast, and with a monster crocodile that wouldn't stay dead. Happily, there was a spare can of gas on board, which Jason poured into the main tank, but with the fuel line sucked dry, the engine wouldn't fire.

For tense, heart-pounding minutes, the starter motor groaned without effect and then inevitably, buzzed to a stop. The battery was dead and we were trapped in the smothering darkness of a moonless tropical night.

Oomo had somehow found a paddle and began digging at the water with determination, but the shore was an hour or more away and there would be more hours of walking to camp. Hiking through wild animals' watering place in the dark of night is not a friendly exercise. There would be lions there, and leopards, elephants, and Cape buffalo. And snakes. While I was thinking these thoughts, Jason was digging through some gear in the back of the boat and presently made a joyous announcement. "Look, see, new battery, see," his black face was invisible in the darkness but his smile shone like a beacon.

At the same time Jack Atcheson's years of experience in hunting situations was making itself known. During all the years I've known Jack I've never ceased to be amazed at the things he carries in his ever-present knapsack. A flashlight I would have expected but when he dug deep and came out with a set of battery jumper cables, we all nearly dropped our teeth. It's hard not to like Jack Atcheson, especially at moments such as these.

Looking up to thank my lucky stars, I was dazzled by a shooting star, then another.

"Look Jack," I said, "there's a meteor shower. No wait, those aren't meteors, they're stars spinning around us."

The cause of the celestial phenomenon was Oomo at work with the paddle. Having no idea how to use a paddle, he was simply clawing at the water from a rear corner of the boat, causing us to spin in a manmade mini-whirlpool. We'd been so preoccupied with our problems that we'd failed to take notice of the considerable RPM's Oomo had achieved.

"Knock it off, Oomo," Mike commanded. "If you want to be useful, put your mouth over the gas tank pipe and blow as hard as you can. That will force some gas into the carburetor so we can get started."

So with Oomo balancing himself on the gunwale while blowing into the fuel tank, Jack holding the cables, Jason grinding the starter, Mike cursing our luck, and me wondering where I'd gone wrong, we bobbed and drifted across the black waters of Lake Kariba.

Despite Oomo's hearty blowing, the fuel line remained empty so we had to do something else. Our next effort was to uncover the engine, remove the air filter, and hope to fire the engine by pouring gasoline into the carburetor.

Of course, this would not normally be a very smart way to deal with a sluggish engine in a crowded boat, but after all we'd already been through, the possibility of an explosion at sea wasn't all that disturbing. Just to be safe however, I crouched behind the upturned engine cowling when Jason hit the starter. The engine caught for a second but sputtered and stopped.

"Pour more gas in the carburetor," Mike ordered. "It wants to start."

Again I crouched behind the cowling, scarcely noticing that my backside was only inches from the croc's mouth, and again the engine sputtered and died. The effort was repeated a dozen times, each time more despairing than the last, when suddenly the fuel pump went to work and the engine rumbled to life. Again we were off toward camp, and hopefully a stiff drink and a hot, if late, meal. Surely, nothing else could go wrong.

"Shine your light on the croc, Jack," I asked. "Let's see how it's going."

I can't remember exactly what made me want to see the croc just then, but I'll never forget what happened next. The instant Jack's beam hit the monster, two things became terrifyingly clear: first, its eyes were open again and second, the rope was gone from around its mouth! Brought to instant life by the light, the crocodile roared mightily, opening its mouth wide, bloody slime streaming from rows of teeth. Again Jason was in the back of the boat, leaving the throttle open and the wheel untended so that we careened across the water.

"You grab the wheel, Mike," I yelled. "I'm going to blow the bastard's head off."

But as I fed a round into the chamber, a feeling of helplessness possessed me. I couldn't blow its head off. Already I'd blown its brain to mush. *Where else could I shoot it? Was it unkillable?*

The only possibility was putting the muzzle behind the creature's head and blowing the spine apart. But to do that, I'd have to shoot almost straight down. If the bullet exited, would it make a big hole in the boat? Big enough to sink the boat?

The croc kept inching toward me, squeezing through the bulkhead, backing me against the engine cowling where I couldn't retreat any farther. The croc's teeth were less than two feet away and coming closer.

"Shoot, shoot, shoot," voices pleaded.

Jason and Oomo were hanging over the stern, ready to let go when the monster broke through the bulkhead, more willing to give themselves to the black lake than to the crocodile.

Somehow I felt like a schoolboy facing the town bully in a fight I knew I would lose.

"Okay," I yelled in its face, "that's far enough. Cross this line and I'm going to shoot no matter what."

With the rifle's muzzle, I traced a line six inches in front of the snapping mouth. This had something of a calming effect on everyone, and for a moment even the crocodile closed its mouth and backed off a couple of inches.

"Hold the light steady, Jack," I said. "I think I see the rope."

The loop of rope was barely visible under the croc's chin. *Could I reach it?* Reaching forward with the rifle, I snagged the loop with the muzzle and slowly, inch by inch, worked the rope free. Finally, the rope was in my hands but too tangled to be of any use. Knot after knot I untied the wet rope until there was enough slack to tie a loop with a slip-knot. Next, I slipped the loop over the croc's snout, using the rifle to push the rope under its mouth.

"Get around behind the croc's head, Mike," I whispered, afraid to speak loudly. "When I throw you the end of the rope, pull it tight. That will keep his mouth closed so we can hog-tie him."

"Just throw me the rope," Mike answered, already scrambling around the edge of the boat. "I'll hold his head up so he can't open his mouth."

And for the next half-hour that's how we traveled, Mike astride the giant reptile like a rodeo rider, heaving its head back so it was relatively harmless.

At last in camp, we called for reinforcements and after considerable struggling succeeded in locking the crocodile's mouth with heavy wire.

News of a giant crocodile travels fast in the African bush, and by noon the next day a considerable crowd of natives had collected to see the monster. Even then, the croc was still twitching and trying to move. An old black man puffed at his gourd pipe and shaking his head, spoke softly in his native tongue.

"What did he say?" I asked.

"He said it takes them a long time to die."

*"The leopard is impossible to explain. Not because of what he is, but because of what he does to men's minds."*

# Chapter 8

# Kill the Leopard

ou do not hunt leopard; you plot confrontation. It is a chess game of will and patience; you make a move and he makes a move, over and over until a wrong move is made. Then you win or he wins.

We had been making our moves for over a week, somewhere in western Tanzania where a parched scrub plain is split by the Rungwa River. It is not an unexplored region; perhaps avoided is a better word. Livingston passed near there, and Stanley and Speke and possibly Baker. But they all went on, leaving the land veiled behind its curtain of bloodsucking tsetse flies. Few men come there now except nomadic bee-hunters seeking wild honey and treasure hunters who wander the forests in search of teak and other rare woods.

When they have chopped their tree or robbed the killer bees of their honey, the men do not remain. That's why this savage and beautiful place is one of the richest hunting lands on earth. Tanzania is a new name. When great books were written about the place, it was known as Tanganyika. It is the land of Kilimanjaro, Ngorongoro Crater, and the Serengeti. It is also one of the last hunting areas in Africa where the traditions of great safari still live. If you turn off the electric generator, the adventure of safari life is the same as when Britain was an empire. Lions roar at night, hippos grunt, and barefoot black men in white coats say "Morning B'wana" when they bring you tea.

That's why we were there. I wanted the first safari for my wife and friends to be like those I had experienced nearly a generation ago when I first came to Africa. There is still plenty of good hunting in Africa, but the days of the classic safari are numbered. The reason is simply because there are so few professional hunters of the old school remaining. These were the professional hunters of legend, educated and cultured gentlemen who organized and guided safaris for sportsmen and sportswomen of, presumably, similar tastes and backgrounds.

Their exploits were the stuff of storybooks. On a normal hunting day, a Finch-Hatton or a Von Blixen would track elephant from dawn to dusk, oversee the camp and staff, discipline rebellious porters, save his client from a charging buffalo, then appear starched and polished for sundowners, ready to knock off a decanter of gin and determined to take all necessary precautions to protect his honor and reputation from a spoiled and determined heiress.

No one in the safari business better fills this description than Michael Rowbotham. Born and educated in England, and a Scots Guard officer in World War II, he was a natural for the professional hunter business. Landing in Kenya after the war, young Rowbotham signed on as assistant hunter with some of the great professionals of that era, including Tony Henley and Harry Selby. Those he didn't work with he at least knew and learned from. In time, he earned his PH license and a reputation as a tough, resourceful hunter who not only brought his clients home alive, but got them great trophies as well.

When *King Solomon's Mines* was filmed in the early 1950s, Rowbotham was hired as a hunter-in-residence to look after the well-being of the movie's stars. Who better than the dashing Rowbotham to guard Deborah Kerr's tent and bedstead from marauding lions and other African rascals?

Today, after more safaris than one can imagine, Mike Rowbotham is owner of Hunter's Tracks Safari Company and one of the very few members of the original East African Professional Hunter's Association still practicing his craft. If your idea of a PH is some galoot with elephant hair bracelets on his arms, a gold chain with lion's claws dangling from his neck, and Banana Republic labels on his kit, Rowbotham is not your man.

To Rowbotham, Swahili is the language of his trade and his tool is a double rifle. I'd hunted with Mike before and insisted that he take personal charge of this safari. Since there were three hunters in our party, plus two non-shooters, he arranged for PH Lew Hallimore, a savvy Rhodesian, to share the guiding chores. Mike's son, Ian, came along as assistant hunter.

Our KLM flight from Amsterdam touched down before dawn at the Arusha airport, and while customs officers busied themselves counting our rifles and ammunition, we witnessed the spectacle of an African sunrise. The first light glinted from a golden crown floating above the plain. Then the light gathered around the crown, causing it to take shape and grow higher. As the sun rose higher, the crown of gold became a mantle of shimmering white. *Kilimanjaro.*

Driving into Arusha, we passed herds of cattle tended by Masai tribesmen, their robes pulled tight against the morning cold. It was July, the time of cool days and dry air—the hunting season.

I'd hunted Africa before, plenty of times, from the Nile to the Cape, each time with a manic determination to explore the land, study the game, and earn the trophies. I was a student of the hunting rifle and Africa was my classroom. But now I wanted to relax with good friends, sharing with them the discoveries and exultations of a first safari.

There was my wife, Linda, Don Crow, Allen Harris, and Stanley, his daughter. Don, a pal since college days, is into more business ventures than I can list, while Allen is one of the world's largest manufacturers of hardwood flooring. Stanley is a pixy to whom the world is a beach ball and life a garden party. Her first safari will not be her last.

Life in a safari camp soon settles into a relaxed daily routine. Since we were not hunting any particular species, we spent the days scouting the plains, watching the game, and occasionally putting a stalk on especially good trophies. The area had not been hunted for several years, so it was not difficult to find record-class animals.

Some days we lunched in the field, but more often we would meet back at camp at midday to unload whatever game we had taken. After lunch and an afternoon nap we would hunt until the sun touched the horizon. Then it was time for sundowners by the fire and happy talk about the day's events while waiting turns in the shower. Dinner was followed by bed and soon a new hunting day would begin.

The hunting had been easy and most likely would have remained so, had not Saleem, one of our trackers, found a track in the sandy bottom of a dry riverbed.

"*Chui,*" he said in Swahili, "Leopard."

Leopards change things. When the presence of a leopard is discovered, you can try to ignore it, which is impossible, or you can try to hunt it. When you hunt leopard, it changes everything about your day. It changes the way you think and the way you act. Your schedule revolves around the leopard. The deadly chess game begins and the first move is yours.

The leopard is impossible to explain. Not because of what he is, but because of what he does to men's minds. It is difficult to look at a leopard and then, looking away, quite remember what you saw. Instead, your memory flashes images from your subconscious. The leopard's eyes are mirrors that reflect things you do not want to see.

When we understand fear, we will understand the leopard. In African culture the leopard is the symbol of savagery. Whereas lions are the symbol of bravery, leopards signify invincibility. Warriors wear leopard skins as a display of their strength and witch doctors invoke the spirit of the leopard to cast magic spells. Even in death the leopard is a force to be reckoned with.

I once knew a professional hunter who could have been one of the best. But he became afraid of leopards. Not ordinary sensible fear, but the kind of fear that rots a man's mind. I haven't seen him for over a decade, but I hear he hangs out in the lobby of cheap hotels in Harrare, swilling gin and selling elephant hair bracelets to gullible tourists. Strangely, he was never attacked by a leopard.

The leopard is one of African's so-called Big Five trophies. If size were the only measure, the leopard wouldn't qualify because a big tom will seldom weigh over 180 pounds, females smaller. But what it lacks in size is more than made up for in savage efficiency. Pound for pound and inch for inch, it is one of the most cunning and efficient killers ever to stalk the earth. His power is difficult to describe, because the measures of strength we ordinarily use simply don't apply. But to give you an idea, let's say that you weigh 200 pounds and stand six feet tall, and possess such superhuman strength that you can make a standing jump onto a ledge a foot or two over your head, landing gracefully on your feet. If you were a leopard you could perform the same feat carrying 200 pounds of dead weight.

You kill a leopard by using *his* rules: The only honor is deceit and quickness, the only measure of sportsmanship. Glory is survival.

The only reasonable chance of killing a leopard is from a blind, and that is the most difficult hunting of all. Building a proper leopard blind is probably a professional hunter's greatest challenge. It's based on several key skills—and luck. All too often leopard hunting is described as being a simple matter of hanging a bait in a tree and waiting for the stupid beast to come looking for an easy meal. But leopards aren't stupid and they aren't easily tempted by free food. That's why a leopard hunt is carried out in stages, not at all unlike a battle plan or a game of chess.

It is exceedingly unusual to see leopards during daylight. The pretty pictures and television documentaries we see of leopards are made in game parks and reserves where their normal habits have been radically altered. Filming a truly wild leopard in his natural environment would be virtually impossible, because they remain hidden during the day. That's why leopards are almost always shot at first light or just before dark.

The only evidence a hunter has of the leopard's presence is the track. Everything else about the leopard is an abstraction, pieces of a spotted puzzle scattered in the thorny bush.

The first stage of the hunt is hanging bait, not just one but several. And not in just any tree. Each hanging site must be just right, in a number of ways. It must be a fairly large tree with limbs thick enough to support the leopard without swaying. It must offer a clear line of fire from the blind, and the area around the tree must be open so the leopard, dead or alive, can be seen. Too, the tree has to be situated so the bait and the leopard are outlined against the sky.

It's usually impossible to find the perfect tree, so compromises have to be made. But one compromise no smart hunter will ever make is safety. A wounded leopard is a professional hunter's worst nightmare, so the selection of bait trees is made with this worst-case scenario uppermost in mind.

The next stage is actually hanging the bait. Just about any meat will do, but it must be hung with exacting care. Hung too low, it will be ripped away by hyenas; too high and the leopard might not take notice. The bait has to be tightly bound to the tree, so the leopard can't make off with it. Mike's technique is to secure the bait with a chain passed through tendons and bone. Sometimes we could use the truck to hoist the bait in place, but more often we simply muscled it into the tree, working as quickly and quietly as possible to leave as little human scent and sign as possible.

It all takes time; hours that might be pleasantly filled hunting other game are now spent killing and hanging bait and searching for additional trees.

Our safari was scheduled to last three weeks, plenty of time for a relaxed general bag hunt, but the leopard demands extra hours and perhaps days while other trophies go unhunted. Many is the hunter who has used up his safari hunting leopard. It is always a gamble. You gamble your money, your time, and your effort. Then, at the moment of payoff, you may gamble your life. The leopard becomes an obsession—nothing else matters.

At the beginning we hung baits in two trees. When nothing came, we baited more trees, hanging small antelope among the branches and slitting their bellies open so their gut stench would drift to where the leopard hid, tempting him out. Leopards are eaters of foul, rotted meat. It's an unspeakable irony of evolution that a creature of such charismatic beauty should bury its face among maggots and feed on carrion.

Every morning we would check each bait, approaching the trees silently and with caution, looking for sign that a leopard had come, searching for a track, a ripped bait, or a claw mark. Each day the baits rotted more, stinking so that it was hard to come near. Flies swarmed and rotted strips of flesh fell among pools of maggots. And then, one night the leopard came.

We did not see the leopard and unskilled eyes would never have known he had been there. There was no track on the hard ground and the bait was not eaten. The only sign was a slit in the tree's bark and three honey-colored hairs snagged in a broken twig. It wasn't much to go on, but it was all we had. The leopard had made a move, so now it was time for the hunt's second stage. Time to build a blind.

When a leopard is feeding on a bait, he is vulnerable, but that is only because he has convinced himself, utterly, that he is in no danger. Until then, he moves like a nervous shadow. Each step is an exercise in caution; the eyes consider everything, searching for any reason to flee. The bait is not natural to the leopard and he is bewildered. It is free food, but whose? Did another leopard put it there? If so, he is trespassing and risking a savage fight. Perhaps he has seen a bait before and even felt the hot breath of a bullet. Every instinct tells him the bait is danger.

A hunter almost never knows when he has spooked a leopard. That's because he remains hidden as he approaches the bait, often freezing into total stillness as he considers everything about him. If he sees or senses something he doesn't like, he retreats as carefully as he came.

The blind must be built so no trace of the hunter is visible. But hiding the hunter isn't the only consideration. The blind has to provide the hunter with a clear view of the bait and surrounding area. What's more, it has to be situated so any wind will not alert the leopard and—because the hunter must remain virtually motionless for hours at a time—it must be relatively comfortable.

Reason tells us that a blind should be a good distance from the bait—a hundred yards or more. This reduces the risk of a leopard detecting the blind, and the hunter himself is safer from attack should he only wound the cat.

Distance, however, is a luxury the professional hunter cannot afford. His single overwhelming concern is that his client's bullet be dead-on target. To this end, he risks all else and puts his skill on the line by putting the blind as close to the bait as possible. I've heard of them being closer than ten yards, especially when the professional hunter didn't have much faith in his client's marksmanship. The longest shooting distance I experienced was some 80 yards from where I nailed a leopard a few years ago in Zimbabwe.

A similar situation now existed because the area around the shootable side of the tree was open and packed hard. That meant the blind had to be about 60 yards from the bait and situated on a slight knoll covered with scrub brush. The distance was acceptable to both Mike and me, and the scrub would help conceal the blind; what was not good, however, was a deep, dry wash just behind the tree. Beyond that was a flat plain of thorny bush that stretched out of sight. If I wounded the leopard, he could instantly disappear into the wash or the dense thorn. Either way, there would be hell to pay.

We've all read those wonderful stories about how brave hunters, armed with shotguns and buckshot, wade into the brush after a wounded leopard.

Shooting a leopard on the wing with a load of buckshot is a chancy business at best, but the only sane way (if it can be called that) to deal with the cats when they're wounded and lying in ambush.

We didn't have a shotgun, and thanks to a bureaucratic snag, Mike's double rifle was being held by customs officials wanting more paperwork. If the leopard didn't die in his tracks, we would have to go into that thorny hell armed only with scope-sighted, bolt-action rifles. In other words, I would have only one chance to do it right and my bullet had better be dead on the mark.

Leopards are tough; they die hard. They have been known to absorb two slugs from an elephant gun and still have enough fight to kill the hunter. It has happened before and it will surely happen yet again.

Mike didn't say much about the danger, but I could tell he was bothered. While the blind was being built, I would see him studying the dry wash and the endless thicket of thorn beyond. It was like looking at a pair of dice and trying to decide whose number would come up. Nothing he saw could give him consolation. Professional hunters like to have faith in their clients, but those who have survived as long as Mike have learned that it is best to put their faith in themselves.

This time he had to put all his faith in someone else because some bureaucrat, hundreds of miles away, had decided that paperwork was more important than a hunter's safety.

The blind was some consolation. Designed by Lou Hallimore, it was made of woven bamboo slats fitted around a box frame. Its advantages, other than being quick to set up, were that it offered somewhat more comfort than a typical blind made of brush, while at the same time almost totally hiding the occupants. The risk of any blind is that the leopard will decide it is not part of the landscape, so we piled green brush around the front and sides so it looked more natural.

When everything was in place, I went inside and propped my rifle on a forked shooting stick. Leaving nothing to chance, I wanted to make sure that I had a steady rest and a clear line of fire. While Linda and Ian piled more brush around the windows so that no light could reflect off my rifle and scope, I studied the situation and tried to anticipate problems that might arise.

One difficulty I spotted immediately was a large, leafy branch that formed a curtain behind the bait. In bright daylight I could see well enough, but in dim light a leopard would blend into the foliage, making it difficult, if not impossible, to see his outline and aim at the vital area. I wanted to see the leopard clearly outlined against the sky so I ordered the limb to be cut. Saleem climbed the tree and hacked at the limbs with his hook-bladed panga until I could see the sky beyond.

The way I had it figured, the leopard would leap from the ground to a low limb, and from there to a thick, horizontal branch just under the bait. When he began feeding, he would be in a broadside position, giving me a clear shot at his heart. Even in dim light, his sky-outlined silhouette would offer me a reasonable target. A reasonable chance is all a leopard hunter can ever ask for.

"Come look here," said Mike. "We need a failsafe plan. When the leopard falls, he may very well drop into that depression beyond the tree. We won't be able to see it from the blind, so we must get out quickly and run to where we can see better. When you fire, I'll dash to that little bluff to our right. You be right behind me, ready to fire again."

Twice we practiced the maneuver; if the cat was still alive, speed would be vital. With luck, I could put another bullet into him before he disappeared.

The last thing I did that morning was go back into the blind and try, once again, to imagine what could go wrong, how I could fail. Linda came in and sat beside me, looking through the hole to see what I would see. She had been with us all along, helping select the trees and hang the baits. She is a professor of literature and has read the hunting stories of Hemingway, Ruark, and Faulkner. Now the stories would have a new focus, a special meaning all their own. She took my hand and we went out of the blind together, counting out 57 paces to the tree. An easy shot?

That day at lunch there was news of another leopard. At least we hoped it was another. Mike and Lou decided that the second track was so far from the first that we were dealing with two different animals. Yet, if the whim strikes them, or if forced out of their territory, leopards will relocate miles away. *Is this what happened to my leopard?* We'd soon know.

Anyway, the immediate plan was for Lou to proceed with selecting trees and hanging baits as if they were onto a different leopard. If it was the cat I'd been working for, there was nothing I could do except hope Don or Allen could get a crack at it. Soon after lunch they left to begin killing and hanging baits. It would keep them occupied for the next couple of days. Would it be possible to bag two leopards on one safari? *Too much to hope for*, I decided. *It takes a lot of luck to get even one.*

That afternoon we stayed at camp later than usual. There were tasks to do and thoughts to be thought. Sleep would have been a blessing, but there was no chance of that. Mike and Ian spent time alone and talked about the things a father and son talk about when they are about to do something dangerous. They talked for a long time. Linda tried to read, but mostly the book lay closed in her lap while she thought about what women think about when their husbands go to kill leopard. I suppose they are the same thoughts born of women whose husbands go to do battle, to race fast cars or to fight bulls. Men force on themselves the luxury of being killed grandly, in a single spectacular instant. Women are seldom granted such an opportunity.

Near our camp I set up a target and paced off 57 steps. The purpose was to learn where my rifle would hit in respect to point of aim at that exact distance. When rifles are sighted in for long-range hunting, as mine was, the short distance point of impact can be somewhat off point of aim. The first bullet was off the mark a bit, less than an inch, so I adjusted the scope slightly and fired again. This time the 250-grain Nosler bullet split the aiming mark.

Sebbi, a camp worker, and Saleem watched with rapt attention, their ebony faces twin studies in solemn concentration. It takes powerful magic to kill a leopard and they wanted to know if any bad spirits were lurking in my bullets. The target was carried back to camp, where a small crowd gathered to discuss the magical power of my rifle. It is a .338 Winchester Magnum built on a Mauser action by the David Miller Company. A veteran of many hunts, the rifle's blue is wearing thin in places and the stock wears a few dents and scars, but it still had all its magic.

"Sebbi," Mike bellowed, "bring tea," and instantly there was the rapid slapping sound of bare feet on packed earth, quickly followed by a rattling of pots and china in the cook tent.

Within moments fresh tea came to the thatch-shaded dining table, and Mike, as only an Englishman can, presided over the service. For a while we sipped the hot brew silently, our thoughts very much on what we were about to do. In the background I could hear the truck being loaded, the tank being filled with gas, everything being done with cautious quietness as if the leopard, miles away, could hear us.

"Linda," Mike broke the silence, "what are your plans? Will you stay in camp or are you going with us?"

"I'm going."

"Very well then, you'll stay in the truck with Ian. The flies will be bad before dark so take your bug jacket. The way I have this figured," he went on, speaking to me, "this fellow should cause us no trouble. But if we should get in a mess, and he gets at you, try to get on your belly and cover your head with your arms. And for God's sake, if he is on me don't shoot unless you're absolutely sure."

One of a professional hunter's greatest fears is being shot by a companion who is trying to save him from an attacking lion or leopard. It has happened often enough that some hunters warn their clients to never use a gun, no matter how bad the situation looks.

"And another thing," Mike continued, "the leopard may be close by, guarding the bait, so we need to slip into the blind quickly and quietly. Ian, you will drive, and Jim and I will be in the back. Drive close to the rear of the blind but don't stop. Just slow down enough for us to step out and you keep on going. If the leopard is watching, his attention will be on the truck, and he'll think it's just passing by. Then circle back and park.

"When you hear a shot, come like bloody hell. Otherwise don't come until full dark."

After that, we finished tea and tried to talk about other things, but the image of a clawing leopard raged in my mind.

In the back of the truck was a large chest I hadn't seen before but I knew what it contained. It was a hospital kit with bottles of powerful antiseptics. Leopards are horribly infectious; their bites and claw rips almost always lead to infections, fever, and even blood poisoning. That's why first aid for a leopard attack is drenching the wounds with antiseptic. The chest would also contain surgical equipment, sutures, and hypodermic syringes. For the pain there would be morphine.

Ian slowed the truck a few feet from the blind and Mike and I were quickly inside, he carrying two canvas camp chairs and a hemp bag of water, and me with the rifle, a small leather case of extra cartridges, and the one other thing a leopard hunter always needs: a book. Quickly we went to the small windows and searched the landscape, first with unaided eyes, then again, more slowly, with binoculars. Finally satisfied the leopard was not there, we unfolded the chairs and made ourselves comfortable for the long watch. It would be more than two hours until dark, and I knew from past experience that time would creep by with excruciating slowness.

My book was *The White Nile,* Allen Moorehead's great story of hunter-explorers who came to Africa searching for the source of the great river. I'd read it before, twice, and now was the time to read it again, because some of the adventures on its pages happened just where we were. Probably some of the explorers had passed by the very place where we were sitting. I looked out the window and wondered if what I saw was different from what Livingston might have seen when he came this way. Probably not.

My routine was simple; I'd read a page, then carefully survey the bait tree and surrounding landscape, tracing every branch, every bush, every feature, straining to detect anything different from the last look. Then I would read a page and begin another search.

It was a warm day with no wind to drive away the tsetse flies and within an hour they had found us. The tsetse flies on silent wings and they have feet like padded snowshoes. They can land on your face so softly that you won't feel a thing until they bore under your skin. Then there is pain like a bee sting and the voracious bloodsucker is gone. They bite through clothing; no repellent yet made will deter them and no insect is more wary. That's why killing one is a victory. A slap won't do it. You have to roll them under your fingers until they pop open and the blood spurts out. It's your blood and you're amazed at how much they can hold in their accordion-pleated bellies.

So you sit there, squashing flies and praying for the leopard to come and end the waiting. *Why in hell doesn't it come? Where is it? Will it come?*

Gradually the shadows shifted, giving a new perspective to every outline. The sky faded from blue to pink, then erupted in a blaze of such brilliant color that the sun seemed to be pouring itself across the earth. Then the sky cooled and became burnished copper, against which the leopard tree was a solitary black outline. Now was time for the leopard to come.

Moving with breathless caution, I eased the rifle through the window and settled it on the shooting stick. The crosshairs of the 4X Leupold first found the bait, then moved cautiously through the tree, inspecting every branch.

"Can you still see?" Mike whispered.

I nodded the affirmative. If the leopard came soon, I would have a good shot. Though I could no longer see into the shadows, the big limb was clearly outlined. The cat would be easy to see if it came in the next 10 minutes, 15 at the most. The minutes ticked by, covering us with darkness, and the leopard did not come.

Next day there was plenty of excitement in camp. The other hunters had made an early morning check of their freshly hung baits and found where a leopard had been feeding. We had checked our baits too and found nothing; layers of maggots sucked at the rotting meat, but no leopard had been there. It had been two days since the leopard had come and even then he had not eaten any of the bait. I did not believe he would come again.

We had already lost too much time, and I felt we should resume our normal hunting and salvage what we could of the few remaining days. It was a disappointment, though what would hunting be if there were no failures. I'd hunted leopard before and lost, but this was a first time for Linda. She had been involved from the beginning, had shared time in the dark, had suffered the tsetse flies, had hoped the hardest, and would most keenly feel the sting of failure. She doesn't give up without a fight.

"Here's what we'll do," I announced at lunch, "we'll try my leopard one more time. Win or lose, we'll dismantle the blind and bring it back tonight. You guys can set it up in the morning and be in business by tomorrow evening."

It was agreed. That afternoon we were in the blind again. The tsetse were particularly vicious, but in a way I suppose I welcomed them. Hunters have a way of rationalizing discomfort that suggests that we are somehow convinced that if we work harder, climb harder, suffer more cold, withstand more heat, and endure more physical torture we will be rewarded. So the tsetse bored into my hide, bug repellent stung my eyes, and I waited for my reward.

Like the day before, the afternoon crawled by with only the occasional cackle of a francolin to punctuate the monotony. Then time gathered speed and the sky turned cold and dark. There was no leopard, no reward. But there was the satisfaction of having made a final effort. I was glad for that. We had played the game the best way we knew how and had been beaten by an opponent who played the game better. There's no disgrace in that. So we took the blind apart in darkness and arrived in camp ready for a tall drink. I toasted the leopard and wished him a long life.

The next day was a good one; it was a relief to have the leopard episode behind us. After a long and difficult stalk, I shot a hartebeest that will rank high in the record book and looked forward to three more days of good hunting. Don and Lou had even better luck.

As easy as you please, they had set up the blind near their working bait and waited only an hour or so for a leopard to appear. Don knocked it off with his .300 Winchester Magnum, and they were back in camp, sipping gin and tonic, before sundown. The whole affair had been so quick and easy that Don wasn't especially impressed. He had been incredibly lucky and didn't even know it. Anyway, it was good to have a leopard in camp. Including the two lions taken by Allen and Don plus our exceptional plains trophies, the safari had been a fantastic success.

We would never have gone back to the bait tree had not Mike needed to retrieve his hanging chain.

"Hurry," he ordered Saleem as we drove near, "climb up there and take the bolts out." We were on our way to a distant *vlei* where we'd seen roan antelope two weeks earlier. It would be a long drive and we didn't have time to waste.

Saleem, running ahead of the truck, never made it to tree, because suddenly he reversed direction and came racing back, pointing over his shoulder as he ran.

"*Chui, chui,*" I recognized the Swahili word again and again in the rapid exchange between the hunter and tracker. *Leopard!*

They were talking about leopard.

"Here's the story," began Mike, using his best British phrasing to hide his excitement. "Saleem says a leopard has been eating the bait. We may have spooked it just now, which is good because it will still be hungry and want to come back. What is your pleasure?"

"Let's go back to camp and get the blind. We'll hunt roan another day."

There hadn't been time to camouflage the blind as carefully as before. A few withered branches were propped here and there, possibly blurring the outline, but if a leopard looked twice he would see us. Looking out of the window with my binoculars, I could see ripped strips of flesh hanging from the bait. Very little had been eaten. I was confident the leopard would come back. I was more than confident, I was certain. Everything around me whispered the cat's presence.

Could a creature be possessed of such powerful presence that it radiates around him like a charged current? I could feel it. Linda in the truck a half-mile away felt it. It was like standing in the wind that comes before a thunderstorm, all of nature bending to its force. Yet not a leaf moved. From somewhere in the bush came a sound I'd never heard before, like a small dog crying in pain. It did not stop for a long while. Mike raised his eyebrows and shrugged his shoulders in silent questioning. The noise was strange to him also.

A hyena came, whimpering the eternal frustration of his species, ugly, his back hunched and his crooked little hind legs scurrying after the larger, more powerful front legs. He stopped under the tree and studied the bait for a long minute. He could see it, he could smell it, and desperately he wanted it. But he could not reach it. Such is the lot of a hyena's existence. Suddenly he seemed to realize he had no business there, and like a frightened thief, spun around and disappeared.

The leopard was close. So very close, I knew it. He was just over there, or over there. The certainty of the leopard's presence was so overpowering that I could resist no longer. My hand went to the rifle and guided its muzzle through the window, the butt touching my shoulder at the exact instant the leopard appeared.

It was there! Walking slowly, utterly confident of the force it radiated, the biggest wild leopard I'd ever seen. It moved toward the tree with unmistakable arrogance, each stride a study in measured power. I could have killed him at any one of several moments; my finger was tight on the trigger, but I wanted that moment to be the best moment. We'd waited too long and worked too hard for me to botch it now.

Suddenly I was aware of Mike close beside me.

*My God,* I realized, *he doesn't see the damn thing!*

Mike's concentration was so intently focused on another spot he hadn't seen the leopard.

*He should be watching the leopard when I shoot. What should I do? The hell with Mike!*

The leopard stopped, looked up at the bait, and then, to my total disbelief, sat down! Sat down just like a dog begging a tidbit. Until that instant, I'd been convinced that I would shoot the leopard once he was in the tree. That's how leopards are killed; it's the time-honored way, the way hunting books are written. It's the safe way. A cat on the ground is not a clear target; one leap and he'll be out of sight.

The cat moved, I could see his muscles tense. *Was he going to leap into the tree or was something wrong? Was he about to run? It was my turn. Now!*

The blaze of muzzle fire reached out like a long arm, torching the landscape like lightning. Momentarily blinded by the fireball, I could not see the leopard. *Where was it? Was it dead?* Then I remembered our practiced routine and charged out of the blind and ran to the knoll. Mike was already there, his eyes, like mine, struggling to see again.

"Shoot again," he commanded. "He's under the tree. Shoot."

The leopard was very still. It was dead, and I knew it. Its heart was gone, and so was its magic. There was no need to make another hole in its magnificent hide.

"Shoot."

I raised the rifle, aimed casually at a spot on the tree and pulled the trigger. Harmless shreds of bark showered the lifeless form.

"Good, now he's dead."

Moments later headlights were darting through the brush. Linda was coming, laughing and crying, Ian shouting. Mike and I stood in the glare of the lights so they could see we were safe. We would go to the leopard together.

Saleem turned the leopard over and poked a finger into the hole where a heart had been. He tried to act casual, unimpressed, as if killing a leopard was just part of a day's work. Later, when he thought we would not see, he knelt beside the leopard and looked at it for a long while. Then he took my rifle and held it close, letting its power—its magic—flow into his body.

On the way to camp, a foraging hippo charged the truck, we got lost and arrived very late. Linda held the leopard all the way. And Mike never asked why there was only one hole.

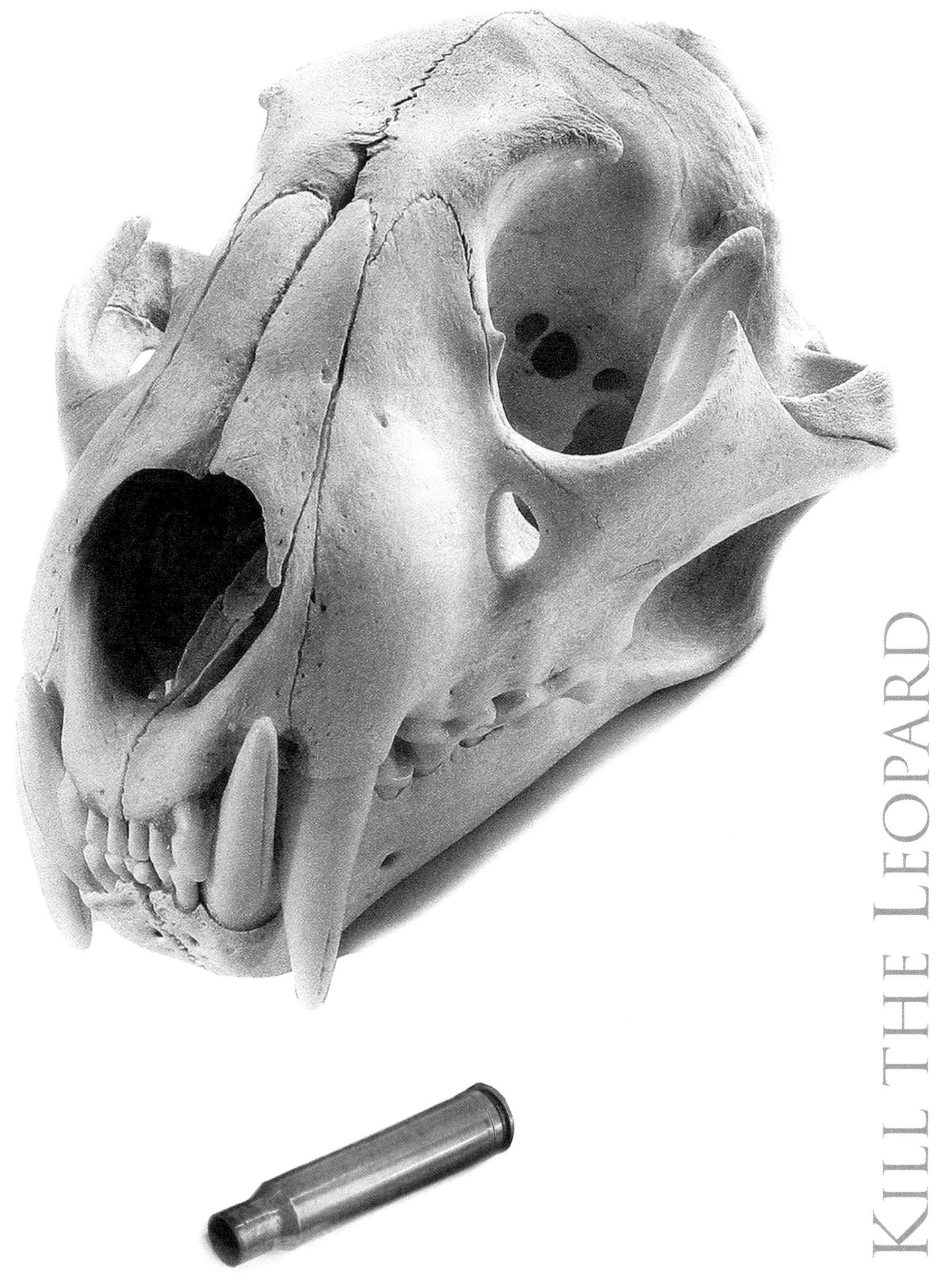

# Kill the Leopard

*"For a long while it seemed like Saturday night at the ol' waterhole, with the three bulls butting and chasing each other around like schoolboys."*

# CHAPTER 9

# AFRICAN (MIS)ADVENTURE

o,” I whispered, shaking my head from side to side and jabbing at the ground with my finger. “We’re staying put right here.”

This sudden decision was in response to Kevin’s hand signal in the direction he’d wanted us to continue crawling across the spiked, uneven ground.

Like every African professional hunter I’ve ever known, Kevin was a believer in getting as close to the quarry as possible. Ordinarily that’s a smart policy, endlessly reinforced by nervous and inept clients who somehow manage to miss unmissable shots. Which is why Kevin responded to my unexpected decision by shrugging his shoulders and slumping lower to the ground. The resignation in his face and body language told me we were probably blowing the best, and so far the only, chance of bagging a prime trophy. It was my call, and I’d have to live with it. If I blew it, it wouldn’t be his fault.

Normally, I would have agreed with my PH and tried to get closer, but to my thinking, trying to get closer would have increased the chances of the

three waterbucks we were watching either scenting or spotting us and making their getaway.

If they did, they could head off in any of several directions, and I'd have to make a running shot, if there was any chance for a shot at all.

I was betting that if we sat tight and didn't disturb the bucks, they would retrace the route they'd followed to reach the waterhole. And if they did, they would pass through a narrow but relatively open space in the rolling plain about 300 yards away. But I'd have a clear shot.

Each of the heads was surmounted with horns longer and thicker than any waterbuck I'd taken before, and one had forward-sweeping horns that were inches longer than either of his pals. From what I could see, the three bulls seemed to be in no hurry to leave, so I settled into a slightly more comfortable position to wait them out.

As the minutes crept by, I thought back on the past several days of a safari that had not been at all what I had expected. I hadn't even planned to hunt waterbuck. Rather, I'd hoped to take a better kudu than the three I'd bagged on earlier hunts. In Africa, though, what you seek and what you find are often not the same.

My rifle was a sweet 7x57 built on a Mauser action by legendary riflemaker Al Bieson. I'd topped it off with Leupold's then spanking-new and unorthodox

looking VX-7, which has a pie-cut in the big 50mm objective bell that allows it to be mounted lower on the rifle than other scopes with big objective lens.

Generally speaking, the modest-looking 7x57 would be in the last row in a lineup of today's popular hunting calibers, but back in its heyday it was hot stuff. During the Spanish-American war, it made such an impression on the Americans that the U.S. military abandoned the .30/40 in favor of a cartridge more like the zippy Mauser. It was also the cartridge used by South Africa's Kommandos during the Boer War. Indeed, just mentioning the 7x57 to an older generation South African will cause his craggy face to light up with admiring recognition. In England, the 7x57 is known by the more impressive-sounding .257 Rigby, and accounted for scores of elephants killed by famed ivory hunter W. D. M. Bell.

I had neither Bell's nor the Boers' motivations, and whereas they had favored 175-grain, full-jacketed non-expanding bullets for the 7x57, my ammo was hand-loaded with 150-grain Nosler Partition bullets to a less-than-awesome velocity of about 2700 feet per second.

Most shots at African game are at fairly close range, usually less than 100 yards, so I'd sighted-in my rifle to hit dead on at 200 yards. Thus zeroed, all I had to do was aim where I wanted to hit out to that distance and my bullet would strike within a couple inches.

Waterbuck are thick-bodied antelope that weigh upwards of 360 pounds and stand a bit over four feet at the shoulder. They are powerful swimmers and get their name from their preference for watery places, for which they are well adapted. Run your hand over a waterbuck's shaggy, waterproof coat and it will come away covered with a smelly oil. I've been told they are poor table fare, tasting something like a blend of bubble gum, hog lard, and rancid peanut butter, which is why I've never tried it. But they are a handsome animal, with the ringed horns of a trophy-class bull measuring over 30 inches. I wanted this one badly.

I was hunting in the Lemco Safari Area, an 850,000-acre game conservancy in southern Zimbabwe, about a three-hour drive out of Bulawayo. The earliest recorded hunt in the area was in 1836 by W. C. Harris, a British sport and intrepid adventurer who explored what was then the domain of the fierce Matabele and their treacherous king Moselekatse.

Game was so plentiful, he recorded, that herds of eland and other antelope species sometimes blocked his ox-drawn wagon. Seventy years later a Baron von Lieberg bought up some million and a half acres of the area for a ranching venture, upon which there eventually were well over 100,000 head of cattle. Naturally, with that much beef for the taking, lions and other predators were a constant menace, plus the added problem of countless thousands of wild animals competing for the same, sometimes scarce grazing. The rancher's solution was to kill off the competition. The wildlife was systematically reduced with such determination that by the 1950s, the endless ocean of game described by Harris was little more than a distant memory.

Over the years the vast Lieberg lands had been broken into smaller holdings, and in the 1990s a group of landowners came to the realization that there was more money to be made from hunting than ranching, and the Lemco consortium was born.

Water, always vital to maintaining a huntable game population, was plentiful even during the rainless half of the year, thanks to a network of borehole-fed tanks and dams built for the cattle operations. Thus, game populations that had previously been held in check slowly rebounded to include 30 huntable species, among them the Big Five.

It was mid-2006, the dry wintertime south of the Equator, and I was there with some big shots from Leupold-Stevens optics. The following year would be the 100th anniversary of Leupold scopes, and they had come to Africa to collect photos and background for the company's safari themed anniversary catalog. Altogether there were six hunters and a professional hunter for each of us. Of course, finding six PHs with suitable vehicles can be difficult, which explains how I wound up with Kevin, a farmer who only guided part-time and had never been to our hunting area. Neither did Loveface, the smiling tracker, gunbearer, and all-around righthand man Kevin had brought with him.

To make up for our combined directional deficiency, we were assigned dour-faced M'tue, who lived on the Lemco. I think his name was actually

Matthew, but he didn't talk much, and when I asked him his name, it came out M'tue. He didn't seem at all happy about joining our group, probably because of Kevin's safari truck, a Toyota Land Cruiser well past its prime.

Our camp was situated on a high bluff overlooking the Bubye River, which is known for the kudu that hang out along its wooded banks. But as it turned out, the Bubye was as dry as an old shoe and the kudu had scattered, which meant we had to travel a good ways from camp. Even so, our safari went pretty well.

On the first day I took a steenbok, a dainty little member of the antelope clan, and on the next I shot a warthog with nicely curved tusks. The area proved to be warthog heaven, and on the fourth day I shot another one—the biggest I'd ever seen, with enormous tusks.

That was the day something came loose or fell apart in the ancient Land Rover's cooling system and water came dribbling from somewhere under the hood. After a long inspection from above and below the engine compartment, with Loveface and M'tue looking on with grave expressions, Kevin declared the problem unfixable in the field and for the rest of the day we dashed from one waterhole to the next, refilling the steaming radiator at each place.

The leak proved to be unfixable at camp as well, resulting in our leaving camp each morning with jugs of water and planning the day's route to intersect with water holes where we could replenish the radiator and jugs.

During these interminable stops the increasingly gloomy M'tue would end his silence and badger me to buy his braided elephant hair bracelets. While the intricate braiding was indeed beautiful, the "elephant hair" turned out to be plastic. I bought a couple anyway because of their fine craftsmanship. Every day thereafter M'tue would display even more bracelets, and then silently brood and pout if I didn't buy any.

Meanwhile, we had pretty well memorized routes from one waterhole to the next—except for Kevin, who remained somewhat directionally challenged—and we spent a good part of each day leaking along dusty trails, hoping to find game along the way.

By the end of the first week, the only animals we'd delivered to the skinning shed were the steenbok and warthogs, plus a battle-scarred zebra we'd bumped into. So as the days dwindled away, it was beginning to look like my only hope for any kind of decent trophy was somewhere near a waterhole where a few head of game had been gathering during the bottom part of the day.

Normally, a watering spot offers fairly easy hunting, but not this one. Years earlier an earthen dam had been built to catch and hold water during the rainy season, which had formed a sloping floodplain about a half-mile across. The plain was bare except for a cluster of tree stumps. A wide four-foot-deep cleft had been cut to drain water to the lower end of the plain, and it was being used as a thoroughfare for game visiting the waterhole.

The day before we'd seen a couple of smallish kudu bulls and a half-dozen waterbuck, but pulling a sneak on them had proved hopeless because of the open ground. Thus our plan for the day was to try to get closer to the waterhole and hope for a shot if a good head happened by. But to do so meant crawling across a quarter-mile of open ground, taking whatever advantage we could of the slightly rolling contour, and using tree stumps for cover when we got up on our knees to glass the area and mark our progress.

Loveface, meanwhile, had been left behind, which he seemed quite happy about, and M'tue seemed gloomier than usual at the prospect of crawling across the baked earth. But I was glad to have him because he was the first to spot the three waterbuck. To get closer, as Kevin wanted to do, would have meant crossing ground that offered almost no cover, which led to my decision not to advance any farther lest we spook them. So we settled down to wait them out.

For a long while it seemed like Saturday night at the ol' waterhole, with the three bulls butting and chasing each other around like schoolboys. But as the sun sank lower and lower, they settled down and at last started back in the direction from which they'd come. So far, so good, in just another 30 yards or so they would be in a swale where I would have a clear shot. Already I could see more and more of their bodies . . . just a few more steps.

Very carefully I rose to a kneeling position, blending my profile with the snag as much as I could. The two leading bulls were almost in the open now, and the third close behind as I leveled the crosshairs.

*Oh, No! Why does something like this always happen to me?*

The bigger bull was on the far side of his companion and almost completely blocked. All I could see was his head and two long horns. No chance for a shot. None. With a few more steps they would be past the cleft and hidden in a streambed beyond.

I had only moments to make a decision. Should I take the second largest bull? He was the one behind in the open for a clear shot. For sure, he had longer horns than any waterbuck I'd ever taken before. *But still, was there a chance the bigger bull would return the next day? Would I be pushing my luck—which had been none too good so far—to come back tomorrow, the last day of the hunt?*

Then suddenly, something happened that I still have trouble believing: an unbelievable, last-second change in my luck. The biggest bull spun around and charged the one behind.

Apparently they were having a territorial dispute and the bigger bull was objecting to having his space invaded, which was probably the cause of their jousting around the waterhole earlier. The lesser bull, intimidated by the other bull's sudden fury, turned and ran. Satisfied that he'd rid himself of his rival, the bigger bull stood watching the other's departure. Broadside and in the open!

The crosshairs landed on the bull's shoulder at the spot I wanted to hit, then went about eight inches higher to account for the 7mm bullet's drop at my roughly estimated distance. I never heard the bullet hit but I knew the shot was good.

Kevin and M'tue were instantly on their feet running toward where the bulls had been. I would have run too except when I tried to rise, I fell over backwards because my leg had gone to sleep. It took me a while to limp to the bull, but when I got there M'tue was holding the bull's head and almost smiling, and Kevin was measuring its horns by overlapping his bridged fingertips the way guides do when something outstanding is on the ground. The horns were long, longer even than we had estimated when we first saw him, topped with the magnificent forward curve of very old bulls.

While Kevin went to fetch his truck, I paced the distance back to the snag where I'd shot and it turned out to be a few paces short of 300 yards.

M'tue sold me a couple more of his fake elephant hair bracelets and when Kevin arrived in his steaming Land Cruiser, the sun was dropping below the far rim of Africa, turning the fluffy clouds to pink cotton candy. We snapped a few pictures in the remaining light, and we had to stop for two radiator refills so it was long after dark before we finally got back to camp and dropped off the waterbuck at the skinning shed.

As I settled myself into a canvas chair beside the big campfire, someone handed me a tall drink and asked, "Anything happen to you today worth telling us about?"

*"As we sat glaring at each other and contemplating an escalation of the Cold War, Hans relieved the growing tension by asking if we would like to go upstairs and see the money."*

# CHAPTER 10

# THE $100,000 RUSSIAN STAG

id I ever tell you about the time I paid a hundred thousand dollars for a deer? The money wasn't mine of course, and it was in rubles, Russian money, but that's what the tab came to in American money.

The whole thing happened several years ago, before the fall of Soviet communism, and the Russians wanted to do some trading with an American computer manufacturer. *(I'm going to leave out some names, and change those of the Russians involved, because for all I know they could still get in trouble over what happened.)* What they wanted were not the type of high-powered computers used for strategic military purposes or stuff like that, and in any event we couldn't sell to them anyway, except for ordinary PCs for innocent chores like library retrieval and medical records.

As it happened, there was at least one U.S. maker of such computers willing to do business with the Russians, but the catch was they didn't want Russian money. The reason being that Russian bucks—rubles—were virtually worthless out of Russia, and for that matter not worth much inside Russia either. But more about that later.

So what the Russians had in mind was swapping some of their products for our computers, and among the items they wanted to trade were guns. Mainly sporting shotguns. The U.S. computer company was interested in trading for guns, but they didn't know anything about Russian shotguns or the American gun market. And that's how I came to be involved.

The deal they offered was irresistible: two Americans, my good pal John Amber, the legendary editor of *Gun Digest*, and myself, accompanied by a trade specialist from the computer company, would visit some of the Russian gunmakers and size up what they had to offer, then give our opinions as to what appeal Russian guns would have for American hunters. In return for our services, they would treat us to an exclusive hunt for Russian stag, plus some waterfowl hunting in one of their preserves.

On top of that, they promised a private tour of the fabled gun collection inside the Kremlin itself. I would have been happy to go just for a peek at the gun factories and Kremlin tour, so the hunting was gravy. But first I had to be convinced that everyone was on the up and up about the computers to be swapped, that they were not to be used for strategic purposes, and that I would not be aiding and abetting our Cold War enemies.

As it turned out, even our State Department was in favor of the deal, so I agreed to go and it came to pass that on a drizzly November evening, I found myself in the dark and dreary bar of a Moscow hotel in some rather mixed company.

Aside from Amber and myself, there was the American trade specialist, whom I'll call Dave, and another American, Roger Barlow, whom I'd met before. Barlow, in addition to being a firearms expert in his own right, was a cinematographer who had been hired to make a promotional movie of our tour and hunting.

The other members of our suspicious-looking group were Hans, an Austrian who looked after the computer maker's affairs in Europe, and Viktor, a Russian whose English-printed business card proclaimed him a "Consultant for Technical Product Trade Alliances," or some such hopelessly unfathomable bureaucratic title.

Viktor and I hadn't hit it off very well at first, beginning with my rather discourteous inquiry if it were possible to get a gin and tonic in Russia, followed by his scowling admonishment that they were not uncivilized bears. As we sat glaring at each other and contemplating an escalation of the Cold War, Hans relieved the growing tension by asking if we would like to go upstairs and see the money.

"The what?"

"The money," he replied, chuckling at my befuddlement, then began explaining the peculiarities of doing business with the Soviet government.

As the ancient birdcage-shaped elevator creaked and bumped its way to the top floor, Hans let us in on the strange fact that the Soviets paid cash in their international trade deals. The catch to paying rubles on the barrelhead, however, is that the money is almost worthless and besides that, it couldn't be taken out of the country. Which is why their so-called cash business had to be propped up with trades for Russian goods, such as the guns Amber and I had come to have a look at..

As a result of such dealings, so much Russian money had been accumulated by his company that Hans had rented a hotel room to store it in. In fact, the entire top floor of the hotel!

"Why bother with a bank," he further explained, "when rubles aren't worth stealing."

And having thus explained what we were about to see, Hans produced a key and swung open the door of a large room. And there, in great piles in the middle of the floor and terraced against the walls were big bundles of rubles, all in large denominations.

Astonished by so much money lying around relatively unguarded, I was somehow reminded of the Donald Duck comic books I'd read as a kid, in which Donald's Uncle Scrooge McDuck hoarded huge piles of money that he played with like a child in a sandbox.

"Part of my job," Hans went on after my companions and I had recovered our collective breath, "is to look after this money and keep inventory. Fresh piles of rubles come in pretty often."

"But what will become of it?" I had to ask.

"Who knows," Hans answered with a shoulder shrug, as if he had no particular interest. Shrugs, as I was to learn in coming days, are part of the Russian language. Especially in official circles.

Over the next three days we looked at guns, were escorted from place to place like dignitaries, indeed saw the Kremlin gun collection, and ate some awful meals (I'll tell that story another time). We also did some skeet shooting with Eugene Petrov, the Olympic gold-medalist shooter (I let him beat me because it was the politically polite thing to do), saw the changing of the guard at Lenin's tomb, and took in a wonderful performance at the famed Bolshoi Ballet.

After the ballet, we attended a fancy reception at one of the gilded and chandelier-hung government palaces. Most of the attendees were military types, each of whom was festooned with yards of gold braid and acres of service medals, so I figured they must be important guys. They seemed to be bored with the affair and indifferent to their American guests, eagerly consuming vodka and caviar with the same single-minded diligence I've observed when dealing with American bureaucrats.

Meanwhile, Viktor and I were hitting it off better. He spoke American English with a New York accent that he picked up when he was a member of the Soviet delegation to the U.N. He was a man to be liked, I discovered during our jaunts, but also a man to be feared.

I found this out late one afternoon, after he and I had been on a walking tour of Moscow and decided we were too far from the hotel to walk back and had better take a taxi. There were plenty of empty cabs going by, but none seemed interested in stopping, apparently because their daily quotas had been filled and they were just joy riding. After several minutes of fruitless cab hailing, Viktor calmly stepped into the lines of traffic and held up his hand so the oncoming cabs could see what he held in his palm. From my angle I couldn't see what he was holding, but it was powerful stuff because a half-dozen or so taxis screeched to a halt, their drivers tumbling out and jerking the rear doors open for our entry, all grinning and bowing like boys caught misbehaving.

We selected the cleaner looking and best repaired of the taxis and once inside, I took a long look at Viktor and suddenly KGB flashed in my mind like a fluttering neon sign—the dreaded Soviet Secret Police.

*So that's it,* I realized, *Viktor's job is to keep an eye on us and make sure we don't get into trouble.*

He must have sensed my questions in the making because before I could speak, he simply shrugged and settled back for our silent ride through the darkening streets of Moscow. When we arrived at the hotel a light snow had begun to fall, and I wondered if I was seeing the beginning of the Russian winter. It had defeated Napoleon's might and a vast German army. Would a couple of American gunwriters fair any better?

According to our schedule, we were to fly to the city of Krasnadar several hundred miles south of Moscow, and from there, drive to a camp where we would hunt the fabled Russian stag. None of us, Viktor included, had any idea what a Russian hunting camp would be like or what services it would offer. So, to be on the safe side, we figured it would be wise to stock up on some caviar, smoked salmon, and other such nutrients vital to survival in a hunting camp. And a few bottles of vodka wouldn't be a bad idea either.

To pay for these necessities, we raided Han's hoard of rubles at the hotel and filled a scuffed and ancient crocodile suitcase we found in one of the rooms. But as it turned out, the foodstuffs we needed were not available at the bare-shelved peoples' markets. In order to buy caviar and other such desirable Russian goods, we had to go to relatively swanky, state-run shops that catered only to foreign currency, preferably U.S. dollars. When we flipped open our ruble-stuffed suitcase and offered to pay in local greenbacks, the husky saleswoman scowled and slammed the lid closed.

"Nyet."

But when Dave produced an American credit card, she brightened instantly and dazzled us with a galaxy of gold teeth.

The catch to shopping at these stores was that they charged at the government-imposed exchange rate, which was then about $3.50 U.S. for one ruble. The illegal street exchange rate, however, was about ten rubles for a single dollar. The ridiculous exchange rate, as it turned out, was to bring our hunt to an almost unhappy conclusion. The shopping tour was a lesson in Soviet economics, but not particularly a surprise because after the previous days in the capital city, I was getting a clearer idea of what Winston Churchill had meant when he said "Russia is a riddle inside a puzzle wrapped in an enigma."

When we got back to our hotel, laden with our survival foods and finished packing for departure for the airport, another Russian mystery presented itself: Viktor's almost psychotic fear of flying. Only he didn't tell us of his fearful distrust of flying on Aeroflot, the Soviet State airline, but rather, lied about the airport at Krasnadar, our destination, being closed for repair and that we would have to go by train. His explanation about the closed airport seemed a bit thin, but no one questioned his motives except to ask if train reservations had been made.

Viktor shrugged, "We'll take care of that when we get to the station," and I had visions of us crammed into a drafty boxcar filled with smelly peasants and chugging across a frozen landscape like in a scene from *Doctor Zhivago*.

The reality of the train we were to take was pleasantly different. It was huge, with tracks of a wider gauge than ours, and pulled by a gigantic, gleaming engine surmounted by the symbolic hammer and sickle of Soviet Communism. But very uncommunistic, for a supposedly classless society, was that the train offered four classes of travel. Upon learning this, we naturally hoped that we could get First Class seats, but without prior reservations it seemed doubtful.

"I'll see what I can do," Viktor shrugged and casually approached a pudgy, cheerful-looking young woman, dressed in what looked like a stewardess uniform, standing by the steps of the yacht-like First Class car. He spoke quietly to her for a moment and was answered by a vehement shaking of her head and a flurry of negative hand gestures. Clearly, there was no First Class space available, and I was resigning myself to travel among the deodorant-challenged masses when Viktor gently took the stewardess by the arm and walked her a short way down the platform with their backs to us and out of hearing. When they returned, she climbed into the First Class coach and Viktor walked over to our apprehensive group.

"It will be a few minutes . . . she is reassigning the First Class compartments, and then we will get on board."

Viktor's mysterious badge had again worked its magic.

The trip to Krasnadar lasted 28 hours and as the giant train roared through miles of primeval forests and across seemingly endless plains, I saw firsthand the abject failure of communism: wheat fields big enough to feed a nation were littered with abandoned farm machinery, while in the villages, horses tugged carts along muddy streets. Wandering through the crowded lower class coaches I saw only sullen faces until I reached Fourth Class, where some turbaned Kazaks were cooking over tiny alcohol stoves. A woman, probably younger than she looked, with her head tightly swathed in a patterned shawl, smiled at me with government-issue stainless steel teeth and invited me to eat with them by pointing at a steaming pot and patting her stomach. It smelled delicious.

The only other sounds of gaiety I heard as the hours passed were uproarious laughter and shrill giggles from a compartment near mine that was inhabited by two Soviet generals and a couple of women who looked too young to be their wives. On the few occasions any of them emerged from the compartment, they wore faces of solemn dignity, but when the door closed, the giggling would resume. In our own compartments the supply of caviar and salmon diminished at a steady rate, and was completely gone by the time our train arrived in Krasnadar.

Which was just as well because our hunting "camp" was a villa once used by the Czars of Imperial Russia and their hunting buddies. It was fully staffed by cooks and maids and gamekeepers who wore the traditional European gamekeeper's insignia of oak clusters, but entwined in their gold-embroidered leaves was the hammer and sickle.

After many introductions to officials whose names I couldn't possibly understand or remember, we were ushered into a small meeting room with a podium over which hung a portrait of Lenin, sitting by a campfire, shotgun over his knee, and apparently haranguing a cluster of fellow hunters. A white-uniformed maid, as sour looking as she was fat, served scalding tea and marble-hard biscuits after which the chief forester welcomed us briefly in passable English, then went about the serious business of explaining the rules of Russian hunting.

His main concern, it seemed, was that we understood their trophy scoring system and, using charts and diagrams, detailed the measurement methods and how a monetary value was attached to various trophy points. At the time I was under the impression that I was a non-paying guest and paid little attention to the price tags attached to various parts of a stag's antlers, but I couldn't help but note the distinctly capitalistic way they were intent on profiting from their deer herd.

That evening, over a meal better than anything we'd had in Moscow, the vodka left over from our train ride disappeared and as it did, the stony-faced local officials became increasingly convivial and the foresters who would be our guides on the morrow raised endless toasts to our coming success.

The Russian stag we were hunting is more commonly known throughout Europe as red deer and is a cousin to North American elk, though somewhat smaller and with a rather different antler configuration, typically branching into a cluster of points at the upper ends. On the better trophies these upper points may palmate into cuplike formations called chalices. The Soviet pricing schedule put a high value on fine chalices.

On the morning of our hunt we were issued our rifles, which were Baikal Medveds. (Baikal is the trade name applied to most Russian sporting arms, being more or less their equivalent to Remington or Winchester.) The gas-operated Medved autoloader, even with its checkered, sporter-style stocks, has distinctly military parentage with an over-the-barrel action rod and military-style sights similar to the Simonov and AK systems. The caliber was 9mm and looked something like a .35 Remington but a bit shorter.

When I asked for ballistic details, I was answered with a shrug and told it was called "deer." Another sporting caliber, I learned, is called "bear." Which probably means that Russian big game hunters don't have much to debate or choose from in the way of calibers. Only one of the rifles had a scope—a stubby, low-power model that looked to be of WW II sniper vintage, which John Amber opted to use.

The vast woodland around us was known as the Red Forest, which was no surprise as they attached the color of revolution communism to about everything (Red Square in Moscow, for example). The deer are hunted from stands with beaters driving the game toward the guns.

The stands turned out to be impromptu hiding places selected by our individual guides. My chain-smoking guide spoke no more English than I spoke Russian and carried a battered bolt-action rifle of ancient origin. Despite the language barrier—or because of it—we got along pretty well with the sign language that hunters communicate with the world over.

On the first drive we spotted a jackal zigzagging in our direction. I wasn't sure if it was on the shooting menu and raised my eyebrows in the universal questioning expression. He responded by nodding in the affirmative, touching my rifle and making a shooting gesture. So when the jackal came within about 25 yards, I killed it with an easy shot. This pleased the guide immensely, who pantomimed that he would take the skin and make it into a fur cap.

When I fired at the jackal, the front sight fell off my rifle and was retrieved by the guide after a brief search in the leaves. He slipped the sight back onto the muzzle—still as loose as before—and smiled with satisfaction at the repair.

Now it was my turn to shrug, and I made a mental note to recommend that the Medved not be imported for American hunters. There were two drives that morning and on the second drive we heard a couple of nearby shots followed minutes later by a running Viktor, explaining that he had wounded a stag and asking if it had come our way. We had seen nothing.

On the second day of our hunt, I was stationed at the edge of a vast, recently plowed field. Two deer had been bagged the previous afternoon, plus the wounded one Viktor was still tracking, but I had seen nothing. More and more I was blaming my poor luck on my guide's incessant cigarette smoking, which was probably spooking any deer headed our way. Just as I was contemplating a complaint to the head forester, the guide made a hissing sound and nudged me toward the open field. There, coming in from an angle that would bring them within 75 yards, was a gang of five or six stags running in a loose bunch. All had good antlers, and as far as I could tell, each was good as the others so I simply swung the loose sights of my Medved ahead of the lead stag and pulled the two-stage trigger.

The shot had no effect that I could see except to turn the deer toward the safety of the forest. Just before they disappeared, I fired again, with no apparent effect. I was disgusted with my bungling shot and with myself even more for being so dumb as hunting with a rifle without having had a chance to check its zero.

But just as I was beginning to utter my disgust, the guide put his cupped hand behind his ear, pantomiming hearing a distant sound, then pointing in the direction where the stags had disappeared. Then he broke into a big smoky grin and made a downward motion with his hands. I had hit the stag and it was down!

The next morning the Russians turned out in their best medal-bedecked suits and uniforms and presented us with rather elegant-looking certificates, which on closer inspection turned out to be scorecards tallying the points of our trophies. Handshakes and solemn congratulations were offered and at the conclusion of the ceremony, a calculator was produced and it was obvious that rubles were being converted to U.S. dollars.

After considerable whispering among themselves and a bit of smug giggling, they presented us with our individual bills. Mine came to something a little over a hundred grand, and the main bureaucrat who handed us our bills stood in front of me in smiling anticipation, as if he thought I had that much cash on me and was going to hand it over.

The night before, Dave had warned us that the Russians would probably try to milk us for a bunch of dollars and outlined what our response was to be. Since I was the first of our group to be presented with the outrageous bill, I was the first to speak and I savored the moment.

"You wish to pay in American, no?"

*"Nyet,"* I replied, returning the bureaucrat's smile and ignoring his proffered bill for American money. "We'll pay in rubles . . . your money."

"Viktor, open that old suitcase so we can pay these guys off and let's get out of here."

*"He was quartering toward me,*
*dropping his head occasionally to snatch*
*a mouthful of whatever it is ibex eat*
*in those vegetation-less areas . . . "*

# Chapter 11

# Pursuing the Persian Prize

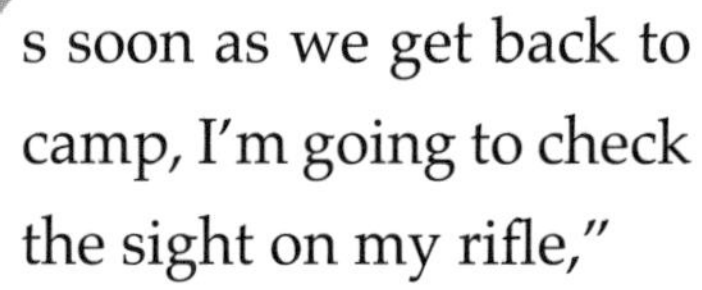

As soon as we get back to camp, I'm going to check the sight on my rifle,"

Hooshang wearily nodded his agreement.

Other than my one terse comment, our lunch of thin, cardboard-like *labosh* layered with the tart white cheese Iranians called *paneer* and cups of scalding tea were downed in silence.

Dog tired, the usually garrulous Iranian shepherds, now serving as guides and porters, gazed silently into the Asian distance. I had the distinct impression that their not speaking nor looking my way was an act of politeness lest I take their words or gaze as a sign of reproach for having muffed a hard-earned shot a half-hour before.

I did not apologize to them for the errant shot because missing, like hitting, is part of hunting, and apologies and explanations are neither required nor expected. Yet as I sipped my tea Iranian fashion with a lump of sugar held behind my teeth, I felt miserable—as only a hunter who has busted a gut trying to get a fine trophy then lost it at the last moment can be miserable.

The hunt had started out with fine style and high prospects. Fred Huntington, the Oroville, California, manufacturer of RCBS Reloading Equipment, and I had left Los Angeles on the last day of 1973 and rang in the New Year somewhere over the North Atlantic in the cozy comfort of a Pan American Clipper jet. Somewhere along our route the captain announced we had crossed a time zone that put us in the new year and amid some sleepy cheering in the cabin, Fred and I hoisted glasses of champagne to the New Year, each other, and our plans for a terrific hunt in Iran.

Fred had hunted in many parts of the world, including several African safaris, but like me, this would be his first adventure in the land of the ancient Persian kings.

Some months before we had been struck with the notion of pursuing Iran's varieties of wild sheep and fabled ibex, so we had booked a *shikar*, as Asian big game hunts are called. The hunt would include the beautiful Urial sheep in northeastern Iran, the elusive little Armenian sheep and ibex near the Turkish and Russian borders of northwestern Iran and finally, the red sheep found only on the Royal Preserve near Tehran.

Now, with 1974 barely a week old, I was sitting on a mountain so close to the Soviet Union that if I kicked a stone loose it would splash into the Araks River, the dividing line between Iran and Russia. In the distance came an occasional thundering, which I later learned was Soviet artillery practice.

That morning, the first day of our hunt, Fred had elected to go with his guide Manouchehr Abdallahian after Armenian sheep, while my guide, Hooshang Bakhtiar, and I would hunt ibex. Hooshang, whom I had met only the day before, was an athletically built man of about medium height who sported a neatly trimmed Clark Gable mustache on a pleasant face. Though he had told me very little about himself, I later learned that he was from an influential family, which probably accounted for the difference and respect accorded him by other members of the hunting staff. He also spoke excellent English, no doubt the result of a first-class education, and turned out to be very personable over our days together. (Which contrasted sharply with the personality of Fred's guide Abdallahian, who seemed to have a perpetually resentful air about him.)

Besides Hooshang and myself, our party consisted of a government game warden, a tall hawk-faced chap who sported a savage-looking moustache and took great pride in his khaki uniform and the official status it proclaimed. Like nearly all people of that region, he was a fiercely devoted cigarette smoker and kept a long ivory cigarette holder clamped between his front teeth at all times, even when not puffing on it. He also liked to give the impression of being in charge, but since he spoke little English, my dealings were mostly with Hooshang. The warden did, however, exercise his supposed authority on lower ranking members of our party, especially toward a husky young fellow in his mid teens, who carried my cameras, our lunches, and an armload of tin cups and fire-blackened tea kettles. Weighted down as he was, and clad only in low-top shoes and a thin jacket, he galloped through the snowdrifts like a caribou, his face glowing and his black eyes snapping with enthusiasm for our adventure. *A born hunter, someday he will be a terrific guide*, I thought.

Another member of our troop was a grizzled old veteran of the mountains whose age, as close as I could tell, lay somewhere between 45 and 75 (I was never able to tell if the harsh life of the northern mountains made old men look young, or young men look old.) He was supposed to be my gunbearer, but since I carried my rifle myself, he designated himself as my personal guardian and did a good job of it. Whenever I felt myself slipping backward on a steep, snow-covered slope, or got caught in a rockslide, he was always there to help, encouraging me with Turkish phrases and a warm smile, his six or eight remaining teeth lending character to his craggy grin. I really got to like him and the way he ignored commands issued by the game warden.

There were two other guys whose purpose I never quite understood. We had rented a thin, rail-backed horse from one of them, so I reckoned he came along to make sure we didn't mistreat his half-starved horse, and his pal probably came to watch an American try to kill an ibex. At first they had little to say and seemed a bit sulky but as the day progressed, they became increasingly willing, eager actually, to contribute comment and advice.

All things considered, we were a mixed bag as we waved our good-byes to Fred, who rode a steed much sturdier and sure-footed than mine. I put up with my clumsy nag for only a half-hour before dismounting in favor of the greater comfort and security of continuing on foot, even on the uneven, snow-covered trail.

Leaving the mud-walled village where we were housed, we skirted a range of almost vertical cliffs where the mountain-dwelling ibex makes its home. These goat-like creatures, weighing about 200 pounds, wear a rather nondescript coat of coarse, grizzled hair. They also have a reputation for smelling bad, especially the males, so all in all they are not an especially impressive animal until you look at a mature ram's horns—and then your heart skips a beat.

All out of proportion to his body size, the male ibex's horns sweep up and back, ending in a downward curl that becomes more pronounced as they grow older, making them one of the planet's most desired trophies. Golden effigies of ibex have been found in the gravesites of ancient Persian kings, and if the real thing did not exist to this day, one would be bound to suspect that those little statues with the oversized horns were, like unicorns, only an ancient goldsmith's interpretation of a mythological creature.

My first sighting of ibex came about mid-morning when we spotted a small band peering down at us from what I thought to be an unapproachable ledge high in the cliffs. Hooshang, however, as I quickly discovered, was not impressed by either the steepness or the height of the cliffs. After circling a quarter-way around the mountain where we would be out of sight of the wary animals, we launched an Iranian style assault straight up a slope that was about 45 degrees steep at the easy places. Sixty degrees was closer to the average because at some points I could extend my arms straight out and touch the hillside before me.

When we finally reached the top, I found that the mountain leveled out mesa-fashion so that walking was somewhat easier, causing me to get optimistic about getting within shooting range. Such hopes were short-lived, because when we circled around to where the ibex had been earlier, we arrived just in time to see them scamper up a steep, rock-strewn draw and hightail it across the plateau to an even higher ridge. This seemed to me to be something of a blessing because the undulating plateau would allow a less exhausting and certainly safer stalk than creeping along the near vertical cliffs.

I had hoped to avoid the latter situation because, quite honestly, I don't do at all well in high places where there is nothing to hang onto except thin air.

The plateau was about a mile and a quarter wide with the southern rim tilted up a few hundred feet higher than the northern edge. Predictably, the ibex had headed toward the highest part. Hooshang judged they would drop off the high rim, then circle back around the mountainside. Wanting to save me another hard climb, he suggested that I go with the warden to the lower rim and watch for the ibex to come around. Meanwhile, he would climb to the upper rim and keep an eye on the ibex to make sure we didn't lose them altogether.

As we made our way on the lower rim, the game warden stopped and peeked over the edge, then quickly dropped to his knees behind a low sage bush and motioned for me to get down. Crawling up to where he was hidden, I saw a grassy bench some 200 yards wide that sloped gently downward for about 400 yards before dropping off sharply. Along the outer edges of the bench was an even bigger herd of at least 25 ibex. Some were grazing among the rocks and others were lying about in calm contentment. The closest animals were about 300 yards away, a pretty long shot for sure but not too far if I could get a solid rest under my rifle.

I had sighted my custom stocked and barreled Model 70 Winchester, chambered for the .280 Remington cartridge, to be dead on at 300 yards. Fred had also brought a .280 and was using an identical load. We figured this was a smart move in case either of us came up short on ammo.

After arriving at the village where we were billeted, our first project had been to check our rifles for any changes that might have occurred during the long trip from Los Angeles to Tehran. With improvised targets set up at a hundred long paces, we had each fired a couple shots with our rifles resting atop a smelly old saddle. Fred's two shots had hit close to where he wanted but mine had printed lower than it should have, so I had cranked up the elevation to put the bullet a couple inches above the aiming point.

Which is why, despite the range, I felt confident I could drop a slug into a ram's power plant without too much difficulty. The only problem was deciding which ram to shoot at—assuming, that is, that I wanted to shoot at all. Three or four rams carried horns noticeably larger than the others, but without Hooshang to advise me, I had no way of knowing if any were the trophy I'd come for. After all, these were the first ibex I'd ever seen.

The game warden evidently had some strong ideas on the matter and began urging me to shoot. He didn't seem to mind which one I shot at and anxiously waved his cigarette holder in their general direction, repeating what I took to be his words for "shoot now, shoot now!"

Hooshang was not yet in sight, so hoping for a bit of guidance, I looked back at the old man to see if he had any opinion as to what I should do. To make my predicament plain to him, I pointed at a few of the better rams and offered him my binoculars as an indication that I wanted him to look the herd over and see if there were any really good trophies. He just gave me his eight-toothed smile, politely declined use of the glasses, then dreamily gazed off into space as if not wanting to offend the game warden but at the same time subtly indicating that the herd contained nothing worth looking at. This was all the advice I needed, so I laid my rifle aside, indicating that I would not shoot.

The game warden continued haranguing me in Iranian, then switched to Turkish. Finally, deciding that anyone who couldn't understand either Iranian or Turkish must be some sort of imbecile, he backed off, waving his hands and grinding his cigarette holder between his teeth.

Ten minutes later the two horse handlers, who had circled the base of the mountain, appeared on a low saddle beyond the bench where we'd been watching the ibex. They were soon joined by Hooshang and the young porter, and a half-hour later the warden, the old man, and I caught up with them.

Hooshang said that the small band of ibex he had been trailing included a ram with a good set of horns but that he was very wary and would be difficult to stalk. Adding to the problem was that the herd had gone on to the next mountain. We decided to pursue them, figuring by the time we reached the herd, they would have settled down somewhat.

Two hours later, as the thin winter sun passed its midpoint of the day, we reached the rocky crest of the next mountain and started studying the still-distant ibex with binoculars. They had bedded down on a sharply angling rock shelf a good 800 yards away. About midway across the open plain was a rock outcropping, and I told Hooshang if he could get me to those rocks, I could handle things from there. The challenge would be in covering about 400 yards of completely exposed territory. If the wary ibex spotted us, they would light out like a bunch of turpentined cats and we'd never catch up with them before dark.

It was the game warden who saved the day. He was as familiar with the terrain as the end of his cigarette holder, and when Hooshang told him I wanted to get to the rock outcropping, he grinned and motioned for us to follow. The rocks, he said, were part of a backbone outcropping that ran around to the backside of the hill we were on. All we had to do was drop back down the back side, circle around to where the backbone began, and stay behind the outcropping until I found a good place to shoot. By the time I got the translated version, it all sounded too easy to be true. It was.

About halfway down the offside of the mountain, the steep slope gave way to a vertical precipice, completely impassable except for a tilted, snow-covered ledge that snaked around the sheer wall. One look and I was seized by the panic that only an acrophobe can understand. Beneath the treacherously narrow ledge was nothing but 200 feet of open air, below which were piles of razor-edged rocks.

Since I couldn't see the other end of the ledge because of the rock wall's curvature, I assumed it to go on many yards, hundreds perhaps, with every inch an invitation to certain death. Oblivious to the danger, the game warden started across the ledge as casually as if going for a stroll, and Hooshang was about to do likewise when I told him to wait up for a moment while we discussed alternate routes.

"Not for me," I explained. "Tippy-toeing around icy, foot-wide ledges is not what I came for, so we're taking another route . . . any route but this one."

For a long moment Hooshang considered my predicament and finally, with a deep sigh and sweeping gesture toward the chasm below, patiently explained our only alternative: Which would mean going all the way down to the gorge below, then re-climbing the mountain. That would take hours and the ledge route would only take minutes. To him there was only one choice. The game warden thought my apprehension was a big joke. Cocking his cigarette holder up at a rakish angle to show his fearless lack of concern, he offered to carry my rifle around the ledge.

I let him. But before setting foot on the ledge, I snapped a photo of the path so there would at least be a pictorial record of where I met my end.

As the warden had promised, the ledge circled around to the outcropping that jutted into an open plain where the ibex were feeding. Keeping low and out of sight, Hooshang and I belly-crawled to a low shelf-like rock where, using my thick wooly cap to rest my rifle, I settled the scope's crosshairs high on the chest of the biggest ibex. He was quartering toward me, dropping his head occasionally to snatch a mouthful of whatever it is ibex eat in those vegetation-less areas, then nervously jerked it erect to survey the surrounding countryside. Most of his buddies were blackish brown except for a grayish underside, but this old fellow was gray farther up on his sides and had a grayish patch running up his chest into his throat and ending just under his beard.

His horns were noticeably thicker at the base than those of the other rams and the outer tips tucked under in a more complete curl. After making a final binocular appraisal of the ram, Hooshang whispered that it was not a record-class head, but one that I could certainly be proud of, which was all I needed to know. My rest was so solid that the crosshairs were virtually motionless when I pressed the trigger, and I was so certain that the shot had been a good that I carelessly took my time working the bolt and looking back down at the animal.

"Shoot again, shoot again, they're running," yelled Hooshang.

*Had I missed?* I couldn't believe it. The shot had been a dead setup. Bewildered and now thoroughly rattled, I slammed the bolt home and swung the crosshairs ahead of a running form I hoped to be the same ram and was pressing the trigger just as they disappeared over the crest of the slope.

"Too bad, they are all gone," said Hooshang.

"That first shot looked good," I protested, "are you sure it wasn't a hit?"

"No, he ran away very fast, you did not hit. It is getting late now. We will eat and start back to the village. Tomorrow we will try again."

The old man, the boy, and the two horse handlers, who had been waiting on the other side of the hill had heard the shooting and now came running up eager to view my trophy. In a few words Hooshang explained what had happened and then ordered them to start a fire and make some tea. Nothing more was said.

It had been a long cold day of difficult hiking and climbing. We'd made a great stalk and I'd muffed the shot. Now we were bone-tired and too dejected to talk, except for a brief conference between Hooshang as to the best route to follow back to the village. One being the direction from where we had come, which I vetoed immediately as I had no intention of twice tempting fate on that heart-stopping ledge. The other being to take a longer but safer path. So in addition to muffing what should have been a certain kill, I was making matters worse by insisting we take a longer and more tiring route to the village that would get us there hours after dark.

When the tea was finished and the pots were gathered up, we trooped down the mountain single file in the direction the escaping ibex had taken. Then, just as the game warden dropped over the brow of the slope, he let out a shout and started galloping down the mountainside, followed an instant later by Hooshang and the others. At first I couldn't understand and then I heard their laughing and cheering.

"Come see, come see," Hooshang was yelling and waving his arms. "Come see, come see."

When I caught up with them, the cluster of men parted so I could see the cause of their jubilation. The big ram was lying on his side with a bullet hole almost exactly where I had called the shot.

"That was a very good shot," grinned Hooshang. "We are all very proud of you."

The old man smiled, the boy continued whooping with unrestrained delight, and the warden, cigarette holder at a jaunty angle, ordered the horse guys to lead their animal closer and load the ram onto it. After more smiles and laughter, and what I took to be praise of my great marksmanship, the old man suddenly became serious and produced a slender-bladed knife, which he offered to Hooshang with a somewhat beseeching expression on his face.

At first I failed to understand, and then Hooshang explained that the man wanted to perform a *zibah*, the ceremonial Muslim practice of rendering the meat edible.

"He knows to be very careful and not ruin the cape," Hooshang noted.

While the brief *zibah* was being performed (which actually left no mark that I could find), and with the ram loaded on the now useful horse, I retraced the recent turn of events. We had been drinking our tea not more than 300 yards from where the ram gone down but had been unable to see where it had fallen under the brow of the slope. Had we taken only a slightly different route, we probably would have missed it entirely. Hooshang's explanation as to why he had been so positive I had missed was the fact that the ram had run so fast and so far without showing any sign of being hit, truly a testament to the amazing toughness of wild ibex.

The sun was dipping low and a bitter wind, bringing snow, swept down out of Russia as we made our way off the mountain. I let the old man take my rifle, which he slung over his shoulder with a warm and grateful smile. There would be a lot to tell Fred tonight.

*"All in all, it was the hardest day's*
*hunting in my career—*
*and probably the luckiest."*

# Chapter 12

# Yankee Luck In New Zealand

ave you ever noticed how steady you can hold the sights on a target when you're only "dry firing" with an unloaded rifle? Let me tell you a story about it:

We were high in the "Alps" of New Zealand's South Island, not too many miles from the western coastlands. My hunting pal was Jeff Veronese, a metal-fabricating contractor from Christchurch and one of the keenest hunters I've ever met. We'd spent the past couple days working our way above the lush farm valleys and had set up our hunting camp in a narrow valley between two snow-blanketed granite ridges.

The ridges that walled the valley were so high and so steep that the summer sun only peeked in for a few hours a day. Where the walls came together, there really wasn't a valley floor, only a surging torrent of icy blue water. The cataract began at the maw of a cloudy blue glacier, which formed the third wall of our valley. After churning downhill for three miles, the water plunged into space and fell hundreds of feet into a river basin below. What I'm calling a valley was actually only a notch, a tiny, glacier-carved pocket cut into the side of the mountain eons ago. For spectacular ruggedness, I've never seen its equal.

Despite the steepness of the valley walls, they were covered with a dense green layer of ferns, mosses, grasses, and rock-clinging vines and bush. Moisture-laden sea air collides with the glacial atmosphere to create a terrific annual rainfall that when combined with the mild, year-round temperatures, results in incredibly lush vegetation. Unbelievably, though, throughout the history of the islands there had been no animal life of any consequence to take advantage of this lush and abundant garden. That all changed in the early 1900s when game species such as deer, wapiti, red stag, chamois, and exotic tahr were introduced.

The rest is hunting history. The super-abundant food supply, plus the total absence of natural enemies, resulted in a virtual tidal wave of game growth. By mid-century some of the deer species were so numerous that the government proclaimed them to be "noxious animals." Everyone was encouraged to hunt them as often as possible and some hunters were even paid by the government to help reduce their numbers.

The stories told by New Zealand's professional deer control hunters would sound incredible to North American hunters, but they give you an idea of just how dense the game population had become by 1930 and later. One hunter, for example, bagged more than 1,500 deer in one year and another chap actually killed three deer with one shot! I've heard of a hunter that killed 25 tahr without moving from his position, and there is an eyewitness account of a hunter who dropped a deer and found that his bullet had exited, ricocheted off a rock, and then killed a second deer!

Game is not so abundant these days because commercial meat-gatherers, spurred by high prices and shooting from helicopters, have accomplished what the control hunters couldn't, and as a result, game is harder to find. The days of the professional hunter are over but even so, deer and some other species are still officially considered noxious beasts, and you can bag all you want any time of the year. There's still no such thing as a hunting license.

With the pressure from helicopter shooting, chamois and tahr have retreated into remote areas, and that's why Jeff and I had hiked into the high peaks. I was to do most of the shooting while he took motion pictures.

We had barely set up camp when Jeff spotted a small band of about six chamois on a 50-degree slope about 600 yards above us.

I was using a Model 70 Winchester of recent vintage, in .270 caliber and topped with a 6X scope of unfamiliar make. I'd borrowed it from a friend in Christchurch and hadn't had a chance to give it a try, but according to the owner, it was sighted dead on the money at 200 yards with his 130-grain Sierra bullet handloads.

We worked our way to within about 450 yards of the sunning chamois, and I set up a solid rest on a boulder while he readied his camera. What with the unfamiliar rifle, the rather longish range, and the somewhat diminutive target, I wasn't at all sure of making a hit. But if I did, it would make a great

movie sequence.

The chamois of New Zealand is the same mountain-dwelling animal of the European Alps. Looking something like a cross between a goat and an antelope, chamois weigh up to 80 pounds and stand a little less than a yard high at the shoulder. Both sexes grow horns, with those of the buck often exceeding ten inches in length. The brownish-black horns grow straight up from the brow for a few inches, then curve over somewhat like those of a North American pronghorn, only on a smaller scale.

I had just squirmed into a solid shooting position and chambered a round when Jeff ordered me to hold up.

"What's the problem?"

"I can't figure it out," he replied. "This camera was working an hour ago but now it won't run."

"Well take your time and get it fixed. While you're monkeying with it, I'll try a few dry shots to test my hold and get used to the rifle's trigger pull."

With that I opened the bolt, took out the cartridge and closed the action. At that range and angle, I figured the bullet would be about 12 to 15 inches below the point of aim, so I held some six inches above the shoulder of the biggest animal, which was quartering toward me on a granite outcropping. As always when dry-firing, the crosshairs were virtually motionless, the wind was calm, and the trigger break was clean and crisp.

*Blam!*

I recovered from the recoil—and my acute astonishment, just in time to see the buck topple from the rock and the others scurry into the undergrowth.

"Hey Jim," Jeff wailed, "why didn't you wait for me? That would have made a terrific movie."

"You're not going to believe me, but I didn't know the gun was loaded," was all I could say. "When I took the cartridge out of the chamber to dry-fire, I overrode the magazine and picked up another round without knowing it. I'm really sorry if I ruined your chance for some good pictures."

"Don't worry about it; the batteries are ruined so I probably couldn't have made a movie anyway. Too bad though, that was really a terrific shot for a Yank. Let's go find your trophy."

His comment "for a Yank" irked me a bit because he'd already been making some scarcely veiled references to his own marksmanship. New Zealand hunters feel, with ample justification, that they are the most able rifle marksmen in the world. There's no question that they get more practice. Jeff has bagged literally scores of big game trophies, which I guess he figures gives him bragging rights.

Actually, Jeff is an Italian lad who sailed to New Zealand during the 1950s and, like every Italian I've ever met, he's a fanatical hunter. Even as a small boy he dreamed of a land where he could hunt every day of the year, and coming to New Zealand was the answer to his wildest imaginings. He told me that he wasn't sure what he would be hunting when he got to this new land but suspected that his quarries would range from tigers to cannibals. He really didn't care what it was just so long as he was hunting something.

I had met Jeff in Christchurch in February of 1974 through Bennie Williams, the guy who had loaned me the rifle. Williams runs a gun shop and is also a distributer of reloading equipment, which is how he came to know Fred Huntington, the founder and owner of RCBS, the widely known and highly respected line of reloading tools.

Fred and I were on a round-the-world hunting spree and during the past month we'd hunted sheep and ibex in Iran, buffalo in Australia, and stopped off for some sight-seeing jaunts in Spain, India, and Hong Kong. New Zealand was our last port-of-call before returning to the U.S. and I hoped to bag chamois and tahr while we were there.

The roaring season for red deer was still a couple of months away, so chamois and tahr were my only options, with not much hope for tahr. Since Fred had business calls to make and wouldn't have time for hunting, I teamed up with Jeff and we'd struck out on our own.

Getting to my chamois proved more of a task than I bargained for. The rushing stream was too deep and fast for wading, and the boulders were a little too far apart to risk rock-hopping across. We hiked the three-mile length of the valley without finding an easy crossing and finally had to settle for wading across a wide but fairly shallow pool near the glacier. Even there the current was so swift that Jeff and I had to lock arms and brace each other to keep from being swept off our feet. The rocks in the streambed were so sharp that we had to keep our boots on and the water was so cold that I was completely numb from the hips down after only a few seconds. I didn't know water could be that cold without being an ice cube.

After crossing the stream we came to another obstacle: Despite the steepness of the mountainside, it was covered with a peculiar sort of brush that grows as thick as a jungle and has long, narrow, tendril-like branches that tend to droop downhill. The growth is so dense that you can't even see the ground, much less put your foot on it. You just have to thrash your way through the thicket, actually walking on top of the vegetation wherever possible, hanging on with hands and—above all—trying to keep from losing your balance. The slopes are about 60 degrees in places, and one slip will send you crashing to the valley floor. Imagine trying to get through an Alaskan alder thicket that has been tilted up on its side and you'll get the idea.

The chamois had been less than 500 yards away when I shot, but getting to it involved a six-hour trek through freezing water, sweltering jungle, glacial ice fields, and sheer granite cliffs. I've hunted on five continents but this was the most rugged terrain I've ever set foot on. During our frequent rest stops, I gazed in wonder and awe at the spires of granite soaring into the heavens on all sides. Several years before, these same mountains had served as a training ground for a New Zealand beekeeper, Edmond Hillary, as he prepared for what was to be the first successful assault on Mt. Everest.

I mused to Jeff, "I wonder if Hillary found Mt. Everest to be any tougher than these New Zealand Alps."

"I've often wondered that myself," he nodded, quite serious.

To reach the outcropping where the chamois had fallen involved a circular route behind it, which took us above the spot and then down from the opposite side. A direct approach was too steep and dangerous—not that our option was all that much better. The brush was especially high in the area and it was impossible to plan ahead for more than ten yards. Sometimes we would emerge from the brush to find ourselves standing on the sheer edge of a 100-foot drop-off. Thus our already pitifully slow progress was further hampered by considerable backtracking.

During one of my increasingly frequent stops, Jeff went on ahead to find a workable route. From where I stood I could plainly see the exact spot from where I'd fired that morning and I reckoned that we were within a hundred yards of the downed chamois. Five miles of Georgia swampland would have been easier and faster. In a couple of minutes Jeff was back, breathing hard and wide-eyed with excitement.

"A bull tahr, just ahead," he panted.

As if by magic, my aching muscles were healed and my lacerated hands and knees forgotten. Since it was February—mid-summer in New Zealand—Jeff had figured the tahr would be considerably higher in the mountains and we probably wouldn't see any. By some luck, however, we had stumbled across a "lowlander" and, with more luck I might get a shot.

Sometimes called Himalayan tahr, animals from the mountains of northern India had been introduced in New Zealand in 1904 by the Duke of Bedford. I don't know much about the duke, but it's a good guess that he wanted to expand his hunting territory. He picked a perfect place for his tahr because by 1936 his original stock of eight animals had multiplied to the point that the government had to commence shooting operations to control their numbers.

A bull tahr is a sight unlike anything a sportsman is likely to encounter in North America. It stands some 40 or more inches at the shoulder and weighs more than 200 pounds. The shoulder area is heavily muscled, as would be expected of a mountain dweller, and the head is more or less like that of a goat. The coat is about the color of an old penny, and the silky hair, especially around the neck and shoulders, may grow to a foot or more in winter. Try to imagine an American bison, in miniature, with a coppery coloration, the hide of an angora goat, and the head and hoofs of a mountain goat and you have a fair image of the tahr. The thick and stubby horns curve to the rear and seldom exceed a foot in length.

When we arrived at the place where Jeff had jumped the tahr, there was nothing to be seen but brush and scattered boulders. To get a better view we shinnied to the top of a dump truck-sized boulder and at once spotted the tahr about a hundred yards off. At the same instant he winded us and made a spectacular dive from his perch into a thicket at least 20 feet below. I snapped off a shot at the airborne target and caught him low in the rib cage. He went limp in mid-air and crashed into brush. There was no doubt that I'd hit him solid.

"I don't believe it," whistled an amazed Jeff. "Nobody makes a shot like that."

"Just luck," I shrugged, barely able to control my own amazement. "Just luck."

"That's twice you've been a bit too lucky today Mate. Are all you Yanks that lucky?"

"Sure," I assured him with as bland an expression as I could possibly manage, "Some American hunters are even luckier than I am."

Jeff stared me in the eye to see if I could possibly be joking and I stared back as innocent and truthful as I could. I expect he's still wondering if I was pulling his leg or not, but for the next two days of our happy association he had very little additional comment about the prowess of his fellow New Zealanders marksmen.

To get the tahr off the mountain, Jeff laced the animal's front legs through slits cut in the rear leg tendons and carried it piggyback fashion. I dressed the

chamois and carried the head, cape, and quarters of meat in Jeff's rucksack. Game meat is highly prized table fare in New Zealand and nearly everything is packed out no matter how rough the hiking.

By the time we got back to camp, the last glimmerings of a summer evening had turned the glaciers into glittering cascades of diamonds but I was too weary to hold my head up and look. After some hot beans and sausage, however, not to mention a glass of Jeff's homemade wine, the day's adventure took on a rosy perspective. All in all, it was the hardest day's hunting in my career—and probably the luckiest.

Fred, as I learned when I caught up with him in Wellington, had had some incredible luck of his own. It seems that Bennie had taken him on a motor tour of the South Island and somewhere in the mountains they had spotted a group of chamois only few hundred yards from the road. Bennie had his .243 in the trunk, so Fred, still decked in suit and tie, tip-toed through the brush, got to within shooting distance, and dropped an especially big buck. Such impromptu shooting is mainly illegal in America but not in New Zealand.

Jeff drove me to the Christchurch airport and I was going through the gate when a final devilish urge hit me to get even for his "for a Yank" comment.

"Jeff, come to America and go hunting with me and a couple of my pals. We'll show you some Yank-style shooting like you won't believe."

*"A three-inch margin of error*
*was plenty acceptable for an animal*
*with more than four square feet of chest area.*
*But even so, there was something*
*that made me hesitate."*

# Chapter 13

# The Worst Shot I Ever Made

The shot was well earned and I was determined to make the most of it. The range was long, but not too long, a bit over 240 yards—hard to say for sure because of the uneven terrain and downward angle. I would have liked to have gotten closer, as would any hunter, but we were as close as we could get without crossing open ground and spooking the wary animals. We'd hunted hard for three days, searching for this one special animal, an animal that could very well win a coveted gold medal.

What breeze there was came at a cross angle that barely rippled the lacey tops of dead grass around the animal, not enough to be a factor in my bullet's flight. With the forearm of my rifle nested on the padded fork of a shooting tripod and its butt cupped into my shoulder, I took a deep breath and held it until the crosshairs of my scope slowed their jiggling and came to rest on the spot I wanted to hit.

Given the distance and the known accuracy of my rifle and ammo, I calculated that the bullet would, at worst, hit within three inches of my aiming point. Probably closer if the shot broke clean. A three-inch margin of error was plenty acceptable for an animal with more than four square feet of chest area.

But even so, there was something that made me hesitate. The animal was lying down and I've never liked shooting at game in that position. Not for any particular reasons regarding my sense of sportsmanship, but because the angles and aiming points I normally use for big game are different when the animal is down and its legs are not visible. I've seen enough shots missed at lying game to know it can be a lot trickier than it looks.

Taking my finger off the trigger and thumbing back the safety, I shook my head toward Dirk and Jim. "Not yet," I whispered, and both nodded in agreement while letting out big whooshes of collectively held breath.

Since arriving at our tented camp in Namibia, we had spent three full days hunting from near-freezing dawns through blistering middays, tracking and cross-tracking endless miles of one of the most notoriously inhospitable places on earth—the Kalahari Desert—in search of one of Africa's most exotically beautiful antelope: the gemsbuck.

Although the popular image of a desert is treeless dunes of shifting sand bestrode by Lawrence of Arabia, they actually come in an astonishing range of climes, topography, and geology. Seen from above, as we had when we flew in to camp from Windhoek, the Kalahari appears like waves in a muddy pond, but seen up close the waves become ridges of garnet-colored sand separated by flat valleys about a half-mile wide.

It was winter in the Kalahari, with cold nights that called for layers of blankets on our cots and down jackets in the mornings. We would shed our jackets under the blazing midday sun and then snuggle into them again when we scooted our canvas camp chairs close to the evening's campfire.

Life in the Kalahari is decreed by water, and the past summer's rainy season had dumped record amounts of it. The barren valleys had bloomed richer than even the oldest natives could remember, which had been followed by an explosion of plant and animal life. Now, in winter's dryness, the waist-high grasses stood stiff and prickly, especially one particularly annoying type of grass we'd named "Velcro" because of the way the spiky seeds penetrated our clothes and resisted removal.

I'd hunted gemsbuck before, taking a pretty good one several years before in Botswana. On that safari I had spotted them only in lonely ones or twos but here, close on to Gemsbuck National Park, they roamed by the thousands. We had been seeing plenty of them, some in herds of 20 or more, but none with horns long enough to win the gold medal I hoped for.

Gemsbuck are members of the oryx family and one of the most distinctive of African antelope because of their long, straight horns set atop black-and-white faces that seem to have been painted by surrealist mask-makers. They are powerfully muscled, weighing between 400 and 500 pounds, with thick, wide-hooved legs that are designed more for endurance than speed. But as with any antelope, speed is only relative; gemsbuck are plenty fast when they want to be.

The gemsbuck is perfectly suited to its harsh environment, and every one I've seen looked sleek and healthy. They drink when water is available and don't seem bothered when it isn't. Deep-rooted, softball-size melons thrive in the Kalahari and they offer moisture. Early trekkers who ran short of water when crossing the Kalahari discovered that the stomachs of gemsbuck held a reserve of water. I doubt if it tasted all that great, but few men dying of thirst would have noticed.

A peculiar thing about gemsbuck is that females are virtually indistinguishable from males (unless you look carefully at the right places), with the same size and markings and horn confirmation. The horns of male gemsbuck tend to be thicker at the base and somewhat shorter than those of females. Long-time observers of gemsbuck, like one of our guides, Hannes Steyn, say that the males wear down their horns by rubbing and polishing them in the sand. True or not, the record books list many females.

On our first afternoon of hunting, Dirk, my PH, and I made a scouting run and watched a good-sized herd slowly picking their way across a grassy vale.

"They can't stand peace," Dirk remarked as we crouched under the cover of a sterbos shrub. "Watch how they are constantly fighting."

The females seemed especially ill-tempered toward each other and every few steps one or the other would make a raking slash at one of her sisters. They seem to be constantly aware of their rapier-like horns and like young warriors with their first swords, can't resist using them at every opportunity.

In trophy-book terms, gemsbuck horns longer than 35 inches are pretty good and more than 42 inches are spectacular. Most of the gemsbuck listed in the record books were taken in the general area where we were hunting.

Dirk, who has looked at thousands of the animals, can judge horn length to the nearest inch. He was confident the gemsbuck that now captured our attention would top 40 inches, but it was difficult to judge his perfectly matched horns because he was lying down. As the minutes ticked into mid-morning, the warming Kalahari atmosphere began to boil with mirage, and the bull's horns seemed to wriggle like snakes dancing on their tails.

Although the Kalahari stretches into Botswana and the Republic of South

Africa, it's mainly associated with Namibia, formally known as Southwest Africa. It had been a German colony before WWI, and one of the more modern of Africa's European colonies, with beautiful towns and cities and paved streets lined with airy, well-kept Victorian-style homes. English is the official lingo, but of course a number of native dialects are spoken and a large percentage of the white population speaks German as its first, or at least most preferred, language. Bavarian-style homes and open beer gardens give many towns an unmistakable Old World German atmosphere. If I were to take residence on the African continent, Namibia would probably be my first choice.

My hunting pals were big shots in the shooting industry; Jim Morey, the top honcho at Swarovski USA and Bob Stutler, the head boss man at Sturm-Ruger's plant in Arizona. Rounding out our group was Rob Fancher, who handled PR and advertising for Swarovski, plus my long time co-conspirator Dave Petzal, who habitually sacrifices his talents to scribble for a rag called *Field & Stream*. It was the first safari for Stutler and Fancher, but the rest of us had heard the roar of lions and drunk from a hippo's pool.

Morey had been to Namibia the year before and hunted with Nimrod Safaris, a guiding operation jointly owned by Dirk DeBok and his partners Hannes Steyn and Pieter Stofberg. All are seasoned professional hunters with outstanding reputations. I was assigned to hunt with Dirk because he prefers to pursue trophy-class animals. I had come primarily to take a gemsbuck bigger than the 37-inch trophy that currently hung in my den.

Raised on a farm where he hunted big game since he could shoulder a rifle, Dirk joined the legendary Namibian Special Forces Police at 18 (roll Navy SEALS, Green Berets, and Selous Rangers into one and you get the idea). Using his farm-bred, hunting-honed skills to track down communist terrorists infiltrating from Angola, he'd become the youngest ever sergeant major in the force.

Unless you happen to be one of the nomadic Bushmen who have hunted the Kalahari since before time was measured, pursuing its animals on foot is out of the question. Dirk's technique was to go as far as possible by truck, using what few roads exist, then climbing the sand ridges on foot and glassing the valley beyond. If nothing was spotted, it was on to the next sand ridge and more glassing. It sounds monotonous but isn't because every mile of the Kalahari offers something worth seeing, and every ridge a different vista.

We were seeing plenty of gemsbuck, sometimes in herds but more often in groups of six or eight. Some had tantalizingly long horns, close to 40 inches or more, but after a long look Dirk would shake his head and say, "We'll find bigger." Then off we'd go to the next sand ridge and another climb and more acacia thorns to dodge and more itchy Velcro seeds to pluck from our pants and socks.

Since the three guides were shared by four hunters, Morey and Fancher took turns swapping off with the other two of us. Which is why Morey had come with Dirk and me on that particular day

"Bring some luck with you," I'd said to him as we loaded the truck with cans of water and the extra gas we'd need for a long day in the desert.

"Red sky in the morning, gemsbuck take warning," he replied, pointing at a distant layer of clouds that reflected the ember glow of a Kalahari sunrise.

We headed deep into the desert, using trails that hadn't been driven since the rainy season and grown over with thick-stemmed grasses and thorny brush. The first ridge we climbed was higher than most, steep on one side and sloping off on the other into a wide valley dotted with tall leadwood trees and scrubby acacia. And scattered between the trees were about 20 gemsbuck.

The animals we'd seen on previous days were typically on the move, their ranks of horns pointing skyward like the fixed bayonets of marching infantry, but these gemsbuck were at rest, some standing idly among the trees, others lying peacefully about.

The broken line of trees and scrub on the ridge where we were positioned offered good cover so we were able to take our time and carefully study each animal with the newly introduced 10X EL Swarovski binoculars Morey had brought along for us to try.

"Nice, nice," I heard Dirk whispering to himself as he moved his binoculars from one animal to the other. "Nice."

"What do you mean by nice?" I asked, training my binocs on the herd. Several animals looked like they would go 40 inches or more, but inches can be deceptive, and I respected Dirk's greater expertise.

"A couple will go forty-two, maybe more; there are others I'm not so sure about," he answered, not taking his searching eyes from his binoculars.

"Look below us," he whispered moments later, sucking in his breath with sudden surprise. "The closest one lying down . . . it's turned its head and you can see better now."

"How much would you estimate?"

"It will go forty-three easy, maybe another inch, the shorter horn is only an inch shorter; both sides are beautiful."

Though gemsbuck trophies are judged by horn length, followed by base thickness and width, I prefer well-matched evenness, and the horns we were looking at were perfectly straight and even, thickly ridged at the bases and spread wide at the top—a beautiful trophy in every respect.

"Well?" Dirk whispered, lowering his binoculars and looking over at me, his eyebrows raised in a comical expression, as if to say "Isn't this what we came for?"

"That's the one I came for."

Dirk quickly spread the legs of the shooting tripod he always carried, positioning it so we were mostly concealed by the straggly brush in front of us, but so I'd have a clear shot. A moment later I had cycled the bolt of my Ruger rifle, feeding a .30/06 round into its chamber and balanced it on the sturdy tripod. With the variable-X Swarovski turned up to full power, the shot looked almost too easy, except that the gemsbuck was lying down. So I waited.

Shooting from a tripod is vastly more accurate than shooting offhand, but firing from stand-up tripods like Dirk's takes some getting used to.

A couple times during the previous days I'd practiced and refined my technique with Dirk's tripod by dry-firing at various targets. I was confident the target before me presented no problem, though I was growing tired after a quarter-hour of waiting for the gemsbuck to get on its feet.

Dirk's tripod was a bit short for me, causing me to stoop somewhat rather than stand straight, and after standing in that position for so long, my back started to ache and my legs began to tire, causing increasing amounts of tremor to creep into my aim. It was increasingly clear that the longer I stood there, my aim would be less steady and the shot less certain. Which is why I'd finally given up the vigil and slumped down in a shady spot next to Morey, who later told me that he had been astonished that I'd had the patience to pass on what would have been a relatively easy shot at the lying animal and wait it out for a better shot.

Time dragged by slowly, long minutes made longer because I couldn't see the animals from where I sat. It seemed forever before Dirk tapped my shoulder and motioning with his thumb, whispered "They're starting to get up."

In an instant I was back on my feet with the rifle settled on the tripod, safety off.

The gemsbuck I wanted was the last to get up and when it did, the angle

was bad. One by one the other animals began to fall in line and move away, but for some mysterious reason the gemsbuck I wanted remained still, its body at an angle that offered a killing shot only if the bullet was perfectly placed. With the crosshairs on a spot high behind the animal's rib cage, I visualized the path of the bullet angling downward through the chest area, slicing a lung and into its heart.

*Shoot now,* I told myself, *this a gold medal trophy and you'll probably never find another one as good.*

For a moment my finger tightened on the trigger, but then hesitated when another thought welled up from my memory, reminding me of what I had heard and read about the toughness of the thickly muscled gemsbuck and how they have been known to run for miles and disappear after absorbing what should have been killing hits. The thought of tracking and possibly losing the trophy had no appeal, but neither did the prospect of losing it without trying.

*Would it be smarter to wait until it moved and possibly offered a better angle?* Either way, the seconds were ticking away, and I'd have to shoot soon or lose the opportunity.

I'd about decided to let it follow the herd and try to get in position for a more positive shot later when suddenly it turned almost sideways—a perfect angle. Except it was looking to the rear with its neck bent and head covering the spot I wanted to aim for.

"Don't shoot," Dirk whispered, but I didn't need to be warned because I knew that if I accidentally hit the animal's head, the skull might be split and its medal-winning tip-to-tip width measurement would be lost. But more important than a gold medal, I wanted a solid hit and clean kill. I'd already waited for a clear shot and now I could wait some more.

More agonizing minutes passed before the gemsbuck finally moved his head a few inches, not completely out of the way but enough for my bullet to hit where I wanted. At last, my patience had paid off and the time had come to take the shot I'd waited for.

The *whop* of the bullet's impact was sharp and clear, signaling a solid hit.

*But why was the gemsbuck still standing? Are they really that tough?* I was probably asking myself as I cycled the bolt for a second shot. But when I brought the crosshairs to where it had been standing seconds before, it wasn't there anymore. It was racing to catch up with the rest of the herd that was disappearing over the crest of the opposite hillside.

"I know I hit it," was all I could say, totally dumbfounded and hardly believing what I was seeing.

"I'm sure you hit it too," Dirk answered. "Let's follow after it on foot and Morey can circle around to meet us with the truck. I think we'll find the animal dead on the other side of the dune, but if it's only hurt and still running, we'll need the truck to keep up with it. I've known them to run for miles before dropping."

Despite his optimism that my gemsbuck was down and dead, I still didn't like the tone of what he was saying because it meant a good hunt was going sour. Even worse was the possibility of a magnificent animal being lost and claimed only by the jackals of the Kalahari.

With such thoughts nagging me as Dirk and I fast-walked, almost jogging across the valley, I prepared myself for the worst. The worst scenario being the gemsbuck getting mixed with the herd and hard to identify on the run, or getting into territory where we couldn't follow with the truck.

These dark doubts turned to hope when we topped the ridge and immediately spotted my gemsbuck, easily picked out in the herd by the bright spot of red low on its jaw. What was now clearly obvious was that I'd misjudged what I'd estimated to be ample clearance for my shot and the bullet had hit a hard wall of molars and jawbone. The herd had stopped running and were now moving away at a steady trot. It would be a long shot but there was no choice now. I had to stop the gemsbuck . . . now or perhaps never.

Dropping into sitting position with my elbows on my knees and the sling tight under my arm, I made a quick estimate of how far the bullet would drop at that distance, held the crosshairs high and fired. In what seemed an eternity there was an answering *whop* of a bullet hitting and already the gemsbuck was stumbling, falling behind the running herd, falling. Down forever.

Thinking back on that day and the celebration that followed when Dirk measured the horns at 45 and 44 ½ inches, ranking it well into the gold medal class, I guess I could claim that the worst shot I ever made was rescued by one of the best shots I ever made. But I'll make no such claim; there's a big difference between good shooting and lucky shots.

I was lucky, damn lucky.

# NORTH AMERICA

*"It was a delicious dilemma:*
*whether to take this obviously superior trophy or*
*to pass it by in the hopes of finding one even better."*

# Chapter 14

# The Land of Giants

The moose was mad. Not mad at anything in particular, just mad because he wanted to be mad. He was in the rut and that had him in a doubly terrible mood. He was too mad to eat and too mad to move, so he just stood there with his head held low, swinging his great antlers in wide arcs, and twitching his ears in absolute annoyance. Nearby a cow was nibbling on a willow branch. He looked her way, and she stopped eating and stood timid and still as if not knowing exactly what to do, but certainly not wanting to do anything that would make the bull madder than he was already.

When he looked away, the vast palms of his antlers swinging like barn doors before the wind, she dipped her bucket nose back into the willows and resumed her uneasy browsing. With its nose to her hocks was a yearling calf, long-legged and ungainly.

From where I watched a quarter-mile away, the bull's territory looked like a yellowed lawn, softly undulating, inviting one to walk there. But this was only an illusion of distance. In reality, it was thick willows, higher than a man's head, with tops so dense they formed an even layer over the entangled mass.

A man moving through this snarl of vegetation would have to fight for every step, but to a bull moose it was no more than lawn grass. As I watched, a second bull, nearly as big as the first, came plowing through the dense bramble as easily as a whale parts the seas.

The chill mist had thickened to streaks of rain on the spotting scope eyepiece, momentarily blurring the scene. A squat spruce a few feet away offered some shelter from the drizzle and knifing wind. Jack and Robert had already taken cover there, but the drama I was witnessing through the telescope was one of nature's most spectacular shows and I didn't want to miss a second. Pulling the parka hood over my head and smearing away the droplets with a numb finger, I watched the interloper crash into a small clearing, then stop short.

If I had spotted this newcomer only an hour before, he would have been one of the biggest bull moose I'd ever seen on the hoof. He was a giant with antlers nearing 60 inches on the outside spread with heavy palms and lots of points. Record-class, possibly, certainly a great trophy, but compared to the hulk he challenged, the bull was insignificant.

Even so, he was capable of awesome combat, and with both surprise and momentum in his favor, plus the possibility of a lucky blow, he might have upset the larger, older animal. But he made the mistake of hesitating before offering battle and any chance of a surprise victory was lost.

For now, the bigger bull was moving, gaining momentum, huge tree-polished antlers carried low, driven by a ton of uncoiling muscle. In that single, miscalculated hesitation the challenger became the challenged, now with barely enough time to lower his antlers like a shield before being overwhelmed by a massive force. Even as he was being driven back, rump-first into the brush from where he had emerged, the invader tried to mount a return charge. Faced with overwhelming size and power, however, his hooves could only churn ineffectively at the earth, uprooting chumps of willow and catapulting pan-sized lumps of sod high into the air. Then, losing his footing altogether, he collapsed backwards in an ignominious heap, thoroughly defeated.

For a long moment the victor stood over the vanquished, his snorts echoing across the valley walls, then triumphantly wheeled and returned to his former position near the cow and calf and resumed being mad. Utterly confident that he was the greatest, the strongest, the most gigantic being of his universe. His victory was total. He was dominant. He was King, and he was in the rut and he was mean.

The cow flicked her ears in coy amusement at the whole spectacle, then went back to nibbling the willow. He regarded her again. But what the hell did she know about anything anyway?

Now it was my turn. I had come to Alaska to take a truly great trophy moose, and the bull I was watching through the foggy rain was truly superb.

The outside antler spread was close to six feet, with wide palms fringed with long, upward-curving points. Each palm was as wide as a man's shoulders and, typical of an older bull's antlers, deeply creased and folded toward the rear as if they had run out of room to grow and bent in on themselves. While it added to the overall massiveness of the antlers, this feature also made the spread appear less handsome.

Now Jack was beside me, studying the bull through the scope.

"He's big but he's ugly," Jack said, his opinion confirming mine. "His brow points are massive, but the front palms are uneven. But any way you look at it, he is a magnificent trophy."

As one of the best-known taxidermists and outfitters in the world, Jack Atcheson's assessment of the trophy was valuable, but since I had drawn first choice—or first refusal—the decision to shoot or not was entirely mine. Any decision was complicated by the possibility that once I got close to him, I might not be able to change my mind. In his ill state of mind, the bull might take me for a challenger and come out fighting.

It was a delicious dilemma: whether to take this obviously superior trophy or to pass it by in the hopes of finding one even better. I'd made this gamble before and as often as not I'd been skunked. But I'd never passed up anything this good. True, he was ugly, but the ugly crags and creases of his antlers gave him a primitive magnificence. He was everything a trophy hunter could desire—but was it the moose I'd come for? Besides it was only the first morning out and I felt like hunting.

"I'll pass on this one," I told Jack. "Let's look for a prettier bull."

Jack and I had been planning this trip for over a year. Each of the three bulls I'd taken previously had been a fine trophy, including one I'd even bagged with a handgun. But none was the wall-filling monster I'd dreamed of.

In addition to his taxidermy operation, Jack Atcheson is internationally known as a big game hunter who also arranges worldwide hunts for sportsmen. As luck would have it, about the time I was getting really serious about going after a big moose, Jack was having similar urgings. When I called him about arranging a hunt for trophy bull, he allowed that some extremely big trophies had been coming out of an area guided by Clark Engle, a well-known guide and former president of the Alaskan Guides Association. Engle's territory had produced so many big bulls that Jack was planning to go there himself. If I was interested, he would schedule a hunt for the two of us. In less than two minutes the hunt was agreed on for the coming autumn.

High hopes and fancy plans have a way of getting fouled up, and when Jack and I couldn't get our timetables to mesh, we decided to reschedule the hunt for the following season.

Rendezvousing in Anchorage in late September a year later, Jack and I chartered a small plane to fly us to Engle's camp on the southwestern boundary of Mount McKinley. The spectacular view of McKinley, North America's highest peak at 20,320 feet and Mt. Foraker at 17,400 feet, was worth the price of the charter.

I've seen all sorts of hunting camps, but nothing approaches Engle's main camp, which was more like a small settlement, complete with a generating plant and wood-floored tents. There was even a greenhouse for fresh table fare, and in the mess tent was a pretty young cook making pies, cookies, and cakes. Clark had even installed the ultimate hunting camp luxury—a sauna.

As it turned out, Jack and I didn't get to enjoy the camp's luxuries because as soon as we'd checked the zero on our rifles, we had packed them and the rest of our gear into Clark's Super Cub and were delivered, one at a time, to a rocky river bed on the western base of a range of snow-covered mountains.

Flying there, Clark had pointed out a couple of his spike camps, which like his base camp structures, were high-roofed, house-shaped tents that looked warm and comfortable. But he didn't land at either of these; instead he set the Cub down on a gravelly river bed next to three crawl tents. Situated near prime moose, grizzly, and caribou areas, the camps are set up and stocked to accommodate a series of hunters and guides throughout the season. The camp where Clark left us with Robert Gerlach, one of his packers, was plainly a one-shot affair in the remotest part of his hunting area. There were three crawl tents, a small gas stove, and enough groceries for several days.

"I'll be back in three or four days, depending on the weather," Clark said as he folded himself back into the Super Cub. "By then you should be dining

on moose steaks."

Jack, who had been flown in before me, already had his spotting scope set up and was glassing the distant slopes.

"Look here," he said to me, indicating the eyepiece lens. For a moment I saw nothing but a fairly open hillside spotted with thick clumps of willow. Then just below the snow line I noticed a movement like someone turning the pages of a newspaper. Big white moose antlers! We were in the land of the giants.

Alaskan law does not permit you to hunt big game on the same day you've been airborne, so there was no thought of going after the bull. Just the same, it was wonderful to observe him as he meandered in and out of the brush. I watched until the light was gone, totally fascinated by the massive animal.

Rubber hip-boots are not, in my profoundest opinion, made for hiking, most certainly not for climbing steep, thickly brushed hills. But there is no other realistic footwear in this part of Alaska where every valley is a marsh and miles are marked by the numbers of churning streams you have to wade. Climbing to the backbone of the ridge had raised the temperature in each boot to a steamy broil. Now, as I huddled in a moss tent on the wind-chilled face of the hill, a clammy cold was creeping up past my ankles.

The big bull we had watched earlier was still in sight, but he no longer held our attention. After the brief battle, the defeated moose retreated along a low ridge, which led into a stand of broken timber just opposite our position. Apparently he had planned to take cover in the trees but just before he got there he suddenly stopped and began a strange, stiff legged, side-to-side tottering that reminded me of a sumo ritual.

"There's another bull in there," Jack whispered excitedly, "and there's going to be another fight."

"I see him," Robert said. "He's coming out of the woods."

Unlike the fight we'd witnessed a few minutes before, there was no attempted ambush or charging counterattack. The defending bull emerged from the trees like a steaming locomotive coming out of an engine barn. He was gigantic, but not mound-shaped like the older bull we had watched earlier. This one's mass was centered in his seven-foot hump. Heavy shoulder muscles bulged through his coat and tapered into trimmer hindquarters, a well-conditioned fighter in his prime. His antlers were as wide and as massive as the older bull's, but more perfectly matched, with platter-like front palms and main palms that reached over his shoulders like a fringed awning. This was the bull I'd come for.

Now the bulls were separated by only a few yards but still they continued their sumo wrestler's foot-stomping as if savoring their rage before unleashing it on their opponent. If size mattered, the smaller of the two was about to receive his second defeat of the day, but his comparative lack of bulk and antler size in no way diminished his courage.

Suddenly the ritual bluffing ended, and as if by signal they lowered their heads until the palms of their antlers stood vertical, than charged into each other with a grinding crash. For an instant the lesser bull withstood the impact, but then he was being pushed back.

Sensing he had won, the bigger moose stopped his charging, probably expecting his challenger to break off the fight and beat a hasty retreat. But the rage of the smaller moose was still not satisfied. Backing off a few feet to gain momentum, he again came at the giant. The impact of the antlers echoed across the narrow valley like the splitting of a great tree. This time the challenger knew he was outclassed, and as he turned away to run, the winner gave him a vicious butt in the hindquarters. While the loser disappeared over the crest of the hill, the victor returned to the protection of the woods.

The bull was no more than 400 yards away, but trying to stalk him in the timber would be tricky. Though we had not yet seen them, his harem of cows had to be nearby or he would not have been challenged. Sometimes rutting bulls will let hunters come pretty close, but wary cows can cause problems, especially if they're scattered around the bull. If a cow sights or scents you, she will probably spook and run, causing the bull to chase after her.

As we were discussing possible courses of action, two cows came into view and crossed a small clearing near the bottom of the opposite hill about 350 yards away and quite a bit below us. Seconds later the bull followed, but he was visible for only a moment, not enough time to shoot. A minute later, still heading downhill, he crossed another small opening.

Though we could distinguish only dark forms moving about in the trees, we could track their movements by the sounds of hooves scraping across logs and antlers ripping the undergrowth. Apparently the cows had scattered during the fight and now the bull was rounding them up again.

If the bull crossed another opening, there might be a chance for a shot. Dropping to a sitting position behind a small tree, I worked the bolt of my Model 700 Remington Bolt rifle and fed the big 8mm Remington Magnum round into the chamber. The rifle was sighted to put a 220-grain bullet three inches high at 100 yards. This meant the bullet would strike six or seven inches low at 300 yards. For a moose-sized target, this was virtually point-blank.

Steadying my rifle along the side of the tree, I settled the crosshairs on the opening where I expected the bull to appear, then turned the magnification of my variable power Leupold scope up to its full 8X magnification. This would give me a better look at the target in case he stayed in the shadows.

"Here he comes," Jack whispered, as a dark form stepped into the opening. Tightening my pressure on the trigger, I swung the crosshairs toward the bull before settling them on his chest, all while taking one more look at the antlers.

*It's not the right bull!* My finger left the trigger the same instant Jack almost shouted, "Don't shoot!"

The moose I had almost shot was definitely not the bull we had seen minutes before. His antlers were smaller, barely mature. Perhaps he was a protégé of the bigger bull, certainly not a challenger, or he wouldn't be allowed to remain so close to the cows. Whatever he was, he would have been on the receiving end of a bad mistake had I not double-checked his antlers before pressing the trigger.

Afraid the bigger moose might have given me the slip altogether, I dropped my rifle across my knees and raised my binoculars to scan the timber. Nothing was there—no bull, no cows, no movement. *Were they gone? Which way?*

The crack of a hoof striking a log caused me to look back to where the smaller bull had been standing. He was disappearing into black, heavily shadowed brush, giving me only a glimpse of his rump and hocks. Then the opening was bare. But only for a second. Stepping quietly from the high side of the hill came another form. At first I could see only the legs, then the belly and finally the flanks, neck, and antlers. It was the big bull. I'd have to shoot fast before he crossed the tiny window in the woods.

For a moment the bull hesitated, dead broadside. In that brief moment my crosshairs found the right spot low on his chest, and I was applying the final ounce of trigger pressure when he moved again and angled away, back into the shadows. In that final instant my crosshairs found another spot, farther back on his flank so the bullet would rake through his lungs toward the offside shoulder. The bull's antlers were again lost in the shadows when the Magnum slammed against my shoulder.

The bull didn't go down at once; big moose seldom do. But he was dead on his feet. Slowly, like a stricken battleship, he turned and stepped to the center of the opening.

A second shot wasn't necessary, but as long as any animal remains on his feet, I'll hit him as often and as hard as I can. My next bullet slapped low in his chest, angling toward the heart. Now the bull was sinking, like he was lying down, gently spreading his great antlers on the ground.

The meadow separating the hills from where I had fired and where the bull had stood was so marshy and overgrown with brambles that it took a quarter-hour to cover the 300-plus yards. And then we had to search more minutes to find the trophy. Big game animals that look trophy size to the hunter when on the hoof sometimes have a way of looking smaller—disappointingly so—after they're bagged. Ground shrinkage, it's sometimes called, but my bull appeared even bigger, more massive, than I had imagined.

I hunted with Jack for a couple more days, and though we saw six to eight big bulls each day, nothing was the trophy he was looking for. Clark flew in early on the fourth day, taking me back to the main camp, leaving Jack a final day to hunt. I would have preferred to stay in the land of the giants, but I was scheduled for a bear hunt in B.C. and figured I'd better get to Anchorage while the weather held.

The following day I was stuffing my gear into the charter plane I'd booked when Clark's Super Cub bounced in with an excited Jack aboard.

"Remember that big bull we saw the first day out?' he yelled, even before unstrapping himself from the Cub. "He tried to ambush Robert and me and I had to shoot in self-defense. He measured sixty-eight on the spread. Ugliest moose I ever saw—but what a hell of a trophy. "

*"The rams weren't far below us,
about 300 yards or a bit less, standing in
a bunch, starkly outlined against the black shale."*

# CHAPTER 15

# SAGA OF THE WHITE RAM

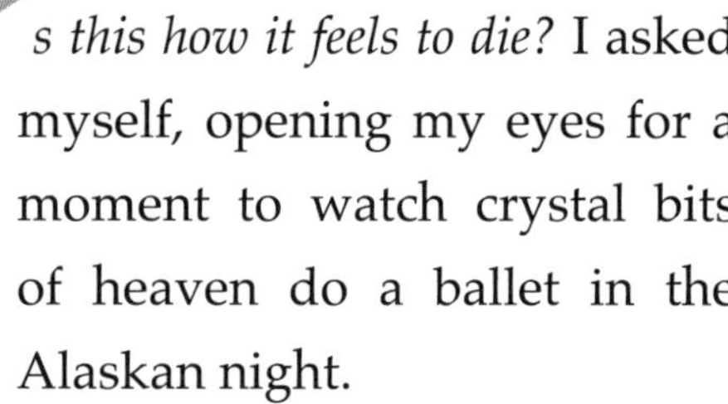

*Is this how it feels to die?* I asked myself, opening my eyes for a moment to watch crystal bits of heaven do a ballet in the Alaskan night.

I can't be dying because this whole situation is too ridiculous; who'd believe it anyway. I even laughed at the thought because who'd believe I'd met my end stretched out on the crest of a no-name mountain? Dead from a combination of twisted guts and Alaskan-style hypothermia.

Hell, why can't I go like a respectable sheep hunter and slip off a thousand-foot ledge or get wiped out by a rock slide? That's the right way to go but this is ridiculous. Then I laughed again, out loud. I guess I laughed a lot that night.

I didn't want to think that I was really going to die, but it was all too plain that I *could* die. Strangely, the possibility of my imminent demise wasn't especially bothersome; the sensation could even be called tranquil. I guess that's how the brain soothes and protects itself when it knows the body is in one hell of a lot of trouble.

Sensible folks don't get themselves in such predicaments because they intend to, but rather because they fall victim to a series of events. That night, spread out on a rock that sucked away my body's heat, I gazed into the heavens and thought back on the chain of circumstances that had brought me there.

The whole thing got started a few years before when my pal Arlen Chaney was taken with a hot idea. Arlen has lots of good ideas; that's why he's president of Omark Industry's sporting division, the big outfit that manufactured Speer bullets, RCBS reloading tools, CC1 primers and ammunition, and Outers accessories. Back then Arlen was a vice-president and one of his jobs was promoting Omark's products. The Speer division had just introduced a line of high-class bullets called Grand Slams, and Arlen's idea was to make sure these premium bullets lived up to their name. He proposed that he and I do this by using the new bullets to bag a "grand slam" of the four species of North American wild sheep, starting with the spectacular Dall variety.

Naturally, I thought Arlen had come up with a heckuva idea and offered to set the program in motion by arranging some first-class hunts. Which meant calling Outfitter Jack Atcheson of Butte, Montana, who never fails to know where to find the best hunting and the best guides. Atcheson said that for white sheep, we could do no better than book with Keith Johnson, who has a prime area in Alaska's Wrangell Mountains and has a reputation for guiding his hunters to big rams. So that's how it came to pass that when August crept around, Arlen and I found ourselves on Keith Johnson's dock on pretty Campbell Lake in Anchorage, shoving our gear into a floatplane. Soon we'd be in the fabled Wrangell Mountains hunting the great white *Ovis dalli*.

The night before we'd dined in a fancy restaurant overlooking the bay. Lifting too many glasses of wine, we toasted our coming success while visions of full-curl horns danced in our heads. There's no doubt we were ready for the mountains. Arlen was lean and fit from a summer of hard play on the paddleball court and I'd been faithful to an unorthodox regimen of swimming hard and fast underwater in my pool until I could do three laps without coming up for air.

The land route from Anchorage to Wrangell sheep country is long, hard, and dusty, which is why Keith spares his clients that particular bit of sightseeing by flying them to a puddle called One Mile Lake near the town Chitina. Unless you happen to be a connoisseur of gold rush mining towns, Chitina isn't worth going out of your way to visit, but during its heyday it would have been a perfect setting for one of Robert Service's bawdy poems.

Like any well-planned Alaskan community, the most accessible building was a saloon, around which reposed an unidentifiable collection of vehicles, all encased in ceramic-hard layers of Alaskan mud. In a weed patch behind the saloon are the remains of a 1920s vintage Fokker airplane. It had either crashed there or arrived by some means that only a born-again sourdough could explain. Which pretty well sums up Chitina's attractions.

Two of Johnson's guides, Butch Houteanen and Bob Pairier, were waiting with one of the muddy trucks, and transferred our duffels and rifles to a dirt landing strip (more rock than dirt) where we stuffed our gear into a ballooned-tired Super Cub for the final leg of our journey. Since our next stop would put us close to sheep country, Arlen and I figured this would be a smart time to check our rifles in case the airline baggage apes had succeeded in rearranging the sights.

Arlen's rifle was his long-time hunting favorite, an elderly Model 70 Winchester in .30/06. My rifle was built around a Model 70 action, re-barreled to .280 Remington and stocked with a gorgeous piece of French walnut by ace stockmaker Clayton Nelson. Actually, I'd retired the old rifle a couple years before, but decided to bring it along for sentimental reasons. I'd lost count of the hunts I'd carried it on, but among the 200 or so head of big game it had accounted for were 15 wild sheep from Asia and North America. So what rifle could be more worthy for Arlen's Grand Slam program?

In accordance with Arlen's plan, I'd loaded my ammo with the new and wicked-looking 160-grain Grand Slam bullets. (Usually I preferred 140-grain bullets for the .280, but 7mm Grand Slams came only in 160 grains and, anyway, the sheep would never know the difference.)

While Keith was ferrying Butch and Bob into our camp, Arlen and I stepped off a hundred long paces of runway, stuck a target on a grocery box and banged off a couple shots. A few clicks of the scope knobs and final confirmation shots put the bullet holes precisely where we wanted. With our rifles ready, we were probably thinking that no hunt had been better organized nor had two hunters been more prepared. But what is it they say about the best-laid plans of mice and men . . .

When it was finally my turn to be flown to camp, it was getting late in the day, which at that latitude in late August is truly late because of the way the sun lingers on the horizon, keeping darkness at bay. Our route doglegged through a cleft between a double row of Wrangell's snow-topped peaks, and I was snapping pictures of the spectacular scenery when Keith reached back and tapped my boot, then pointed out some white specks on the mountainside at about the same altitude we were flying.

"Sheep," he said, trying to make me hear over the engine's roar, but I already had dropped my camera and grabbed my binoculars. Seeing your first Dall sheep can be something of a shock to those of us accustomed to the dull, camouflaged coloration of most big game. Dall sheep stand out almost like the white of new snow, especially when silhouetted against the dark background of a rocky mountainside. Which is why they can usually be easily spotted against almost any background, except snow.

We were at least a mile away from the sheep, too far to make out details, but I was sure I had seen horns before Keith swerved around the mountain and began descending toward a semi-level looking patch of gravel. Flanking the crude airstrip was a plain log cabin with the inevitable stilted Alaskan meat cache to one side.

But plain as it was, situated on the edge of the Lakima River plain and walled on three sides by sheepy looking mountains, the scene before me looked like paradise when I unfolded myself from the Cub's cramped back seat.

No sooner had I gotten my legs straight enough to walk when Arlen, who'd flown in before me, started waving wildly and pointing at something high on the steeply sloping side of the nearest mountain.

"Look through this thing, Pard, and tell me what you see," indicating a spotting scope he'd set up in front of an upturned bucket.

I could tell by the size of his grin what he'd seen, but at first I saw nothing but a black wall of shale somewhere near the mountain's peak. Then, as I twisted the scope's focusing ring for a clearer picture, a narrow, grass-lined depression came into view, in the center of which were two white forms.

"Rams, too far to judge, but they're high and lonesome and might be big ones," Arlen said.

About then Butch came out of the cabin, where he and Bob had been taking turns cussing whatever it was that had gnawed into the grub box and carpeted the floor with several pounds of pancake mix.

"Take a look at these rams," Arlen said. "Do they look familiar?"

For a long moment Butch gazed up at the distant slope, then took a look through the scope. Butch has a way of looking at sheep, his family came from Iceland and his eyes are like polished pieces of blue glacier ice.

"Yeah, I think I know them . . . there's been a good ram hanging around there for the past couple of seasons . . . usually has one or two smaller rams with him."

"Hey, Bob," Arlen called toward the open cabin door, "how about you and me strolling up that way tomorrow and get a better look at those rams."

Bob appeared in the door and studied the mountain, his eyes tracking the routes they would have to follow to make a clean stalk.

"That's what we came for," he finally said, smiling at Arlen's enthusiasm, but also offering fair warning of what obviously would be a challenging climb. "We'd better take a tent and grub for two days. That's a lot farther and higher than it looks from here."

"What about us, Butch?" I asked. "I hope you've got a big ram spotted somewhere on a gentle hillside."

"I think I know where we might find a really big ram, Jim, but he's in a tough place and it might be a gamble going after him. I spotted him from the air a few times last year. Sometimes he was there and sometimes he wasn't. I think he has a secret hideout, because I'd see him in the same place and then he would disappear. If he's still there, he's well worth the effort, but if he's gone, it's a hard two-day hike for nothing."

"That's the story of my life, Butch. I've never taken a sheep the easy way. Maybe I'm due for a lucky break." And I think I meant it.

Later, after Keith had headed back to Chitina and we were sorting our duffels and rifle cases, the inevitable subject of shooting came up. What caliber rifle had I brought, Butch asked, and how much shooting had I done with it? It's a fair question, one that guides almost always ask because it gives them some idea as to what to expect in the way of rifle and shooter performance. It's also a question I look forward to when hunting with a guide I've never hunted with before because it gives me chance to pull their leg a bit and create a somewhat more informal relationship.

Though I'd actually sighted in my .280 to put 160-grain Grand Slams dead on point-of-aim at 200 yards, the rifle was easily capable of accurate 300-yard shots.

"Oh, about fifty yards I think," I answered with a straight face but slipping a wink at Arlen. "If we can get within fifty yards and the sheep is standing still and if I can get my rifle braced on a solid rest, the odds are better than half I'll hit what I'm shooting at."

Butch chewed on this bit of news for a while, not sure what to make of it because we'd only met that day. Bob, allowing that he might have a similar problem, turned to a straight-faced Arlen: "What about you, Mister Chaney? How far can you hit a sheep with your rifle?"

"Oh, about the same as Jim I guess, or a bit less. He's shot more than me."

With these revelations to ponder, Butch and Bob didn't have much else to say and went about fixing supper. Arlen and I spotted a couple of moose on a nearby hillside and watched them amble about, twitching their ears, until an evening mantle of blue shadows settled over the white peaks.

By lamplight the next morning Arlen and I reduced our gear to the lightest possible pile of necessities and filled our backpacks. Whenever I pack my duffel at home, it seems there are all sorts of gear that I can't possibly get along without, but when standing at the bottom of a mountain I'm about to climb, it's amazing to find how many I can do without.

The sun was just warming the peaks, turning them to gold, when Arlen and Bob shouldered their pack-frames and headed toward the mountains and the sheep. I walked with them as far as the first stream-crossing and tossed over Arlen's boots after he'd waded across barefoot, howling at the icy water and rocky bottom.

Back at the cabin I set up my spotting scope and again looked at the distant sheep. They were in the same pocket where we'd seen them the day before, golden-fleeced in the early light. *Were they trophy rams?* I hoped they were but sometimes it takes a lot of climbing to learn for sure. Arlen was on his way to find out.

As it turned out there would be no actual hunting for me that day because of a last-minute change of plans brought on by Butch's description of the big ram and my eagerness to go after it. Our revised plan was for Keith to return today and fly Butch and me to a dry gravel bar where we could set up a spike camp. I heartily approved of this tactic, not just because it put us within striking distance of where Butch had been seeing the big ram, but also it saved us a day of hiking and climbing to get there.

The only drawback was that we would not be able to immediately start hunting after landing there because Alaska game regulations prohibit flying and bagging game on the same day. Even so, I considered the lost time a smart tradeoff as I'd be rested and ready on the following day when we'd begin our climb to where the mystery ram made his on-and-off appearances.

Our prospects looked even brighter that afternoon when I discovered that the area where Butch had been seeing his big ram was close to where we had spotted sheep when flying to camp on the previous day. *Was it possible that I could have already seen the very ram I wanted?* I remembered thinking how I'd hoped to get a crack at them and now I'd get my chance.

Basically, I'm a pretty good rock-climber and the scenery in sheep country is always spectacular and the air exhilarating. What I don't like one little bit is struggling through the alder and spiky devil's club that grow in tangled barriers around the bases of Alaskan mountains. The thickets Butch and I struggled through on the following morning were some of the worst I'd ever encountered and it was late in the day before we finally broke out onto open ground. By then we were so sweaty and exhausted that we decided to pitch our tent on the first level piece of ground we could find. That turned out to be a narrow bench on the mountain that put us almost in sight of the high meadow where Butch had been seeing the mystery ram. But just as we got there, the sight that greeted us was not what we had hoped for. I'd never seen anything more sickening.

For a moment I just stood there, not understanding what we were seeing, but Butch knew immediately and scorched the air with a volley of Viking oaths. "The bastards are after our sheep."

An airplane was making tight circles over the ram's high meadow, sometimes swooping so low that its wings almost touched the ground. Clearly, he was the chasing sheep from the mountain, no doubt the same sheep I'd seen two days before, not just breaking the law but also violating every tenant of sportsmanship and hunting ethics. But why? Possibly it was an outlaw hunter or outfitter trying to chase the trophy ram and the other sheep out of Keith Johnson's area into another area where they could be hunted by someone else. Or was it some anti-hunting group trying to spook the sheep so they'd be impossible to hunt? They had tried that before during another season, even using helicopters to harass the sheep, but what they had actually done was slaughter several magnificent rams as well as ewes and lambs by forcing them to make suicidal leaps off high cliffs.

Whatever the plane's purpose, it was certainly evil, but there was nothing I could do except kick the ground and describe the pilot's ancestry in ways that would have caused an Arab camel jockey to quiver with envy.

The next day we hiked back up to the high meadow, then climbed the mountain that lay beyond. There were no sheep of any size at all, not even puffs of white scampering into the distance; the bastard in the plane had chased them all away. During the day's climbing my feet had become increasingly sore but I hadn't thought much of it. My boots were broken in and had never caused any trouble, but when we made it back to spike camp, I discovered I was in trouble.

When I tried to peel my socks off, they came away crusted with blood and strips of skin that had been the soles of my feet. During the day my feet hadn't seemed to hurt all that bad, but come morning I would probably be out of commission entirely. What a hell of a way to start—and end—a sheep hunt. Two days before, my prospects for a great hunt couldn't have been brighter, but thanks to a criminal in an airplane and two tender feet, my hunt was over. Next morning I hobbled off the mountain and met Keith a day later.

A big part of my disappointment was not being able to see Butch's big ram. A sheep hunter can get himself psyched up for a particular ram and when it can't be found, a lot of enthusiasm for the hunt is lost. I was a fairly dejected piece of humanity when Keith's Super Cub bounced to a stop on the sand bar where Butch and I waited. My spirits were quickly lifted though when Keith jumped out of the plane and excitedly described the tremendous ram that Arlen had bagged. More than a full curl, the tips of its horns spanned out like a gull's wings. It was a magnificent beginning for his Grand Slam promotion, but I'd let him down on my end of the deal.

Two days later, my feet too swollen to wear shoes, I was on a plane back to the Lower 48, my dreams of a great white sheep shattered. I figured the story ended there—but it hadn't, not by a long shot. A new saga was just beginning.

Two years later, when I hooked up with Keith Johnson again at a convention of wild sheep hunters in New Orleans, he asked, "How's your tender feet?"

"Not as tender as last time," I answered, "and they're ready to climb another mountain."

"Well then, you'd better come back up this August. There's a big ram still waiting, and Butch still wants to get you within fifty yards of him."

Just then Butch himself walked up.

"Is that right, Butch?" I asked. "You're still willing to guide a gimpy old hack like me?"

"You bet, and we'll get your ram next time . . . I promise."

So come August we were fighting our way up another mountain.

The devil's club guarding the base of the mountain was, if anything, even denser and more savage than what we'd fought two years before. And this time the going was made even worse by a steady rain that seeped through our parkas and soaked our clothes, our gear, and our souls. Of particular worry was my beloved .280, which again I'd brought along, more determined than ever to crown its retirement with a spectacular trophy.

After years of hard hunting, much of the stock's original oil finish was worn away, exposing patches of barely protected dry walnut that soaked up water like a thirsty blotter. By the time we pitched our tent and downed a freeze-dried supper, my tired old rifle was showing the bad effects of the rain, with the stock's forend so swollen that the barrel was squeezed partially out of its channel. This upward pressure would surely cause my shots to hit higher than normal, but how much? *A foot? Five feet? Was this hunt to end in disaster too, only because I wanted to take a favorite old rifle on one last hunt?*

The dawn came clear and cool, ideal for hunting wild sheep. The savage devil's club was below us now and above was only grassy earth and stone, my favorite climbing terrain. Anticipating that the day would soon be warm and that the climbing would keep me warm anyway, I wore a flannel shirt and a hunter orange vest. I had stuffed only a light down jacket in my pack along with my usual cameras and film, some candy, a folding cup, and a plastic tube for sucking water out of snow puddles. I also had a little packet of some stuff recommended by long-distance runners that was supposed to supply a jolt of energy. Butch didn't carry much either, his oversize cargo pack almost empty except for his spotting scope, a snack, and two sets of white "sheep's clothing." Both of us figured we'd be back to our spike camp by nightfall.

By midday we were above the grass line and had topped out on a ridge of black shale that went more or less straight and level for a couple of miles, then crested so sharply that it was impossible to walk on the very top. Doing so would have been like attempting a balancing act on a slippery two-by-four. It was a lot easier and safer to walk a foot or two below the crest, following a faint trail made by years of sheep traffic. The sides of the ridge sloped away sharply, then disappeared completely, meaning they were edged in vertical cliffs. Even so there wasn't much danger, because if one of us fell, there were plenty of rocks to grab before going over the edge.

The mountain scenery was wonderful and I felt great. Not far away soared 16,000-foot Mt. Blackburn, the second highest peak in the Wrangells.

Even with the sheep path to follow, our progress was slow—like walking on a railway rail. Before long we came to the edge of a steep-sided saddle that dropped nearly a thousand feet. Butch and I crawled the last few yards along the trail so we wouldn't be skylined at the edge. Cautiously, Butch looked first then ducked back and dug into his pack for the spotting scope.

"Four rams," he whispered, "a couple of good ones. There, on the left side of the saddle."

Wiggling forward on my belly, I stuck my nose over the brow of the ridge and scanned the shale slide through my binoculars. For such magnificent animals, wild sheep can sometimes look and act remarkably stupid. These rams looked for all the world like a quartet of good 'ol boys hanging around a pool hall waiting for something to happen. All were mature, shootable rams, and two sported full-curl horns nearly wide enough and heavy enough to make a sheep-hunting addict get light-headed. But "nearly" does not a trophy make and even before Butch had propped his spotting scope on a rock and focused on the bigger rams, I'd double-checked them with my binoculars and decided to give them a pass. The day was still young and there were more days of hunting before us. There might be four rams, then four more. The ridgeline climbed beyond the saddle, and I felt like hiking.

Crossing the saddle, however, presented something of a problem. We wanted to get across without spooking the rams. After all, in a few days' time, those two with the full curls might look pretty good, and we didn't want to chase them out of the area. Our dilemma was that the right side of the saddle fell away too steeply to cross safely. That meant we would have to cross on the left side, in full sight of the sheep.

Butch had the answer with his "sheep's clothing"— two ankle-length white smocks and white caps. Donning the clothes and walking single file in a more or less bent-over position, we simply ambled across the saddle within full view of the rams. They stared at us with big-eyed curiosity but didn't spook. Butch says he has used his sheep's clothes ploy to stroll almost within touching distance of wild sheep.

The ridge beyond the saddle broadened out into a grassy bench with a shallow, meadow-like saddle just beyond. There, we found three more sheep, a young sickle-headed ram and two mature rams with full-curl horns, though the largest was barely equal in horn length to those we'd seen earlier. The grassy bench was a good place to rest and eat our candy bars while watching the rams as they went about the peculiar business of being wild sheep.

Though hiking the ridgeline was about as easy as sheep hunting ever gets, crossing the saddles could be murder. The shale was as soft as sand, sucking our feet so deep that every step was a chore. Every mile or so the ridge collapsed into a saddle, but there were sheep in every saddle. By the third saddle we'd counted 11 rams, including five with full curls.

By the time we'd looked at so many rams, and sneaked by them in Butch's sheep suits, the day was getting on. We had only enough daylight to make it back to camp, but the ridge trail lay tantalizingly ahead, and we couldn't resist looking into one more saddle. After all, the route to camp was fairly straight and we could find our way back in the dark. The decision to go on was almost my last one.

The last of the trail led us to a sheep hunter's dreamland. All day the ridgeline had angled slightly upward so that now we had a view that cannot be described—or understood—by anyone who has not looked down on the world from a high and wild place. The crest was becoming so sharp and the sides so steep that soon it would be too dangerous to continue. Even if we saw a good ram, it might be too dangerous to attempt a stalk.

Sheep hunters live with danger; it's part of the game. Just a stroll in sheep country might be considered death-defying by flatlanders so when a hunter says he's in "bad" country, he's talking about a place that can kill you. We weren't in a bad place yet, but we were getting close and it was getting dark. That's when we saw more big rams than I've ever seen in one place.

Eight big boys were standing proud and wild with their horns curling deep and heavy, then flaring out like wings. One old ram was the one I knew I'd come for. He wasn't that much bigger than the others but his horns were engraved by the years, perhaps past his peak, and probably only a winter or two from death by nature in this high place.

The rams weren't far below us, about 300 yards or a bit less, standing in a bunch, starkly outlined against the black shale.

"Can we get him out of here if I shoot him?" I whispered.

"Don't worry about that," Butch whispered back, "you get him down and then we'll figure a way to get him out."

Under normal circumstances, the shot would have been fairly easy, because we were lying prone on the off side of the ridge where I was resting the rifle over my pack. The difficulty was the water my rifle had absorbed the previous day. It had dried some, but the barrel was still partially squeezed out of the channel and I had no doubt it would cause my shots to hit high above where I aimed. But by how much? All I could do was shoot and find out.

To allow for this anticipated elevation, plus the extra elevation caused by shooting downhill, I held the Leupold scope's crosswire just at the bottom line of the ram's chest. It was a gamble but this way the bullet could hit nearly two feet above where I aimed and still be in the right place. I had already explained the problem to Butch and told him to be watching for the bullet's impact in case I missed. All I could do was press the trigger and hope.

"Missed!" he said. "Right over him and looks about two feet high."

Alerted by the shot but not sure of the danger's direction, the sheep milled about for a moment, then joined in a tight band. At first I couldn't see the big ram but then he stepped clear and stopped. Now I put the crosswire level with his hooves and fired again. He was dead before he hit the ground; the Grand Slam bullet performed beautifully.

It took us the better part of an hour to get to the ram because we had to scramble across a jumble of razor-edged granite that slashed through the double-thick leather of my boots. After snapping a few pictures in the fading light, then caping and cutting off the sheep's haunches, there was very little daylight left.

There was no way down the mountain; all we could do would be to make it back to the crest of the ridge before darkness came. This didn't seem to be too much of a problem because once on top we could take our time and pick our way back to camp. After all, we had our sheep and could sleep all next day.

I carried my rifle and the sheep's head and horns rolled up in the cape, while Butch lugged his cargo pack full of heavy sheep haunches. We followed a long winding sheep trail to the top of the ridge. It was a hard pull with lots of panting and stops for rest, but we made it to the top in time to see the royal purple of an Alaskan twilight. Then stars filled the night, just out of reach.

I felt pretty good after our climb, except for being hungry enough to eat at least two of the sheep quarters in Butch's pack, and I dearly wished I'd packed an extra candy bar or two. That's when I remembered the packet of "quick energy" stuff in my pack. Following the instructions on the packet, I poured the powder into my folding cup and let it bubble and fizz for a moment before drinking.The bubbling solution hit my stomach, then came right back up, bringing everything else with it. The next instant I was doubled over in agony, desperately trying not to pass out.

When Butch, who had been a couple of minutes behind me, caught up, I was flat on my back, unable to stand, fighting to hold on to my consciousness.

"Jim! What happened? Are you hurt?" His first impression was that I was having a heart attack and probably in my death throes. For terrible minutes I couldn't speak; every time I opened my mouth my insides tried to climb out.

"It's that damn quick-energy stuff," I finally gasped. "It's killing me."

"Can you walk?"

"No, let me lie here for a while."

After a while the pain went away, but I was so weak I could barely sit up. Walking seemed impossible but I had to try.

"Let's go," I said, trying to sound positive, but when I tried to stand, I staggered and fell to my knees. Then I got up again and lurched along the trail, falling and getting up over and over.

When we came to the first saddle, I knew it was no use. The steep shale slide may as well have been Mount Everest.

"I can't go on, Butch, I'll have to rest here 'til morning. Tell you what. Why don't you leave your jacket here and go on to camp. I'll be okay here and you can bring some food in the morning. If I can get some food down, I'll make it out."

"No way . . . couldn't leave you even if I wanted to. A guide can't leave a hunter stranded. I'd lose my license."

"Well, this is a hell of a place to spend the night," I said. "We'll both freeze."

Then my legs gave way and I collapsed on a bed of cold, black shale. There was no grass or even bare earth to lie on and the shards of stone dug at my body in a hundred places. But worse than the discomfort was the way the shale sucked away my body's vital heat and my thin down jacket was little help. Other than being in water or wind, there is no more deadly way to lose body heat than lying on a rock, but I had no choice. Without the strength to stand or even sit, there was nothing I could do but lie there and feel the last of my life's energy seep away into a nameless mountain.

Digging into his emergency kit, Butch found one of those thin aluminum-coated sheets that are supposed to help retain heat.

"Here, lie on this, and let's get as close together as we can. If we lie together like spoons, we'll help each other stay warm."

For a while we lay together, front to back, but it was impossible to stay in one position for long because the sharp rocks would dig in and become so painful one or both of us would have to move. Then the trapped heat would disappear and I'd feel colder than ever.

For an hour we lay huddled together, but I began shaking so violently that it was impossible for us to lay close enough to do any good. Butch was my only source of heat but he couldn't help me because I literally shook him off like a dog shaking off water. Finally, I just turned over on my back, opened my eyes and gazed into the beautiful Alaskan heaven. With my head resting on my pack, I was strangely at peace and the cold didn't seem to matter. This, I've been told, is the onset of a more serious phase of hypothermia.

The trembling had stopped. It takes energy to tremble and now even that was gone. Strangely, my hands and feet didn't feel especially cold, but I felt a kind of cold I'd never before experienced. It went deep in my vitals, outlining each of my body's organs with a hard coating of cold. I could feel my heart, my liver, my kidneys, and my lungs as separate parts and feel each reacting to the cold. I considered each part with idle curiosity, as if only a bystander to my death.

*If I die here will they name this mountain after me?* I wondered. Not bad, Mount Carmichel—a place where wild sheep live. Better than Carmichel Street or Carmichelville. I couldn't help laughing at the idea.

"What the hell's so funny?" Butch asked, nudging me with an elbow, surely I seemed mad.

"Nothing much, just thinking." Then I laughed again, louder this time.

"I wish you'd tell me what's so funny so I can laugh, too."

"Oh, I was just thinking about what a hell of a job you're going to have packing out my carcass."

"That's not funny."

"I've got it," I said, laughing even harder, "why not wait 'til I freeze solid, then saw me in half so you can take me out in two loads."

"Don't talk like that," he said, very quietly.

I'd heard that the last stage of hypothermia is getting sleepy. I'd tried to avoid the feeling but now it came. I was too sleepy to resist, nothing mattered anymore. It was so peaceful. The stars came down from the heavens and touched me, dancing all around, incredibly bright.

"Butch," I said, nearly dreaming, "it's a hell of a good ram, isn't it." If he answered I never heard it.

Minutes, or hours, later, I don't know which, I was awake, alive! The sky was lighter, the night nearly over. I tried sitting up and for a moment my head reeled then steadied. Then I stood and took a deep breath. Alive! I'd made it. The outline of my head was sharply traced on my pack by a thick layer of frost.

Butch was already on his feet, "How are you feeling now, partner?"

"Great," I think I answered, or something like that, wondering if the past hours had been a dream. "Let's go for a hike. Let's go to camp and get some grub. I'm ready for a dozen eggs and some sheep meat."

"Butch, how many sheep did we see yesterday?"

"Nineteen rams."

"It was a great day, don't you think?"

*"Our plan for the next day was to ride the rims of the tributary canyons leading to the Grand Canyon and glass the ledges for bucks."*

# Chapter 16

# Canyonland Trophy

ey pardner, you look so good they won't know who you are or what you're up to," kidded Dan Wolfe, holding Red's head as I pulled up the cinch.

"That's the whole idea," I answered. "I figured a bath and shave would change my luck some. What's for supper?"

"Cowboy beans and steak, what else?" he grinned. "That's unless you just happen to come leadn' ol' Red back with one of those big bucks tied across the saddle and want some fresh liver and onions."

"And miss your steak and beans? Not a chance."

With that I stepped into the saddle and turned my mount's head south, toward the Grand Canyon.

I've hunted in some of the most wildly beautiful and vastly forlorn terrain this planet has to offer; from glaciered peaks to scorching deserts, but for spectacular scenery and eerie endlessness, nothing is quite like the land where I was now hunting mule deer—the fabled Arizona Strip. The almost completely uninhabited rectangle of territory is bordered on the south and east by the great gorge of the Colorado River and to the north and west by Utah and Nevada.

The Arizona Strip is famous for the unbelievable growth of its mule deer antlers, but it's also the scene of one of history's most tragic examples of the evils of trying to overprotect a deer herd—the great Kaibab Forest debacle of the 1920s.

In 1920 as many as 100,000 deer lived on the Kaibab plateau, but this inflated population, brought on by a no-hunting regulation and strict predator controls, led to an era of starvation and forest destruction that wiped out nine out of every ten deer within the next two decades. A tragic lesson, and one that's too often ignored by wildlife "preservationists."

Today, thanks to sound management practices, which rely on a yearly deer harvest by sport hunters, the Kaibab is once again producing trophy bucks. West of the Kaibab plateau where we were hunting, there has always been a healthy mule deer population with big bucks that display absolutely awesome antler growth. For example, the antlers on a one-year-old buck may have three or even four points on a side! Of course, feed conditions can have a lot to do with antler growth, but after a buck is four years old or so, his antlers are likely to be of the non-typical type with literally a dozen or more points growing and twisting in all sorts of weird directions and shapes.

Arizona deer hunting is by drawn permit only, but the area where we were hunting, known as Management Unit 13, is so vast that some 2,500 permits were allowed there in 1974. Even with this many permits, there's very little likelihood of seeing many, if any, other hunters because the area covers something like 3,500 square miles.

I was hunting with outfitter and guide Hunter Wells of Prescott, where he operates a year-round, lion-hunting guide service as well as hunts for Arizona elk, pronghorn, desert sheep, and deer. Wells' clients have taken such fine trophies out of the strip country that I signed on for the late fall hunt.

In addition to Hunter's father, Fred, and two brothers, Rube and Fred Jr., who helped out with the guiding and camp chores, our group included head cook and wrangler Dan Wolfe and rancher Eddie Balmes who helped with the wrangling and claimed to be the resident poker expert. The other hunters were Carlo Von Moffie, who came all the way from Canada, and Californians Dan and Donnie Smith. Dan had hunted with Wells the year before and was so enchanted with the size of the bucks he saw that he vowed to return every year.

You can hunt the strip without a guide, but the country is so vast and remote that a miscalculation in direction could result in becoming hopelessly lost. Also, the services, especially the horses, offered by Arizona guides such as Wells greatly enhance the likelihood of bagging a trophy buck. A hunter on foot can't see over and around the scrubby pines and junipers nearly as well as a man on horseback.

When the strip country deer season opened, I was hunting whitetails in Maine's north woods, so by the time I arrived in Arizona, the hunt was well underway. I met Eddie Balmes in Prescott and we flew to Kanab, a little Utah town just over the Arizona border. We were met by Rube Wells, and after picking up some fresh grub plus a few extra bales of hay for the horses, headed into the strip country.

When we were still several miles from camp, I told Rube to stop so I could check the zero on my rifle. I'd waited a long time for a crack at the big strip country deer and had no intention of muffing a shot because of a bum zero. Eddie paced off about 150 yards and set up a citrus box with a picture of a brightly colored orange on the side. Using a bale of hay for a rifle rest, I drilled three seven-millimeter holes along the top edge of the fruit. The zero was dead-on.

My rifle was a Nelson-stocked Model 70 Winchester in .280 Remington, topped with Leupold's new 2.5-8x scope. I'd used the rifle in Africa, Asia, and Canada but never in the United States. For the medium- to long-range shots I anticipated in the strip country, an accurate, flat-shooting rifle is necessary and a good bolt-action .280 is about ideal.

When we got to camp late in the afternoon, I learned that Dan Smith had already bagged a big five-point (Western count, five points on a side) buck and passed over several bucks that would be "takers" most anywhere else. In country where the next hill or dry wash might produce a record-book trophy, one tends to think twice before filling his license with even a good four-point buck.

Camp had been pitched on a gentle slope near a protective stand of junipers. Water was available for the horses in a shallow basin less than a mile away and atop the hill was a ring of large stones put there hundreds of years before. About 15 feet in diameter, the circle had been the foundation of an Indian dwelling. The floor of the affair had been dug down several inches as added protection against the bitter high country winters and also for a measure of coolness during the parching summer months.

The entrance had faced due south, no doubt to let in the maximum amount of light. The ancient campsite was probably a treasure trove of Indian artifacts, but other than examining a few bits of pottery scattered on the surface, we did not disturb it.

That evening, as the Arizona sky splashed itself with hues of gold, lavender, and scarlet, Hunter filled me in on the hunting situation. There was more water than usual for that time of year and as a result, the deer were not traveling very often or very far. Finding a really good buck, he maintained, would be a matter of digging him out of one of the rock ledges or canyon-side overhangs where wise old bucks prefer to hide out. Our plan for the next day was to ride the rims of the tributary canyons leading to the Grand Canyon and glass the ledges for bucks.

"Hey Dan," he yelled as soon as we'd gone over the next day's game plan, "how about digging up some grub?"

"Hold onto your shirt," Dan yelled back from the cook tent. "I've got to keep stirring these beans so they won't eat through the pot. I'll be there with a shovel when I get good and ready."

"Sounds just like an old time trail cook," I laughed. "But what does he need with a shovel?"

"Just what I said," replied Hunter. "We've really got to dig up our supper. It's buried just about where your feet are."

Before I could answer, Dan appeared with a long-handled shovel and started digging right in front of me. In a few seconds I caught the silver flash of aluminum foil and a moment later Dan lifted a large, foil-wrapped chunk of something from its burial place. In another second the foil shield was peeled back and Hunter was slicing a juicy piece of white meat from a turkey.

"Before we leave camp in the morning," Dan explained, "we dig a hole like this one and line it with hot coals from the campfire. Then we put in that evening's meat, cover it with more coals and a layer of earth, and let it cook all day."

That night, as the November moon rose over the knoll above our camp and outlined the cold circle of rocks that had once been an Indian home, I wondered what kind of man had lived there, and if he had sat by this campfire and dreamed of great bucks with high-reaching antlers.

The next morning, filled to the brim with eggs, bacon, and hotcakes, we saddled up and headed toward one of the major canyons leading into the Grand Canyon. In darkness the world is small, only as wide and as far as a man can see. But with the coming of dawn, the vastness of the Arizona Strip opened up before us farther than the eye can reach. The gently rolling, juniper-dotted hills and knolls seemed to go on forever. *Deer don't have to hide here,* I thought, *they just get so lost no one can find them.*

As everyone who has visited the Grand Canyon knows, there is nothing about the surrounding countryside that indicates that nearby the earth is split by a gigantic rent in the earth's crust. So it was in the area where we hunted. You seem to be riding along an unending plain of gentle swells and valleys when suddenly your horse steps through a dense fringe of scrub cedars and you find yourself on the brink of a sheer chasm. A stone kicked loose by your horse seems to fall for long minutes and you can't even hear it hit bottom.

All day we worked the edges of these and lesser canyons, stopping often to glass a suspicious form or movement in the brush along the rocky rims, but stopping just as often to take in the view.

Here and there the canyon floors would be specked by the sun-blackened remains of a prospector's hut, and holes bored into solid rock showed where miners had gathered the earth's riches a century before.

The closest thing we saw to a deer that first day was two hind legs of a buck or doe as it disappeared into a tight growth of shoulder-high brush. We circled the area and worked our way in carefully, but we never saw it again.

As we skirted one wide but fairly shallow

Carmichel sights on a caribou just below the skyline.

One of the benefits of a caribou hunt is the opportunity to catch big grayling.

On the last hour of the last day, the author took this Northwest Territories bull caribou.

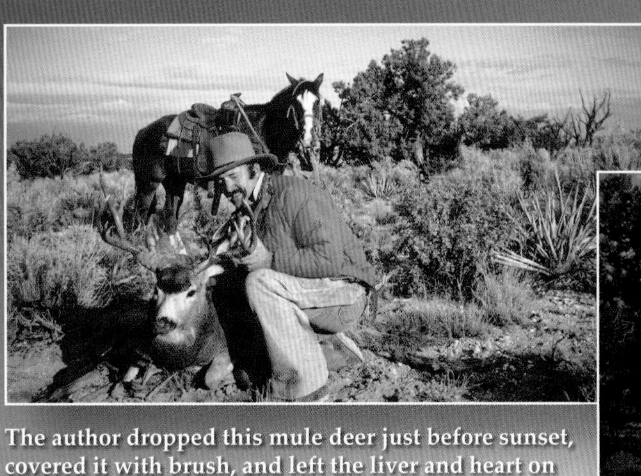

The author dropped this mule deer just before sunset, covered it with brush, and left the liver and heart on top for the coyotes. He returned the next morning at first light with his trusty pack horse to find the heart and liver gone, but his buck untouched.

A stunningly beautiful and gratifying evening, filled with peace and contentment — like a symphony or tone poem by Ferde Grofé or Ottorino Resphiggi.

A fine pair of hard-earned canyonland mule deer.

Scouting along the north rim of the Grand Canyon.

The author will gladly sacrifice distance for a good, solid rifle rest — of any kind.

Carmichel's storied career has taken him across North America in pursuit of nearly every species of big game animal on the continent.

Jim Carmichel and Elmer Keith at Keith's Salmon, Idaho home.

Shooting Editors of the "Big Three" outdoor publications, during the heyday of the magazines.

Left to right, Grits Gresham *(Sports Afield)*, Jim Carmichel *(Outdoor Life)*, and Bob Brister *(Field & Stream)*, on a sporting clays getaway.

Hunting the magnificent Dall sheep of Alaska.

There is no grander animal in North America than the great Alaskan moose — nor a more enthralling big game hunt.

No room in the plane — outfitter and bush pilot Clark Engle secures Carmichel's giant moose rack to the struts of his Piper Cub for transport from spike camp back to the main camp.

Carmichel's quest for mountain goat led him into some of British Columbia's steepest and most challenging terrain.

canyon, I noticed deer tracks going in opposite directions. It appeared there was fairly heavy traffic of deer going to and from some particular place. The well-used trail did not lead to any water or particularly good grazing area that anyone knew of, but I couldn't help wondering where all the deer were that made those tracks. The trail led generally toward the south. I stored this bit of information for later investigation.

That evening Dan dug up some giant T-bone steaks, which must have smelled mighty good to the local coyote population. They howled a few mournful tunes for our dining entertainment and the bones we tossed out were gone the next morning.

The next day we rode west and skirted some limestone bluffs where Hunter had spotted some good bucks during his pre-season scouting. Eddie and I circled a fairly wide area, hoping to jump some deer out of the bluff pockets and possibly move them toward a low mesa where Hunter and the Smith brothers were on the lookout.

About mid-morning Eddie and I heard a quick series of shots, but it turned out to be another hunter whom we never saw.

Early in the afternoon I found myself fairly close to camp, and since I'd lost track of Hunter and the Smiths, and wasn't sure where Rube had taken Carlo, I headed in for a snack and perhaps a shave. Fred Wells and his younger son had gone to check out a few draws northeast of camp, but to my notion it was too warm and still for much deer movement. In other words a perfect time to crawl into the sack for a couple hours of shuteye.

About four in the afternoon, after a nice nap, splash-bath and shave, I headed south out of camp. I didn't have a clear idea of where I was going, but the heavy concentration of tracks we'd seen the day before had given me an idea. The deer that made all those tracks had to come from somewhere and if a fellow got there at the right time, there should be some action.

After riding south for about a half-hour, I turned due east. This would lead me across the heavily traveled trail and if I had calculated right, just in time for the late-afternoon traffic.

Horses are usually good game-spotters, snorting and twisting their ears forward when they see deer, but ol' Red let me down completely this time. I don't think he ever saw the herd of does that broke from cover and trotted up the gentle slope to our left. I counted eight does in the first group and just as I was dismounting, five or six more broke from another patch of juniper and trotted after the first group.

After tying the reins to a bush, I fed a cartridge into the chamber of my rifle and followed the deer on foot. I hadn't seen anything with antlers, but it was the height of the rutting season and I couldn't imagine there would be that many ladies in one place without a suitor close by.

The deer had disappeared over the crest of the hill, and since they hadn't been alarmed, I guessed they would stop on the other side. All I could do for the moment was get to the top of the hill where I could keep an eye on them and see if a buck showed up.

A row of trees along the hilltop made a perfect place for me to keep hidden, and a gnarled tree trunk offered a perfect rifle rest. The does were taking their ease in a shallow draw about 200 yards slightly below me and it would be a cinch shot if a good buck stepped out. Old bucks, though, can be pretty clever and I knew that if there was one there, he'd take his time coming out.

After a few minutes the does started walking up the draw and one by one topped a granite rim and disappeared. Still, I was confident that a buck was close by . . . there just had to be. The safety was off and I had a solid rest. At 200 yards across open ground, a slow-moving deer isn't a tough target, but I felt he'd probably stop a time or two, and I'd have a dead shot.

The last doe disappeared over the rim and there was still no buck. It looked like I'd guessed wrong.

*Oh well, it was a good idea anyway,* I thought, as I stood up and thumbed the safety to the on position. But just at that moment a big deer broke from cover at the lower end of the draw and raced toward the rim where the does had disappeared.

*There was a buck after all!* But now I was caught completely off balance. *Was it good enough to shoot?* There was only an instant to decide. Already I was tracking the deer with my rifle, and through the scope I could see his antlers—wide and high, glowing like headlights in the late-afternoon sun.

The crosshairs pitched ahead of his chest and I pressed the trigger. It looked like a good shot but he didn't seem hurt. Just as he reached the rim, I threw another shot at him, but this time I called it too high.

I followed at a dead run; there wasn't much daylight left and there was a fair chance the buck was hit. My number one rule is to follow up on every animal I shoot at, no matter how wild the shot may seem or how untouched he appears. This time it paid off. Just over the rim the buck had collapsed onto a low cedar bush—completely lifeless. The bullet had hit him squarely in the chest cavity and pulverized both lungs.

After taking a few photos and field-dressing the buck, there was very little light left and no chance of getting him back to camp before morning. But if I left the carcass out, the coyotes would surely get at it during the night. I handled the problem by piling limbs and brush over the carcass and placed the deer's heart, liver, and other morsels on top of the pile. The idea was to give the coyotes enough to eat to keep them away from the deer.

The next morning when Eddie and I returned, the buck was untouched, but the heart and liver were gone. It was a good trade.

*" Our hours in the field were fascinating, with something new to be seen in every direction our boat, feet, or binoculars took us."*

# Chapter 17

# Caribou for Two

*ell, we've done it again,* I thought as I hunkered down and focused my camera on Jack Atcheson and our guide Bruce Football crawling to the crest of a low ridgeline. Just beyond, in easy shooting distance of Jack's muzzleloader, was a really good bull caribou. I couldn't see much of the animal's body from my low angle, only the tips of its widespread antlers turning side to side, but otherwise it seemed to be standing still. The shot would be embarrassingly easy, and the "Golden Boys" will have pulled off yet another of their famous last-day-of-the-hunt successes.

Through our years of hunting together, Jack and I have picked up a reputation for uncanny luck because of the many times we've managed to find outstanding trophies in the last hours, even minutes, of a hunt. It's happened in the lower states time and again, plus Alaska and Canada and several more times on African safaris. Here, in the lonely wilderness of Canada's Northwest Territory, it was about to happen again. Some might call it luck but mostly I credit Atcheson's never-give-up way of hunting. When you hunt with Jack, you hunt until the last ray of the last day.

Jack isn't one to dawdle with his shots, firing quickly when his sights are on target, and after a minute or two I knew something was wrong. Had the caribou turned so he was waiting for a better angle?

The antlers began to move away and then the whole animal appeared, trotting off over a stony ridge and disappearing.

Jack's in-line, black-powder rifle hadn't fired because it actually has two safeties. One works conventionally, and the other is a locking knob on a threaded rod that when engaged, prevents the striker from hitting the percussion cap. Apparently the vibrations of our boat's outboard engine had spun loose the knob and blocked the striker. Jack thought the rifle had simply misfired when he pulled the trigger. By the time he discovered the problem, the bull had spooked and was lost.

*Had our famous luck run out?* The sun had passed its zenith on the last afternoon of a hunt that had held great promise only a few days earlier. Jack was going home without the trophy he'd hoped for and I felt the sting of disappointment as keenly as he.

Six days earlier, when we hopped off the pontoons of the twin-engine plane that ferried us to Little Martin Lake, we had every reason to be optimistic about our prospects. All of the departing hunters who had been in camp the previous week wore happy smiles and their arms were filled with long-pointed antlers. Apparently, every one of them had taken their allowed two caribou so I figured our hunt would be equally successful. With five days to hunt, and the caribou migration in full swing, we'd have the luxury of choosing the very best trophies. I should have known better.

Our luck started going sour the first morning when a cold north wind came roaring down Little Martin Lake. Our assigned hunting area was reachable only by boat, in a direction that took us into the angry teeth of a gale that grew more powerful by the minute and lashed the water into a violently heaving tempest. Head-on waves rattled our molars and alternately catapulted the boat's bow skyward, or drenched us with buckets of bone-chilling water. The waves became so dangerously high that we finally succumbed to common sense and turned back to camp for the day.

As I sat hunched over and shivering in the pitching boat with my back to the wind and my parka's hood fluttering against my ears, the thought occurred that even with our powerful boats and far-reaching rifles, we had no great advantage, if any, over the nomadic hunters who had followed the track of the caribou across these barren lands for countless generations.

The camp we returned to was unlike any I'd ever hunted from before and certainly a lot more comfortable than most. The big wood-floored tents with kerosene stoves were dry and cozy, and the cluster of tents was surrounded by a solar-powered electrified fence to discourage curious grizzly bears.

What made the camp truly unique, however, was its main cook David Vaughan, who was actually on what he called his favorite vacation. The retired owner of a chain of bakeries, Vaughan's idea of a vacation was preparing rich doughnuts, éclairs, cream pies, and loaves of delicious breads for famished hunters. Imagine what a five-star pastry chef can do with caribou loin and you'll have an idea of mealtime at Little Martin Lake.

The camp's manager, David Grindlay, is a former Mountie with a passion for order and keeping everything running on schedule. In addition to hunters like us, the camp also caters to groups that come just to fish and even game-sighting expeditions for tourists, mainly Japanese, who come to view the Northern Lights, which happen to be especially spectacular in the region. The main reason for the electric fence, Grindlay confessed, was to sooth the apprehensions of Japanese tourists who tend to be terrified of bears.

Managing a camp with a dozen or more hunters, plus a guide for every two hunters, requires lots of experience and know-how, and ex-Mountie Grindlay kept the camp working as smoothly as a custom-built rifle. Jack and I were invariably the first hunters to the kitchen tent every morning and as we warmed ourselves close by the stove, stuffing ourselves with Vaughan's freshly made doughnuts, Grindlay would show us on a big map where we would be hunting for the day. Jack and I especially approved of his plan to put just the two of us in a different area every day. That way we'd be seeing and hunting a new territory every day and not interfering with, or being interfered by, any other hunters.

As it turned out, the other hunters in camp were a group of Mexican-Americans from South Texas on what had to be the grand adventure of their lives. They were old pals and apparently knew by heart every Mexican serenade ever written and sang them long into the night. Which is why Jack and I enjoyed the refuge of a two-bunk tent on the opposite edge of camp, where even the loudest notes of the Mexican chorus were no more disturbing than the midnight wails of a Texas coyote.

Hunting caribou around Little Martin Lake is a mixture of boating and hiking. Skirting the rugged shoreline in flat-bottomed wood boats and threading around the countless inlets and islands is an efficient and relatively comfortable way to spot caribou, but eventually, the hunter is obliged to set his boots on the rocky terrain and search beyond the shoreline ridges.

On the second day our route took us on a half-hour journey by water, and then miles overland to a long, glacier-gouged waterway where a second boat had been strategically placed. This saved us miles of hiking and landed us on a shoreline that rose to a boulder-strewn ridge some two miles distant.

Our plan was to make it to the crest of the ridge and from there, glass the surrounding hills and valleys. It would be an ideal place to spot the almost constantly moving herds of caribou and hopefully get my crosshairs on a trophy bull.

I'd won the first shot coin toss. Football was leading the way and just as he reached the crest and peeked over a Volkswagen-sized boulder, he dropped back and silently hand-signaled Jack and me with a downward patting motion.

Keep low, the signal said, and with a curved finger motion he indicated that caribou were just beyond the ridge.

*How close,* I wondered as I slipped the backpack off my shoulders and bolted a cartridge into my chamber.

Dragging my backpack behind in case it would be needed for a rifle rest, I bent low and made the final yards to where Football was peering over the bolder. Scattered across a saucer-shaped valley was a herd of about 30 caribou, the closest animals about 200 yards away and most of them a good bit farther. Most were cows, along with a few young bulls, and three or four adult bulls. The largest of these was a good, but not great trophy—I'd taken better on earlier hunts—but he had a fairly wide shovel, good points, and an exceptional coat.

If I'd had only one license, I probably would have turned him down in hopes of finding a better one. But since I had two licenses, I'd have a chance for a better one and I didn't want to be too choosy and keep Jack from getting his chance at an early shot. My other option was to forfeit the shot to Jack, who by then was beside me with his binoculars focused on the largest of the bulls.

"If you want him, I'll pass," I whispered.

"It's a pretty good bull but too far for my muzzleloader," he whispered back. "If I were you, I'd take him!"

That was all the persuasion I needed, so I carefully eased my backpack to the top of the boulder to use as a soft rest for my rifle. The rifle I slid onto the pack was my old .280 Remington built by Ultra Light Arms back when the company, which would become famous for its lightweight but accurate rifles, was first getting started. Even with a 3-10X Swarovski scope the rig is only six pounds and the tough fiberglass stock is a match for northern Canada's arctic rigors. Turning the scope's power ring up to full 10X, I made a quick calculation of the range, about 260 yards, briefly considered and dismissed the effect of a quartering breeze, snuggled the stock tight against my shoulder, and with my left hand pressing the forearm firmly into the makeshift rest, began putting pressure on the trigger.

I'd brought two different batches of handloaded ammo: one with my old favorite 140-grain Nosler Partition bullets and the other with the new, sleek-looking 150-grain Sciroccos made by Swift Bullet Co. My intention was to shoot a caribou with each of the bullets and compare the results. A limited comparison to be sure, but such comparisons are what make gunwriters tick and for this first bull I'd chosen the Scirocco.

The bull was standing almost broadside, headed to my left, and for a long moment after the Scirocco hit, he seemed untouched. So much so that I quickly bolted another round into the chamber. But there was no need for a second shot, because what I saw when the crosshairs came back on target was a fist-sized hole low in the bull's chest where his heart had been. He was literally dead on his feet and a moment later he collapsed where he had been standing.

On the first day of our hunt, when the weather stranded us in camp, I'd had a chance to pleasantly pass the hours devouring a plate of Vaughan's pastries and getting to know more about our guide with the funny name. Bruce was of the Dogrib Dené, he told me, a people whose existence has been intertwined with the caribou from an age when time was measured only by the seasons.

When early missionaries came to the Canadian Northwest and set the natives' names down in writing, they could not find letters that mimicked the sound of Bruce's ancient family name so it was recorded simply as Football, and the name stuck through following generations. Bruce, as I was to discover during the days we hunted together, is stolid and quiet, befitting the dignity of his hunting heritage, with an almost mystical, perhaps even genetic, understanding of caribou and their habits, and a reverence for his people's timeless relationship with the caribou. After my bull was skinned and boned and we'd packed the best cuts in cloth bags, Bruce reverently covered the remaining bones with a piece of hide. Offering, I think, the traditional prayerful thanks for the caribou's bounty. He gave no explanation for his brief but solemn ceremony, and I expected none. White men need not know.

The following two days brought little except occasional blowing rain, miles of hiking and endlessly searching the horizon with our binoculars. Even though we found no trophy caribou, our hours in the field were fascinating, with something new to be seen in every direction our boat, feet, or binoculars took us.

Twice we spotted two packs of wolves following the herds, chasing hard but giving up when the caribou took to water and swam to the safety of a distant shore. Another time we watched two young grizzlies, whose mother had apparently kicked them out so they could learn to get by on their own. Like teenagers set free, they were exploring the wonders of their world, sniffing the earth, turning over rocks, and frolicking on the beach, yet not so certain of their new independence as to dare lose sight of each other.

Once we came within yards of an old snaggle-antlered bull—too old, too tired, and perhaps too sick to continue this final migration. He simply stood there in calm dignity, awaiting the inevitable wolves.

The final day of our hunt arrived bright and calm, with no hint of the wind and rain that had plagued us on previous days. One might assume that with only a few hours left to hunt, Jack might lower his standards somewhat and be willing to take a lesser trophy, but in fact the opposite was true. Since there was virtually no hope of taking two bulls, Jack wanted his one trophy to be a good one. Which was all the more reason we were so keenly disappointed when his rifle failed on his only chance of that final day.

But like I said, Jack never gives up, and we still had a few hours to hunt. Soon we were back in the boat, winding our way between the barren islands of Little Martin Lake. We were passing through a narrow channel, over water so clear I could see the rocky bottom, when Jack, who was sitting in the bow, suddenly spun around on his seat and signaled Bruce to turn the boat around.

"There are three bulls just around that bank where the channel widens," Jack explained as we retreated. "Let's go around to the other side of the island and come up on foot. That will put us above them within shooting distance."

"Do they look like shooters?" I asked.

"They all looked pretty good but I only saw them for a second. I've never seen caribou so spooky . . . it's like hunting elk."

"Yeah," Football nodded in agreement. "It's the wolves."

Twenty minutes later we were belly down on a moss-covered ridgeline looking at the three bulls through our binoculars. They were good bulls, very good bulls, each bigger than the one Jack had flubbed scarcely an hour before, with one spectacularly bigger than the other two. No question, this was the one we'd been hunting for.

The distance was a bit over 200 yards, too far for Jack's muzzleloader, but with the bulls partly hidden in a shallow ravine, it would be easy to closer.

"Make sure that damn safety is off this time," I whispered as I patted Jack on the shoulder for luck and watched him make his crouched way along the winding ravine. I circled back to a higher lookout where I could get a bird's-eye view of events.

Just as I focused my binoculars on the bulls, I saw Jack, followed by Football, come out of the ravine not 50 yards from the caribou. There was no wasted time; Jack raised his rifle and I saw white smoke before I heard the big boom of his .50 caliber rifle. We'd pulled off another one of our last-minute victories! Never say die with Jack Atcheson.

After we'd dressed the bull and loaded him in our boat, Jack broke out his fishing tackle and we passed a fantastic hour hauling in a big arctic grayling on nearly every with Jack catching a big lake trout and an even bigger pike. What a day!

Back at camp, chef David Vaughan treated us to wide slabs of peach pie and afterwards, just as I was pulling off my boots, never-say-die-Jack still wasn't ready to call it a day.

"Hey, there's a couple hours of daylight left . . . let's get Football to take us down the lake a-ways, I'm still feeling lucky."

The direction we took was the same that had defeated us on that storm-tossed first day. Only this time the lake's surface was as serene as oiled silk, shimmering under the slanting rays of a radiant, late-afternoon sun. After an hour of steady cruising, we rounded a bend in the lake and on the opposite shore about a half-mile away we could see the white rump of a lone caribou. The animal quickly passed over a ridgeline slanting up from the shore, but we could see that he was an antlered bull, possibly a good one.

Pulling up on shore where we could approach the spot where we'd last seen the bull, I uncased my rifle and filled the magazine with Nosler Partitions. With the setting sun on our backs, we headed up the gentle rise at a fast walk. Again it was almost too easy, our luck unbelievable.

There he was, loafing along the downside of the slope less than 200 yards away. His antlers were wide and magnificent, not as many points as the one Jack had bagged earlier, but with a tremendously deep shovel of over 20 inches! The Noslers did their work and we grabbed a few pictures in the final glimmers of sunlight, with Football grinning and shaking his head in disbelief that two hunters could be so lucky.

That night, long after the Mexicans had crooned their last serenade, I walked the sandy beach of Little Martin Lake and even the heavens seemed to rejoice, showering their congratulations in the most spectacular display of Northern Lights I've ever seen, glimmering like silver-spun draperies in the chambers of a celestial Kubla Kahn. In the distance I heard a distant howl, a single, lonely soaring note, and I thought of the old caribou that had been waiting for the wolves.

# CARIBOU FOR TWO

*"When you see a really good 'un,
you don't have to count points,
you just know it's good."*

# Chapter 18

# Coues Deer Down Mexico Way

Gimme some numbers . . . can you see eye guards?"

"Only see one, and he's got his head down," Kirk answered Dave's quiet but curtly businesslike question. "Now I can see them—he's got both."

"Length?"

"Maybe three inches . . . maybe three and a half."

"What about G-twos?"

"Left is shorter than the right . . . about six I'd say."

"What's he got for G-threes?"

"Looks like four inches on the right and I'll give him five on the left."

Just three minutes before, we'd been bouncing along a rocky trail when Rafael, beside me in the rear seat, had urgently tapped Kirk's shoulder.

"Deer, Señor," he said, leaning forward and thrusting his arm through the open front window so Kirk could sight along his pointing finger.

"*Macho?*" ("A buck?") Kirk asked.

"*Si, muy macho!*" ("Yes, a big buck!")

Seconds later doors on both sides of the Suburban flew open, and with the orderly precision of a well-rehearsed commando raid, Dave Miller and Kirk Kelso were hunkered at the roadside, with Kirk bringing his giant 30X tripod-mounted binoculars to bear on a distant slope. Through my 10X binoculars I saw nothing but flat-topped trees casting long shadows across frosty grass that shimmered like spun gold beneath a radiant Mexican sunrise.

Touching Rafael's arm for attention, I raised my eyebrows and waved my hand in the general direction where Kirk's binoculars were aimed, saying without words, *I don't see it, show me where . . .*

Then, sighting over his outstretched arm and finger, I picked up a colorless form between distant trees that seemed totally unrecognizable as a deer, except that it was neither a rock nor a bush.

"How about spread," I heard Dave ask, drawing my attention back to their intense dialog.

"Thirteen about."

"Does he wrap around enough?"

"Not quite, fifteen or sixteen at most."

"Give me an estimate on quarter measurement."

"I'll say thirteen!"

"Okay, that comes to about forty-seven or forty-eight on a side—so he's somewhere in the nineties. He's knocking on the door but not going in."

"Yeah, let's go."

Minutes later we are bouncing along the trail again, me looking back in the direction of a near-record-book Coues deer that for most trophy hunters would be the stuff that dreams are made of, while marveling at the efficiency and accountant-like accuracy with which Dave and Kirk had appraised the buck's antlers at a distance of well over 700 yards. More remarkable still was the astonishing fact that Rafael, a Mexican guide who works for Kirk during hunting season, had spotted the deer and determined that it was a buck—without using binoculars.

"*Bueno Rafael,*" I said, patting his shoulder and pointing to his eyes, giving him a thumbs-up sign of my appreciation.

"*De nada (It is nothing), Señor Jeem,*" he replied, smiling with happiness to have pleased me, but also somewhat embarrassed that I would be impressed by something that he did quite naturally.

*I'm going to stick close to this guy*, I told myself.

An hour later we topped out on a mile-high ridge that made all the long hours of travel from my U.S. home to this unnamed place in the San Antonio Sierras of Sonora worthwhile. Valleys and ridges undulated to the horizon like a many-hued tapestry rippling in a gentle breeze. Far off in the distance, perhaps 20 miles, the corrals of a rancho could be seen through the clean, dry air, but the land between seemed as timeless and untouched as when Spanish conquistadors had passed through centuries before.

"This looks like the place," Kirk said, after our eyes had drunk their fill.

"Let's get comfortable and find that big buck we came for."

The day before, Dave and I met four other hunters at the Tuscon Airport and flew to Hermosillo, Mexico. From there, Kirk Kelso had driven us into Sonora's high country over narrow, increasingly curvy and treacherous roads until long after dark. Finally, at the end of a rutted trail, we came to a newly finished adobe bunkhouse with concrete floors, beds, and even running water (sort of).

In our group was Randy Brooks, head of Barnes Bullets (the X-Bullet man) who had come from Utah with hopes of getting a Coues buck that he would mount life-size for his wildlife museum. Another hunter had come from Hawaii and another from Oregon, all primed and eager to go after one of North America's toughest-to-find trophies.

Though I'd met Kirk only the day before and knew him only by his reputation for finding great trophies, I'd known David Miller longer than either of us would admit. But this was our first hunt together. A few years back he'd started pestering me about joining him on a Coues deer hunt, but I hadn't been the least bit excited by the prospect because chasing the spooky critters in their thorn- and cactus-spiked habitat was a form of torture that I could do well without.

Though I once lived in Arizona, the home of Coues deer north of the border, I'd never paid them much attention, preferring to invest my hunting days in pursuit of the record-busting deer that inhabit the arid Arizona Strip or combing the state's ponderosa-crowned mountains for elk.

By comparison, the Coues, a bantam-size member of the whitetail family, seemed short on antlers and meat, and what's more, they hung out with rattlesnakes and scorpions and other unsavory critters in the thorny, cactus-covered wastelands of southern Arizona where no sensible hunter would venture. The Coues also had a reputation for being extremely hard to hunt, which is another reason my buddies and I never bothered with them.

"It's not like that anymore," Dave had promised. "We've developed a whole new way of hunting them that you'll like, and besides that I've got a new type of rifle that I want you to try."

The prospect of trying a new Miller rifle weakened me, and I also have to admit that I'd come down with a case of Coues fever and decided that my trophy room wouldn't be complete without a set of their craggy, tightly curved antlers on the wall.

The final temptation was word that Kirk Kelso, owner of Pusch Ridge Outfitters, had located a Coues deer paradise in the Mexican state of Sonora and that there was an opening for a late-November hunt.

When Kelso talks Coues deer, he means trophy-size bucks, and I knew Miller wouldn't be interested unless there was a possibility of taking a record-class head. Which held a special attraction for me because it meant that I might be there to see him tie the record for the most Coues deer entries in the Boone and Crockett Record Book.

Pursuing the dainty deer with a passion that had already posted six fair chase entries in the B&C book, plus a record-book pickup, Miller needed only one more trophy Coues deer to tie the seemingly unbeatable eight entries held by the late George Parker.

In case you don't know about Parker, he was a crusty Arizonian who is still spoken of with awe in some hunting circles. He was one of the best all-around marksmen who collected several record-class trophies including a legendary string of seven Coues deer. Until David Miller came on the scene, Parker's total was generally thought to be unbeatable because he had advantages that are no longer available.

Bagging his first record-class Coues way back in 1947, Parker did most of his hunting during a laid-back era when seasons were long, licenses were easy to come by, and game animals weren't as intensely hunted as they are today. Parker's other big advantage was that he lived near some of Arizona's best Coues deer areas and had easy access into Mexico, where he took half of his record-book deer.

All of which explains why the chances of besting Parker's total seemed impossible to hunters with less determination than David Miller.

Miller admits that Parker may have enjoyed some advantages in his time, though he is quick to point out that he benefits from certain modern-day advantages that Parker didn't have. They include better hunting methods, high-tech optics, and shooting gear that simply didn't exist in Parker's days.

Old-time Arizona hunters that I've gabbed with tell me that back then the standard hunting techniques for Coues deer was the "flush 'em and bust 'em" approach. Meaning that the hunter, either on foot or horseback, simply sneaked through the thorny cover—seldom seeing ahead more than a few yards—and hoped to surprise a hidden buck and get off some quick shots at the small, fleeting target. An alternate method was to spot deer from a hilltop lookout and then try to stalk within rifle range. In those casual days of lever-action .30/.30 saddle carbines and open sights, a 200-yard shot was a pretty long poke, especially at a diminutive Coues deer.

The technique used by Miller and Kelso to spot Coues deer builds on that old sit-and-look method, but whereas Parker may have thought himself blessed by the luxury of 7X binoculars, modern-day hunters can scour the countryside with optics of much greater power and definition. Kelso uses 30X binoculars with an objective lens as big around as a loaf of Italian bread, while the always mechanical-minded Miller has combined two Bushnell spotting scopes with 30X wide-angle eyepieces into a binocular-like arrangement that sifts Coues deer out of great expanses of territory.

"Let your optics do the walking," he says, along with his favorite phrase, "You can always spot an expert Coues deer hunter because his boots look new but the seat of his pants is worn thin."

Being able to spot and evaluate trophy deer from considerable distances is a great advantage, but that solves only half the problem of getting a record-book buck. The other half of the problem is getting a bullet to the target with a killing shot, and that's why Miller had wanted me try his new rifle.

Among aficionados of elegant shooting ware, it's no secret that the David Miller Company produces what are very likely the finest bolt-action hunting rifles ever made. The company is composed only of Miller and his partner Curt Crum who share a passion for excellence, and despite a frenzied demand for their rifles and year-long wait lists, they refuse to take on extra help. One reason being that every piece of a Miller rifle is hand-finished and scrutinized for perfection. Which helps explain why a Miller rifle once sold at auction for over $200,000, the highest ever paid at the time for an unmatched (not paired) rifle of modern make. Even the "ordinary" Miller Classics start at about $30,000 each, so anyone with a hankering to buy one of his rifles probably won't find it at the local Wal-Mart.

The popular Miller Marksmen, on the other hand, sells for considerably less (starting at $10,500 in case you're curious) and is the end product of Miller's dream of a rifle that best matched his calculated way of hunting Coues deer. As originally intended, Miller's rifle was to be a one-of-a-kind for himself, but before it was off the workbench, visitors to his shop liked what they saw and ordered duplicates. Thus was born the Miller Marksmen.

Though Miller will add extra features such as fancy wood to his Marksmen rifles, he draws the line at anything that will compromise performance. For example, if a customer thinks he can get by with any scope mounts other than the super-strong system that Miller makes, he's politely told that customers have no say in such matters. He's equally hardheaded about choices in calibers, barrels, stock configurations, triggers, and even seemingly trivial items that most of us don't even think about, but are considered by Miller to be essential ingredients of the total performance package.

Beginning with a special type of Pre-'64 Model-70 action made by U.S. Repeating Arms and available only to Miller, every surface is trued and smoothed, and some areas even re-contoured so the action's lines flow into a harmonious whole with the stock, mount, trigger guard assembly, and barrel. A hallmark of Miller's rifles is that all the components compliment each other artistically as well as mechanically.

Unlike most builders of performance rifles, Miller makes no claims about the accuracy of his Marksmen series—he doesn't need to. Each rifle is accuracy tested repeatedly at the benchrest by both he and Crum, and no rifle is delivered until both men are satisfied that it has no bad habits whatever and will put every bullet where it's aimed, even in extremes of temperature and weather.

"When we spot a Coues buck at 400 yards or more, we need to kill him that far," Miller says. He notes that shooting a Coues deer is often like threading a needle, because when they're hiding in heavy brush, you often have to shoot through narrow openings. That's the kind of rifle performance I'd come to witness.

I had wanted to test a Miller Marksmen before our hunt, but time grew short and now my first shot with one would be at a living target—not at all my favorite way to go hunting.

"Don't worry," Kirk had assured me, "the rifle is ready if you are."

By midmorning we'd spotted a half-dozen bucks, with Dave and Kirk adding up their points like fiendish tax collectors. None added up to the magical one-ten, however, or even the hundred points that earns B&C's annual listing. As the deer drifted into deeper shade, we decided to call it a morning and drive back to camp for some grub and a nice siesta before trying again in late-afternoon.

Earlier we'd passed some rough diggings and a bleached lean-to that looked like it might have been used by gold prospectors a century ago, so on the way back to camp I asked Kirk to stop so I could look around for artifacts and take a few pictures. While I was poking at the fallen timbers, the three others took a short hike up a steep trail and had just disappeared around an outcropping of blue rocks when Kirk reappeared, wildly waving his arms and pointing toward the Suburban, then gesturing like someone aiming a rifle.

*Get the rifle and come fast,* he was signaling, and a moment later I was slipping out his Miller Marksmen and grabbing a handful of his .300 Weatherby Magnum handloads. Kirk was about 200 yards above me and somewhere beyond was a Coues buck. Judging by Kirk's excited waving, it was a very good buck, and the temptation to go charging up the hill was powerful, but I knew that if I ran uphill in the thin air, I'd be breathing too hard for a steady shot. It's smarter, I decided, to pace myself and be better prepared to shoot when I got there.

So, climbing at a steady pace, I concentrated on testing the rifle's trigger pull. I'd never fired a Marksmen before and if I had to make a long, carefully aimed shot, I wanted to know exactly when the trigger would break. Two pounds it felt like, crisp and smooth, just right. Next I began feeding ammo into the magazine, closing the bolt, and thumbing the safety to ON, just as I met Dave coming down the path, pointing back to where he'd just come.

"There's a buck in a thick stand of brush only about a hundred yards beyond this rise. Rafael spotted him and says he's *muy grande,* but he's spooky and we can't see for sure how big he is yet. When he comes out, he'll be running so get ready to shoot fast, but don't shoot unless Kirk says to. And good luck if you do."

*Expect the unexpected,* I told myself as I climbed the last few feet to where Kirk and Rafael were aiming their binoculars into a basin covered with thorny brush.

"Get ready," Kirk whispered, "he's moving toward the far side of that patch of brush and will make a break for it any second now."

Even as he spoke I was extending the legs of the Harris bipod attached to the rifle's forearm and getting into a sitting position. Coming up the hill I'd already turned the power adjustment ring of the 6.5x20 Leupold down from 20X to the 10X setting, so I'd have a wider field of view for a running shot. Just as I raised the butt to my shoulder and flicked off the safety, the buck bolted. For a slim part of a moment the deer stood clear of the brush, looking straight at us and then turned and ran. That moment was all it took for Kirk to size up the trophy, and as he later said, "When you see a really good 'un, you don't have to count points, you just know it's good."

"Shoot that buck! Shoot that buck!" he shouted. "Shoot that buck!"

The deer was running up a curving, cactus- and tree-dotted slope that got steeper toward the top, and he had to cover about 300 yards of open ground before disappearing over the crest. I'd found the buck in the scope before he'd covered a hundred yards and swung the crosshairs ahead, calculating lead, and tightening finger pressure on the trigger when suddenly he stopped and whirled around, looked at us again for a long second, then turned again and resumed his dash to the top of the hill. But now he seemed uncertain of why he was running, slowing his pace.

*That buck is going to stop again,* I told myself, *and when he does, he's going to take a long look. Don't rush the shot, there's time, remember what you tell other hunters—that you'll always trade distance for a standing shot. Look! Now! He's stopped.*

Now there was no need to rush; the deer was standing under a gnarled, sparsely limbed tree at about 190 yards, quartering away but turned so his left shoulder was exposed.

*You're in control now,* I told myself. *Put the crosshairs exactly where you want them and touch the trigger. The rifle will do the rest.*

An instant later my ears were ringing from the side blast of ported muzzle, and Rafael was pumping my hand with Latin exuberance.

*"Bueno Señor Jeem, Bueno."*

I didn't see the deer go down, but Rafael's dancing and Kirk's big grin left little doubt that the shot had been true.

"Pardner," he said, "you just shot yourself a deer."

As it turned out my buck "green" measured at 102 3/8 points, not enough to qualify for permanent posting in B&C records, but a lot bigger than I'd hoped for. Dave was the man seeking the record and I wanted to be there when he took it.

By the second day, laser-eyed Rafael had earned the nickname "Radar Rafael" because of his uncanny ability to spot almost invisible deer, sometimes at astonishing distances. (Despite the long-held opinion of many that blue eyes see detail best—Col. Hiram Berdon, for example, would allow only blue-eyed riflemen to join his famed Civil War Regiment of sharpshooters—the best game-spotters I've hunted with all had brown eyes: including Africans, American Indians, and now, Radar Rafael.)

Sometimes when I thought Rafael was pulling my leg about a buck he'd spotted in the distance, I would ask, *"defensia pointe?"* (How high are his eye guards?) and when he showed us the length on his fingers, his accuracy would be confirmed by one of the high-X scopes.

As we were driving through a steep-sided valley on the second day, Radar spotted a buck in an impossibly tangle of brush and cactus at about 450 yards.

*"Muy Grande,"* he said, joining his fingers to indicate lengths of the points. Getting a shot at a buck smart enough to get that big takes some planning, so instead of stopping, Kirk kept driving until we were out of sight and could

stop without being seen by the buck.

The plan was simple: Dave and Kirk would hike back to within shooting distance—staying out of sight in brush on the side of the valley opposite the buck—while Rafael and I kept our eyes on the deer from farther away. The shot would be difficult, not only long but at a steep uphill angle.

"Don't forget to figure in the angle when you're aiming," I reminded Dave as I gave him a thumbs-up signal.

"You bet," he answered, shouldering his Marksmen rifle and disappearing behind some scrubby trees.

When Rafael and I found a lookout position, we couldn't see Dave and Kirk, but I could get a pretty good look at the buck's head. He didn't look as big as Rafael had indicated, only about the size of the one I'd taken the day before. A beautiful trophy, certainly, but not one for the record book, so I figured that when Dave got a better look, he'd let it go.

But the thought had just passed through my head when Dave's rifle boomed and the buck made two high bounds and disappeared over the ridge, apparently unharmed.

*I'm not believing this!* I thought. *He missed!* But then I caught a glimpse of another deer angling down the hillside, crashing into brush, and then lying still. I'd been looking at another deer all along and failed to see a bigger buck that had been so well hidden that Dave had to thread the needle to get in a killing shot.

By the time I'd fetched the truck, Rafael had carried the buck off the hill and Dave looked mighty happy.

"Will he make it?" was my first question.

"He looks bigger than he is, I think, but even if he's not a record, he's still a beautiful buck and I couldn't be happier."

That was a year ago, and by the time you read this another Coues season will have passed and Dave Miller may have put another one or two in the record book.

*"My goat was somewhere far below in a deep ravine, and now we'd have to go after him."*

# Chapter 19

# British Columbia Goat Hunt

e who hesitates is lost," the old saying goes. I hesitated and my guide and I were almost lost for good. Had I pulled the trigger two seconds sooner, there would have been no problem. We could have skinned out a fine trophy goat in warm sunlight and had a pleasant stroll down the mountain. But that two-second delay pretty much ruined my day.

It was the best day of the season for hunting goat in British Columbia. The mountain air, kissed by frost then warmed in morning sun, was like a clear, dry wine. Birch trees, shedding their cares for the winter, showered the earth and waters with shimmering gardens of golden doubloons. The horses stamped and snorted jets of steaming air, eager to go to the mountain, and when I climbed into the saddle, the pancakes and bacon felt just right in my belly. It would be a good ride, eight or ten miles to the mountain beyond the mountain where the big goats were.

I was hunting out of Coyne Callison's main camp on the Turnagain River in one of the best big game areas in North America. Within easy walking distance of Callison's comfortable log cabins are plenty of stone sheep, moose, goats, black bear, and grizzlies. Not only are there plenty of these species, with the populations steadily expanding—especially the number of grizzlies—but big ones. Every season Callison's hunters return with trophies that qualify for the Boone and Crockett record book. I expect there just might be a world record Canada moose loafing around there somewhere. In 1983 one of Callison's clients took the number two moose. I saw three big grizzlies in two days and lost count of the moose.

My hunting pals were outfitter Jack Atcheson and Bob Funk, a boy wonder of the oil industry. Atcheson books most of my big game hunts, and we've come to be known as the Golden boys because of our incredible luck when we hunt together. After arriving in Callison's camp via floatplane from Watson Lake in the Yukon, we'd split up, with Jack and Bob going to separate spike camps for moose and sheep. First and foremost, I was after a big billy goat but I also had tags for moose and grizzly.

To my notion, the North American mountain goat is one of the world's most underrated game animals. Not underrated perhaps so much as ignored. One has only to look at the places where goats live to decide that there are easier things to hunt. Yet a big billy is one of the most magnificent trophies on the North American continent. He is a solitary creature of the high and wild places, a determined and resourceful survivor. A beautiful but stinking and conniving con artist that borrowed his face from the devil and his feet from angels, he survives not by killing his enemies but by luring them to places there they kill themselves. His siren call is the wind and his weapon the mountain.

My guide was Claude Smarch, a savvy young fellow who learned the business from his dad. Claude had been after a particularly big billy all season but hadn't been able to get a hunter within range. The goat had a lookout position near the peak of his mountain fortress that gave him a view of most access routes. That made him all but impossible to stalk, because when he spotted hunters coming up the mountain, he'd sneak off by way of his secret escape route.

But like I said, it was the best day of the season to hunt goat and I was feeling lucky. A feeling that blossomed when Claude and I arrived at the foot of the mountain and hid our horses in a willow thicket. Far above us, the old billy was resting in his favorite lookout spot, though he hadn't noticed our arrival because we'd sneaked in through a back door of our own. If he stayed put for the next few hours, we had a chance of climbing the mountain undetected and pulling off a stalk.

The mountain was steep and tall but I've been on worse. Anyway, a mountain is always easier to climb when there is game waiting at the top. A few weeks earlier, while making a movie for Remington Arms, I'd buggered my knee so that walking was a bit painful, especially when angling around hillsides. For this reason I found it less painful to climb straight up rather than following the usual switchback climbing technique. The result was that even with a bum leg I've never climbed faster. By midmorning we were near the peak and had begun creeping around to the bench where we'd last seen the goat.

Everything seemed too perfect and it almost was. We calculated that we were about 50 to 70 yards above the goat's lookout spot, which was a narrow bench. By simply circling around the mountaintop and not making any serious mistakes, such as causing a rockslide, we hoped to put ourselves almost on top of the wary old billy before he got wise to what was happening.

But something always seems to go wrong when the setup is too perfect. The old goat wasn't where he was supposed to be. That meant he'd either hightailed it over the crest while we were on the blind side of the mountain, or had simply moved one way or the other along the bench. From our position we could only see a few yards of the bench, so after a whispered planning session, Claude and I separated, each working our way around the mountain and keeping our eyes on the narrow bench-like ledge.

We'd been separated only a few minutes when I heard a small pebble land at my heels and turned to see Claude motioning for me to head back. He'd spotted the billy, he lip whispered, lying behind a boulder at the narrowest part of the bench. To get a clear shot I'd have to cross a steep shale face. I'd be in easy view of the goat if he looked up and if I kicked loose a single stone, it would surely spook him. Already we were within 70 yards of him and had to move like ghosts.

Despite the short range, I wouldn't get a clear shot until I was even closer because of the convex curvature of the open shale face. As I worked my way toward the billy, planning each step with breathless care, I could see his horns and head but nothing more. Finally though, after spending 10 minutes crossing less than 20 yards, I settled into a sitting position behind a rock outcropping. Now the goat was too close to miss. *How could anything go wrong?*

Pinching the rifle's safety lever between my fingers so it wouldn't make a sound, I steadied the crosshairs on the goat's backbone. At this downhill angle, steeper than 45 degrees, the 250-grain Nosler bullet from my .338 Winchester Magnum would sever the backbone and drive on into the lungs and heart.

All I had to do was press the trigger, but I hesitated because the goat was lying down. Once I had a foolproof shot at an antelope that was lying down and missed it clean. Never did I figure out how I missed, unless I was fooled by the angles. An animal in its bed can be a deceptive target and, besides, I just don't like to shoot them that way. So I waited. Soon the goat would be on its feet and I'd have a fair shot.

Claude, I knew, wanted me to kill the goat in its bed, and for good reason. If it moved a few steps either way, it would be out of sight. Worst of all, if it went over the edge of the bench, it would fall a thousand feet or more into a deep ravine.

Many trophy goats have been badly damaged by such falls, some lost and never found. But still I held my fire because when an animal gets up, even if it's spooked, it will usually stand still for a moment, determining the source of danger before deciding which way to run. In times past I've spooked deer and elk and other game out of their beds and had ample time to get off a shot while they were deciding what to do.

Already the goat sensed something was wrong and would soon be up. He was moving his head in quick jerks, trying to see everywhere. This gave me a good look at his horns, shining black and hooked at the tips like Arab daggers. If the horns of a Rocky Mountain goat measure nine inches or more he is a really good one. I estimated the old billy's horns at about 9 ½ inches and was having visions of his head on my trophy room wall when suddenly he looked straight at me. He was running even before he was fully on his feet—toward the edge of the cliff!

My bullet caught him just as he dived over the edge and tumbled into space. He was dead in the air, no question about that. Claude and I both saw a bright red spot high on his shoulder.

When I climbed down to the bench and looked over the edge, I could only hope that the goat hadn't fallen far and had been stopped by a tree snag or boulder. But no such luck. As far down as we could see there was nothing. My goat was somewhere far below in a deep ravine, and now we'd have to go after him.

"Okay Claude," I said, trying to sound optimistic, "This is what you're getting paid for . . . let's go find him."

"It's a long way down there," he answered trying to match my optimism with a half-hearted grin, "But one thing's for sure, when we find him he'll be half-skinned."

It was a long way down, but that didn't worry me half as much as the fact that it was also a long way back up. As far as I could see there was no way out of the black ravine, except to climb out. The morning's hike up the mountain would be a cakewalk compared to what lay ahead.

While Claude took a more or less direct route, sliding and falling on the loose shale, I followed a slower course, looking for a way to come back up the mountain. In places the steep mountainside gave way to vertical rock walls, and I'd have to make long detours, stopping often to look back, making certain that I could find a climbable route out.

Though the day had been pleasantly warm, it was cold and dark in the ravine with great sheets of ice clinging to the rock walls. Apparently the sun never penetrated this lonely place.

"Over here," Claude shouted from off to my right, "He's wedged behind a rock."

"Can you climb back up from where you are?" I shouted back.

"No way, it's too steep here. I'll have to keep going down and just hope for the best."

"Wait until I get below you, then roll the goat on down." Not far below a torrent of water surged through the ravine. I wanted to be where I could grab the goat before it was swept away by the current and lost forever.

With each step down, the ravine became colder and darker while far above, the crest of the mountain gleamed in the sunlight. The streambed was a jumble of boulders, torturing the water into a roaring cataract. Finding a place where I had fairly good footing, I shouted for Claude to let the goat slide down.

Moments later there was a crashing from above, a shower of loose dirt and rock splattered around me, and the goat splashed into the water. It would have been swept away in an instant, but I managed to grab a handful of hair and hung on, pulling it onto a flat rock.

While Claude caped the animal, I backtracked up the mountain a short distance, wanting to make sure we had a way out. I'd briefly considered following the stream out of the ravine but abandoned the idea. Every few yards the water plunged over a precipice and fell several feet. What falls I could see could be negotiated without trouble, but it was the falls I couldn't see that bothered me. What if we got into a place where it was too steep to go down and too high or slippery to go back up? It would be a bad way to be stranded. A misstep on an icy rock could mean a broken leg, and then what?

"What are you doing up there?" Claude yelled when I was 50 yards above him, hunting my original trail.

"We've got to go back up this way," I answered, "Because we might get trapped in the ravine if we follow the stream."

"Don't worry," he answered, surprised at my concern, "This way we'll be out in an hour. If we climb back the way we came, we won't be back to camp before dark. Besides, it's safer this way than trying to climb up that loose rock."

"Okay," I said, resigning myself to an uncertain fate, "You're the guide, so start guiding us out of here."

The first few falls were no more than five or six feet high, and could be climbed if we had to backtrack. But as we went farther downstream, the sheer ravine walls squeezed together and the falls became progressively higher. That's when we came to the place I had been dreading. I heard it even before I saw it, the water crashed down for 10 feet, then exploded into spray that froze on the ravine walls.

"Claude, if we go down there, we won't be able to climb back up."

"Don't worry, we won't want to come back this way anyhow. We'll soon be out."

Claude went first, hanging onto my hand, then falling about five feet to the rocky streambed.

"Com'on," he urged. "It's not bad at all."

I tossed our backpacks down, then the goat's head and hide, and lastly, my prized David Miller rifle.

Rolling over on my belly and sliding off the rock shelf next to the falls, I inched down until my feet touched Claude's shoulder and then I was safe.

"See," Claude said, "there's nothing to it."

I was nearly convinced until we rounded a sharp bend and peered over the edge of the next waterfall. It was over 20 feet to the bottom, and there was no possible way to climb around. The rock walls on both sides were straight up and down and covered with ice. There was no way out but down and that meant a long jump. It also meant we'd land in the water below. *But how deep was it? Deep enough to cushion our fall or did the foaming water hide solid rock?*

Clearly, there was no reasonable choice; to jump into the unknown water was too much of a risk. The shock of the freezing water would be bad enough, but hitting a hidden rock would be even worse. The chances of surviving the fall without serious injury, I calculated, were perhaps one in three. Not very good odds. If both of us were injured or knocked unconscious, our chances of survival were next to nothing. *Who would look for us in that dark ravine?*

Our only hope was to go back upstream and try to climb out at the last falls. But would it be possible? For a long while we tried to get a hand or foothold on the slick rock but it was no use. Just as I had feared, there was no way to climb out. We were trapped.

Claude and I knew we were in one hell of a fix, but we never admitted it.

"Let's take a break," I suggested, "No use burning up our energy. After we've rested we'll figure this out."

Mentally, I thought about the equipment I carried in my daypack. There was above five feet of nylon cord strong enough to hold a man's weight. *What else?* I wondered. *My rifle sling, that's four more feet! Can we tie enough sling and cord and strips of clothes together to let ourselves down? Sure! We'd make it out of this hell-hole after all. A bit wet and cold but at least in one piece.*

While I was putting my ideas together, Claude was doing some thinking on his own. "If that tree were a few feet longer we could use it like a ladder," he said, pointing to a bleached length of spruce wedged between some boulders.

"It's long enough!" I shouted. "Let's work it loose and drop it alongside the waterfall."

"But it's too short," Claude protested, "Not more than ten feet. Even with the log leaned up on the ravine wall we still have over ten feet to fall."

"We'll tie my rifle sling to some cord I have and loop it around a rock at the top of the fall. Then we can let ourselves down to the log and shinny down the rest of the way."

After tying the cord to the leather sling, we looped it around the stub of a limb at one end of the spruce log and swung it into position. This was accomplished by lying on the edge of the waterfall, half in the current, and stretching my arms until they ached. Claude held onto my legs to keep me from being washed over the edge. After a couple of tries, and almost dropping the log, I got it leaning against the wall at an angle that I hoped would hold. Next a loop was tied around a rock at the edge of the shelf. This left about five feet of cord and sling to hold onto with another five or six feet to the top of the nearly vertical log.

Claude went first, wriggling off the edge of the rock shelf and letting himself down slowly. When his boots found a hold on the log, he waited a moment to catch his breath, then let go of the sling. For a moment he seemed to teeter in mid-air, then ever so carefully he bent his knees until he could grab the top of the log in his hands. Then he easily slid down the thin log and was safely on solid rock.

Next I tossed the packs and hide down and, holding my breath, let the rifle fall. Claude caught it and I raised my eyes to heaven in thanks

"Your turn Jim. It's as easy as rolling off a log."

"That's not funny," I answered.

The tough leather sling felt strong in my grip as I inched off the shelf and let myself slide down the icy rock. I didn't look down or up, only at my bare hands gripping the leather. "How close am I?"

"Just a few more inches, keep coming."

Then my boot touched the log and it felt good to shift my weight to my legs. After that, it was like climbing down a ladder, and I was beside Claude, looking up at the sheer wall of ice-covered rocks. It seemed impossible.

"That's a good sling up there, Claude," I said, "If you ever come by this way again, be sure and get it for me."

"If you don't mind," he answered, "I'll just buy you a new one."

I guess that rifle sling is still there, dangling from a short length of nylon cord in a deep, dark ravine that the sun has never discovered.

# British Columbia Goat Hunt

*"For all their size and seeming awkwardness, moose have an uncanny knack for dissolving into patches of willow and other brush . . . "*

# Chapter 20

# Days of Wind and Wolves

It was the kind of shot that smart hunters don't like. Not because it was too far—though on the outer edge of certainty—nor too small—it was a moose, a giant bull moose. But because pulling the trigger could be the final, bitter frustration of long days of agonizing disappointment. Cold, wet Alaskan days that had tantalized us with visions of wondrous trophies, yet like the perverse gods of ancient sagas, dangled them beyond our taking. Now before me was a trophy beyond expectation. *Would it be the reward for our labors or the cruelest illusion of all?*

"When I grunt, he'll be on his feet," Ken whispered, "and you'll have about five seconds to shoot before he's over the edge and gone and we'll never see him again. Are you ready?"

"Do it," I answered, tightening my finger on the trigger. All or nothing, the kind of shot smart hunters try to avoid.

It wasn't supposed to be that way, not when Jack Atcheson and I hunt together. We're the Golden Boys, or at least that's what we've been called from Whitehorse to Capetown by professional hunters who've marveled at our golden luck.

Like the time on the first morning of an Idaho elk hunt when Jack and I had two good bulls on the ground within the first hour of daylight. And another time in South Africa, when we were hunting the elusive nyala, not one but two magnificent bulls stepped out of the brush and presented Jack and me with ridiculously easy shots. The list of such hunts goes on, which is why I suppose we became comfortable, smug perhaps, with our luck.

So when Jack called and said let's go to Alaska and hunt some moose and bears, I had visions of vast herds of game stretching across the tundra, a matter of picking and choosing. The last time we hunted for moose in Alaska, we saw a dozen trophy bulls on the first day. Why would anything be different now?

Jack's plan was for us to hunt with Kelly Vrem and Clay Katzmarek, one of the most successful outfitting partnerships in Alaska. During the previous season, seven of their eight grizzly hunters were successful and all of their moose hunters took bulls—the smallest of which had an antler spread of over five feet! And seeing as how their hunting area includes part of the range of the vast Mulchatna caribou herd, numbering over a hundred thousand head, they had a perfect record on caribou as well.

Over the years their hunting area had produced 28 Boone and Crockett trophies, including moose, grizzly, and caribou, plus a host of entries in the Safari Club record book. One of the reasons their partnership had been so successful was the way they move hunters into areas with dense game populations. Rather than staying in overhunted central camps, they put their clients in spike camps that can be moved quickly. When a hunter takes his moose, for instance, he'll probably be moved to an area where there are good caribou, then possibly yet again to a hot bear area.

I'd been itching for another hunt with Jack and this hunt sounded perfect. "So what are you waiting for? Book us right now, I want to go this season."

"I figured that's what you'd say," he responded, "so I've already booked us for the last half of September."

"Great, where do we meet?"

"Ever been in Aniak?"

"Aniak? Where is Aniak?"

"Well, find it on a map and get ready for the town's bright lights. I'll meet you there on the 14th and we'll fly to camp next day."

There are no roads to Aniak. You can get there by boat on the broad Kuskokwim River if you're not in a hurry, but just about everything from groceries to concrete blocks arrive on airplanes into Aniak's high-fenced airport. The fence, visitors are assured, was built by the U.S. Government to keep out terrorists, but one has to wonder why anyone would want to invade Aniak.

When I arrived on the appointed day and piled my hunting gear into the town's only taxi, something else was happening thousands of miles away. Something that would change everything about our hunt. It started with a layer of turbulent air. Heated and expanded by the summer-warmed waters of the Pacific, the air mass swirled and rose, drew in more masses of air and swirled ever faster, gaining power and sucking great gulps of water into the atmosphere. At first it went unnoticed, except perhaps by a few Japanese fishing boats. Then it began to move. Eastward.

In Aniak, everything was calm and unseasonably warm when Jack and I took a stroll along the banks of the Kuskokwim. Native hunters floated by, their boats laden with great quarters of moose meat and piled with antlers, and I was eager to go where they had been. After all, we were overflowing with confidence. Jack didn't confess until later, but he was so confident that we'd get all our game in five or six days that he'd even booked his flight home a week early. His optimistic outlook was reinforced even more that evening when Vrem flew in with a hunter who seemed to be in a state of shock from all the game he'd seen. The man was bubbling with excitement over the moose, caribou, and two bears he's bagged. Next day it would be our turn . . .

Kelly Vrem's plane is a Wilga PZL 104, a high-winged observation plane built in Poland for the Warsaw Pact military. An incredible aircraft, the Wilga (which I'm told is Polish for lark) looks like the forlorn offspring of the mating of a pterodactyl and a giant mosquito. It's not much faster than a dogsled, but with its powerful radial engine the Wilga slingshots itself off the tundra and lands like a fluff of thistle-down. I had yet to discover all this as we circled our spike camp and Kelly dropped its flaps to land.

*Are we landing?* I wondered. *Certainly not here.*

This was no place to land, just the top of a brush-specked knob where some guy stood pointing his arms into the wind, but we were dropping and I braced myself for the crash. Then there was a soft bump, the engine was quiet, and I uncurled my toes. I've flown with dozens of good bush pilots and landed in some gawdawful places, but Vrem and his peculiar looking Wilga were in a class by themselves.

The human windsock was Ken Robertson, who was to be our guide. He'd flown in the day before, set up camp and scouted the area.

"I've been watching a seventyish bull down there," he said, spreading his arms to indicate the six-foot width of the moose's antlers and pointing to a willow flat about a half-mile away. The flat was rimmed by a fast-running creek and just beyond a range of steep-sided hills rose out of a dense boundary of spruce. Halfway up the hills, the trees and brush thinned, giving way to what from a distance seemed to be an endless grey cloak of tundra over which lay an intricate network of trails incised in the tundra by the comings and goings of caribou for centuries beyond reckoning.

Behind us rose another range of hills, also patterned with the paths of caribou, but somewhat steeper and topped with rock outcroppings. The two ranges were separated by a valley of green marshes and gardens of tall willows, now golden in their autumn colors.

Our camp sat on a finger-like peninsula of high ground poking into the valley, putting us in the center of a vast theatre from where we could see both sides of the valley for miles. It was a wondrous place.

"I'll be back in three or four days to see how you're doing," Kelly said, waving goodbye, and a moment later the Wilga's engine snarled and the strange-looking plane bounced into the air.

"How about some chow?" Ken said, pointing at the larger of two tents. "While you guys store your gear, I'll rustle up some freeze-dry and then we'll go spot some moose. Tomorrow you'll be legal (referring to the regulation prohibiting flying and bagging game on the same day), and we'll be on top of that big bull. "

As I watched the Wilga disappear through a cleft in valley, I was taken with a sudden feeling of apprehension. It wasn't the sense of aloneness that outsiders often experience when experiencing the Alaskan vastness. I know that feeling well, but this was different, the feeling we get when everything seems perfect but somehow we know it isn't.

*Why is the air so silent and deathly still?* I wondered, as I picked up our rifle cases and followed a caribou trail that led past our tent.

Many miles to the southwest, somewhere over the ocean, what had been a vagrant current of swirling air a few days before had become an immensely powerful storm of violent air.

The ancient Japanese had given such storms a name: *"Thy-Foon"*, they called them—killers of ships. Modern meteorologists give them friendlier names; this one, the most powerful of the season would be called Typhoon Oscar, and as it grew in size and momentum, its bearing became northeasterly—toward Alaska.

"Have you noticed how still the air is?" Jack commented that evening while the three of us were glassing the valley where Ken had spotted the big moose.

"Yeah," Ken answered, not taking his eyes from his raised binoculars. "Feels strange doesn't it . . . been like that since yesterday, and warmer than I like it too."

With three sets of binoculars at work, we quickly spotted some game in the late-evening stillness. A couple of cows dodged in and out of the spruce, chased by a bull with more ardor than antlers, while higher on the hill, intermittent strings of caribou followed their timeless routes. In another direction a good-sized black bear, his head down like a four-legged vacuum cleaner, gorged himself on blueberries. But there was no sighting of the giant moose Ken had seen the day before.

For all their size and seeming awkwardness, moose have an uncanny knack for dissolving into patches of willow and other brush, not to be seen for hours, then unexpectedly showing up in quite another place. So finding the big bull was a matter of looking until he was located. If not tomorrow, then the next day; with three pairs of searching eyes, it would be only a matter of time.

Even in the wilderness, Jack Atheson is a civilized sort of guy and on that first evening in camp he unpacked a pair of crystal wine glasses and filled each from the spout of a not-too-bad box wine.

"To our hunt," he toasted "and to all hunters everywhere."

Sometime during the night a light wind had begun, and I was awakened by the flapping of our tent's loose fly. When I went outside to peg down the loose end, I scanned the horizon, hoping to see the princess of light, Aurora, dancing in the Alaskan heavens. There was no Aurora, only a strangely warm breeze from the southwest, carrying a sound I had not heard for a long while.

"Did you hear what I heard last night?" I asked over pre-dawn tea.

"Hear what?"

"Wolves."

Ken nodded. "I heard them."

"Could be bad news," Jack added. "Sometimes when wolves move into an area, the game moves out, even moose."

The breeze that had begun during the night had strengthened by the time we'd finished breakfast, and increased even more when the three of us positioned ourselves so we could glass the area in all directions. The big black bear we'd seen the day before was again stuffing himself on blueberries, and I counted 40 caribou splashing across a marshy flat in the valley. There was a trophy-size bull in the band, with a tremendous shovel and lots of points, but they were moving fast and we had no chance of catching them.

Ken is a smart guide who knows that hours of searching with binoculars and spotting scope are well spent, a fact demonstrated about mid-morning when he motioned me over to where he'd set up his scope.

"Take a look and tell me what you see."

I took a long look but saw nothing and said so.

"See that yellow bush in the center of the field next to what looks like a shallow gully?"

"I see it, but what's there?"

"Keep watching."

For a couple of minutes there was nothing, then a dark, round shape appeared, like a basketball with ears.

"I got it now . . . it's a bear. What's he doing?"

"I've been watching it for an hour and it looks like a grizzly on a kill. Every now and then he sticks his head up and looks around. I haven't seen the rest of him, but judging by the shape of his head, I'd say he's only junior size."

About then an excited Jack came running up.

"Did you guys see those wolves?"

"Where?"

"Just over the knoll, four of 'em came running by no farther than fifty yards and never spotted me. One was the whitest wolf I've ever seen, and big, too. Another was pure black. The big white one is a beauty."

That afternoon we watched a steady stream of caribou crossing some distant hills, and Jack spotted what looked like a fair-sized grizzly, though it was far away and too late in the day to go after. A light rain had begun, driven by a wind that steadily gained strength. Alaska weather can change fast—mild days alternating with cold and rain—and that evening we zipped ourselves into our sleeping bags, hoping the wind would blow itself out by morning. But such was not to be, because that night Typhoon Oscar struck the coast of Alaska, hurling boats ashore, smashing buildings, and flooding towns with inches of rain every hour.

By morning the full force of Oscar had not yet reached inland, but already the winds at our camp were gusting to 40 miles-per-hour and the horizontally driven rain made it almost impossible to use our binoculars. Trying to find a spot where we might be able to see better, we'd dropped few hundred yards down the lee side of the knoll from where we were camped. When we left camp the tents had seemed to be well anchored, but when the wind suddenly starting hitting us with quick, violent jolts, Jack and I raced back up the hill, making it just in time to see the canvas of our tent being ripping away from the tie-down ropes.

Dashing inside, we yanked out the center pole to collapse the tent, then scrambled on top to hold it down. Another two minutes and it would have been ripped to shreds. Ken wasn't far behind and quickly stuffed our gear and food into plastic garbage bags.

I'd long thought that it would be interesting to sit out a hurricane, but from a safe and dry vantage point, not huddled in a claustrophobic tent that threatened to take wing with each surge of the increasing gale.

Jack Atcheson is not a believer in the old camper's rule of traveling light. Instead, he travels with a minimum of two—more often three—giant duffels packed with everything from jumper cables to surgical instruments plus nostrums for every known human ailment. On our first day in camp he'd pulled from his magic duffel a turtle shaped, wind-resistant two-man tent. "I'm going to set this tent up," he'd said then, "because we might need it." His foresight was a blessing, otherwise the three of us would have been cramped in Ken's two-man shelter and a bad situation would have been much worse. Even so, there was barely enough room for sleeping and light cooking, so non-essentials such as pack frames, spotting scopes, and even our rifles had to be left outside.

My rifle was a Browning A-Bolt Stainless Stalker in .338 Win. Mag. Jack had brought a .375 Model 70 Winchester, which like my rifle, was built of stainless steel and space age synthetics. Both rifles, along with their Leupold scopes, were supposed to be weatherproof, but could they withstand the relentless pounding of water driven by gale-force winds? At that point it really didn't matter because keeping our tents anchored was of greater concern than the hunting.

I'd brought along a lightweight rain suit made of some sort of material that is supposed to allow air to pass through but not water. I liked its light weight, and when I'd tested it back home, it hadn't leaked so I thought it would be about right for the drizzles I'd experienced on previous Alaskan hunts. But when I put it on and stepped outside the tent, the stinging rain drove through it like cheesecloth. In a minute or so I was soaked from my head down to the tops of my hip-high rubber boots. I made a mental note to send it back to its manufacturer when I got home.

Yet incredibly, even with the wind gusting at what we estimated to be over 60 miles-per-hour (we later learned that inland weather stations recorded winds topping 85 mph) and horizontal rain that stung like a sand-blaster, we still managed to venture out occasionally. Although there was little chance of spotting game during the storm, ours was the spirit that springs eternal in the heart of every hunter. Surely, once the storm eased the animals would be hungry and on the move, easy to find, and we would be ready.

On the third day the wind dropped somewhat and with the rain coming only in intermittent squalls, we figured some moose would be starting to move. But after several hours of glassing, we'd spotted only the same black bear, still stuffing himself with blueberries, and a few straggles of caribou that kept themselves near the tops of the bare hills. *Where was all the game we'd seen on the first day? Had the storm driven all wildlife out of the valley?*

Later in the day, when we gathered for a rest and some candy bars, Ken pointed his binoculars toward the far side of the valley and jumped up with a yell.

"Look over there. Do you see 'em? It's the wolves again!"

Racing among the scattered clumps of willow were four wolves, one black and another one pure white. Now we knew why there was no game in the valley and why even the migrating caribou stayed high on the hillsides. Our only chance now was to move to another area, but we'd need an airplane for that and the wind was still blowing too hard to chance landing a plane, even the agile Wilga. *Had our luck finally played out?*

It was another two days before the wind dropped enough for Kelly and Clay to land and get us back to their main camp. When we heard about the flooding and destruction wrought by Typhoon Oscar, we figured that we'd been pretty lucky after all, thanks mainly to our wind-resistant tents. Other camps had been ripped apart and scattered across Alaska. We tested our rifles and were happy to find—though not really surprised—that our scopes were clear and the rifles still on target.

With half of our two-week hunt lost, we'd have to move fast. A good moose area had been spotted before the storm and the plan was to set up a quick camp there and hunt for three days. Then we'd move to another camp for caribou. Packing only the barest necessities, we were dropped off late in the day and pitched our tents on the lee of a low ridge that sloped down into a flat river basin about two miles wide.

In a stand of birch and stubby evergreens along the river's banks, we spotted three bulls, their antlers flashing in the setting sun like golden wings. For the first time in days the sky was clear and cloudless, but the temperature was dropping fast.

Next morning Ken set up his spotting scope at first light. When we joined him on the frosty knoll above our tents, he pointed to a bend in the river, some two or three miles distance, where he'd just seen a bull cross to our side.

"He looked big but it's too far to say for sure. Let's get some breakfast and go see."

Six hours later we topped out on a high ridge and looked down on a willow-covered bench about a quarter-mile wide. Our route had been tough, and we'd traveled mainly on the crest of ridges that ran in the direction we wanted to go. The climbing had been hard at times, especially in our hip-high

"Alaskan sneakers," and we'd had to scramble down steep-sided gorges and wade cold, fast-running streams, or balance our way across beaver dams like tight-rope walkers. Even so, the going had been easier than slogging through the dense snarls of willows and muddy bogs on the lower ground. By mid-afternoon we'd found a lookout spot just under the crest of a ridge that gave us a good view of the river and surrounding willow flats.

What we saw below made the effort getting there more than worthwhile, because it was a bull with about the widest antler palms I've ever seen. He was standing guard over a cow and around them circled two lovesick bulls who vented their frustration by alternately fighting each other and making charges at the monarch. The cow seemed to be a timid creature who apparently wanted nothing to do with any of the bulls and was mainly intent on getting into a border of thick timber between the willow-covered bench and the river.

The big bull was sufficiently distracted for us to make our way off the ridge without being spotted. The wind was good, quartering into our faces as we made quick downhill sprints to rocks and bushes where we'd take cover and momentarily watch the bull.

At one point we thought we'd spooked them when he and the cow disappeared over the edge of the bench and into the timber, but a few agonizing minutes later he came back, butting the cow in her rump with his great, ivory-colored antlers. The cow knew something was wrong and stared directly at us, the bull's baleful gaze following. But then he turned to charge at the circling suitors and we made a final dash to a low clump of thin brush.

That was as far as we could go. Before us was 300 yards of open ground. If we tried to get closer, the wary cow would surely spot us, and we'd probably never see them again. She kept looking our way and trying to coax the bull back toward the river. Now, and here, was the only shot I would have.

I've often said that I'll trade distance for a steady rest. But would I be trading too much distance for a not-so-steady rest? There was no rock or log to steady my aim, and the only option was to shoot from a sitting position using Ken's pack-frame as a rest. I estimated the distance at roughly 350 yards, with a quartering wind from two o'clock.

My rifle carried 250-grain Bitterroot bullets, hand-made virtually one at a time, with the head cores soldered to the jackets for minimum weight loss and maximum penetration. Despite its punch, the .338 Winchester Magnum is not a flat-shooting, long-range sizzler. Sighted-in to hit three inches high at 100 yards, my loads were on target at 225 yards and about six inches low at 300 yards. At 350 yards I'd need to aim about a foot high to put the bullet where I wanted, and if the bull was just 50 yards beyond the estimated distance, the bullet would hit yet another foot lower—and miss. The wind, I figured, would drift the bullet a few inches to the left, and would have to be accounted for in my aim.

So after days of wind and wolves, rain and disappointment, the moment had come. Two weeks of hunting was now condensed into the instant of a trigger pull. The bull was almost side-on when I centered the crosshairs low on his chest where I wanted the bullet to hit, then counted up—six, eight, twelve inches. *Don't forget the wind,* I told myself, and put the tip of my finger on the trigger.

And at that instant the bull did the totally unexpected—he laid down! Right before my eyes the giant bull almost totally disappeared with nothing showing in the tall willows except the tips of his antlers. The breath I'd been holding hissed through my teeth. "Damn."

"Stay ready," Ken whispered, "I'm going to challenge him. When I grunt you'll have about five seconds to shoot. Are you ready?"

"Do it."

With his hands cupped around his mouth, Ken made a grunting noise, almost like a gruff bark. The bull rose to his feet with astonishing quickness, looking directly at us, then turned to follow the cow that was already running toward the river. At that moment my finger tightened on the trigger and in the next moment I heard the dull thump a big bullet makes on hard impact.

The bull didn't flinch and continued after the cow, but then slowed to a walk, as if undisturbed, his great antlers held high, magnificent.

*Aim higher*, I told myself, slamming the bolt home and putting the crosshairs high on the bull's shoulder hump.

This time there was no thump of impact. *A miss? How? Shoot again;*

*hurry before he runs again.* But my crosshairs found only willows where the bull had been.

"He's down," Jack shouted. "He's down, he's down . . . you got him—you got a hell of a moose! A tremendous moose!"

The willow thicket was much wider and denser than it had appeared from above, and it took nearly a half-hour of searching through the tangled maze to find the bull. I went up to him cautiously, with my rifle ready; if still alive, he would be dangerous. But there was no danger now. One bullet, presumably the first, had torn his heart open and the second had crashed a fist-sized hole through his ribs and shredded his lungs.

In the manner of other moose I've bagged, he'd absorbed tremendous energy without flinching and died on his feet. He was an old bull, with broken teeth and no fat on his ribs and probably would not have survived the Alaskan winter. Or the wolves. While we were skinning him and preparing the meat to be packed out, another moose came grunting and crashing through the willows. It was a young bull, healthy and snorting and full of fight, waving his antlers at us. He would have been a good trophy, and Jack had a license to fill, but the day was growing short, we were tired, and the miles back to camp would be exhausting. Best to hunt him another day.

As we hiked back to camp by starlight, we were challenged by yet another moose and I fell face down in a bog. We didn't arrive until after midnight, giddy with triumph and exhaustion, but not too weary to pour the last of the box wine into Jack's crystal goblets and raise a toast.

"To the moose."

"Yes, to the moose," someone added. "And to hunters."

RUFFIN JOHNSON
CUSTOM KNIVES

*"Getting within shooting range of antelope often requires some tactical maneuvering, especially when the quarry has already been spooked . . . "*

# Chapter 21

# Up Close Antelope

o you see him now? Can you see him now?" Brad's dry whispers were urgent. "He's the one in front."

Crouched above me with his hands on my shoulders, Brad could see the tips of three pairs of pronged horns shadowing through the spiky sagebrush, but I could see nothing from my lower sitting position. It was a curious situation to be in, but the best plan we could come up with on short notice and by no means a sure bet.

"There he is—get ready." I could feel Brad's grip tighten on my shoulder as I leaned into the rifle and fixed the crosshairs where I expected—hoped—the big pronghorn would appear. In a solid position, with my rifle supported by a sturdy bipod, a 200-yard shot would have been a piece of cake and not much of a challenge at 300 yards or even beyond. At my shoulder was an accurate rifle in one of the flattest shooting calibers extant, but distance wasn't the problem. The animal I wanted was too damn close!

Brad Ruddell and I, with our guide Steve Hopkins, were hunting antelope in New Mexico on rangeland that had once been the scene of the state's notorious Lincoln County war. Our hunt had been organized by outfitter Kirk Kelso who is noted for searching out the best areas for good heads. I'd hunted with Kirk in previous years and had taken an exceptional Coues deer in Mexico the year before, so when he passed the word that he was putting together a hunt in one of New Mexico's best pronghorn areas, I'd quickly signed on.

On opening morning, the state was in the midst of one of the worst droughts in history and the parched grass crunched under our boots like burnt toast when we trudged up a hogback ridge in the pre-dawn gloom. We set up our sporting scopes just as the first glow of day outlined a range of mountains to the east.

One of my favorite things about hunting pronghorns is that they live in sweet-smelling sagebrush country, and as the rising sun spread color across Lincoln County's historic landscape, I filled my lungs with big breaths of the sage-perfumed air.

From where we were situated, our spotting scopes reached across miles of ranchland, finding here and there the snowy rumps of antelope. Some were in twos or threes, others in larger bunches, but mostly too distant to pick out the best bucks. The closest animals we could see were trotting along a fenceline a good half-mile away. Apparently spooked by other hunters, three of the bigger bucks split off from the main group and angled our way until the distance was about 600 yards.

Steve's real job is running a bank over in Arizona, but his passion is hunting antelope with an enviable knack for sizing up trophies. He gets his kicks helping other hunters sort out the best heads, which is how he came to be hooked up with Kirk and fell in with Brad and me.

"Sweet Sixteen" is the golden rule for judging trophy-class pronghorns, meaning a buck with horns 16 inches or longer.

One of the three bucks looked like he would easily go 16 or better and our situation looked pretty good for getting a shot. The trio had already slowed to a walk and would probably soon stop. Then, it would be easy for us to drop off the backside of our knoll, and keeping out of sight behind the ridgeline, circle around until we were close enough for me to belly-crawl over the ridge-top and get a clear shot with my long-reaching rifle.

Brad Ruddell is a longtime pal who has done a lot of hunting in a lot of places. He also happened to be vice president of sales and marketing at Weatherby and came to our hunt outfitted with a new rifle model that he wanted to try and show off. It was a spiffy-looking rig with a camo-patterned Fibermark stock; later, he would use the rifle to pull off a shot that earned him some serious bragging rights. I was also carrying a Weatherby rifle, not just because it was the politically polite thing to do while hunting with the company's V.P., but because it happens to be my all-time favorite antelope rifle.

It's a love affair that began back in the barefoot 1950s when my prospects of owning such a rifle were about the same as getting a passing grade in spelling.

The shooting magazines I devoured back then always had an article or two about Roy Weatherby's rifles and sizzling fast cartridges, and I mooned over pictures of the sexy rifles the way too-long-at-sea sailors drool over pictures of sexy pinup girls. Even my first attempts at whittling gunstocks from slabs of local black walnut were inspired by the unmistakable Weatherby profile. While most lads my age collected baseball cards and memorized batting statistics, I stuffed my brain with more useful information, such as memorizing and comparing the trajectory tables of different rifle calibers and bullet weights. Which is why by my calculations the caliber that topped every ballistic chart was the .257 Weatherby Magnum, a conclusion I arrived at by shooting groundhogs in the pastures and hayfields of our Tennessee farm.

With an 87-grain bullet screaming out the muzzle at nearly 4000 fps, the trajectory would be almost as straight as a string stretched tight across a woodchuck-infested alfalfa field. Sighted in with the bullet path only an inch and a half above aim at 100 yards, it would be less than three inches low at 300 yards. In other words, if I could ever get my hands on a rifle in this wondrous caliber, I'd hit any groundhog I shot at simply by aiming at its chest, with no hold-over to worry about.

This was dizzying stuff for a gun-crazy farm boy, and I reckoned the .257 Weatherby was nothing less than a gift handed down from Olympus, which I figured to be located somewhere in California. Such imaginings are the stuff of boyhood dreams.

Dreams have a way of coming true if you keep your fingers crossed long enough, and grown up years later, when my own children were old enough to have their own dreams, I figured the time had at last arrived to own a Weatherby. Not just an everyday Weatherby, but the rifle of my boyhood's wildest wishes, with a glistening stock inlayed with patterns of exotic wood and lavish hand-checkering. The caliber, of course, had to be .257 Weatherby Magnum.

After getting into the gun-writing business, I'd visited with Roy Weatherby several times and we'd become pretty good buddies. He'd had quite a chuckle when I confessed he'd towered above all my boyhood idols, and I think he'd been impressed when I described how I'd once calculated the way to sight in a

.257 Mag. for groundhogs. Or at least he pretended to be, because when I put in my order, he threw in a couple of custom touches that made the rifle one I'll never part with.

As an antelope rifle, it's unsurpassed. I honestly can't remember how many pronghorns I've taken with it over the past quarter-century.

First-time hunters of the American pronghorn are usually surprised at how small they are. Their petite profile, combined with an unsociable habit of putting long yardage between themselves and anything that looks like a hunter, makes them a challenge for both hunter and rifle. They don't need a lot of killing, but they do take a lot of hitting.

Shooting distances tend to be long—often well over 200 yards—and distance judging over the typically flat or rolling landscape can be deceptive. Which is why savvy hunters tilt the odds in their favor by using flat-shooting calibers that forgive errors in distance-guessing.

Bullets in the 100- to 120-grain range have plenty of punch for pronghorn and the accent should be on downrange velocity and accuracy. For the New Mexico hunt, I'd handloaded some of Combined Technology's streamlined 115-grain bullets to about 3400 fps, that when sighted-in to hit 2½ inches high at 100 yards, hit within four inches of point of aim all the way out to 350 yards. Even at 400 yards the drop is only about nine inches, which means aiming high on a buck's shoulder will put the bullet about where it needs to be.

My .257 Weatherby rifle is by no means a lightweight. With its 26-inch, heavy sporter contoured barrel, it's just shy of ten pounds with scope. Antelope rifles don't need to be lightweight since the whole idea is to let your bullet do the walking. Propped on the legs of a Harris bipod, the extra weight adds the steadiness necessary for shots out to 300 yards and beyond. Which is just the sort of shot I anticipated taking once I'd bellied to the crest of the ridgeline.

The best-laid hunting plans have a way of being ruined by unexpected events, and our hopes for a successful stalk were suddenly dashed asunder by the crack of a distant rifle. Although it came from a long way off, the noise sent the three antelope into instant overdrive as they bee-lined for a distant fence along the dusty road we'd driven in on.

"Oh no," groaned Steve, "if they do what I think they're going to do and cross that road, we've got a problem."

Sure enough, the three bucks ran straight to the fence and ducked under it the funny way antelope do, then trotted across the road and slipped under a fence on the opposite side.

Shaking his head with disappointment, Steve explained the situation. "We don't have permission to hunt on that side of the road and those guys hightailed it over there like they knew it. Look at them now."

As though they knew they were in safe territory, the three bucks slowed to a casual walk and looked completely at ease.

With no more antelope within stalking distance and none of the distant specks of white and tan appearing to be headed our way, we needed to find another lookout. Steve had scouted the area days before and had located a few other good spotting positions and we spent the rest of the morning checking them out.

We saw antelope at every place where we set up our spotting scopes, but they were either too small or too far or on "no-hunting" property. As midday came closer, the cool early morning air that had allowed crisp definition and distant trophy-judging had warmed and distorted our images with wiggly waves of mirage.

After a long and fruitless search at a final lookout, Steve suggested we go back to our starting place and see if there had been any movement of the distant herds we'd seen earlier. Back in his pickup, we were heading down the gravel ranch road when Steve slammed on the brakes, shouting, "Will you look at that! It's the three bucks we lost earlier!"

As we watched, the trio ducked under a fence on the no hunting side and crossed the road, once more in our hunting territory.

"Let's just drift by and get some idea where they're headed. We'll go down the road a-ways, leave the truck out of sight, then walk back and try to cut them off at the pass."

As we drove by, the three bucks were ambling down a shallow draw, hemmed on each side by sage-dotted backbone ridges. A quarter-mile down the road we discovered another shallow vale running parallel to the one the bucks were in and converging into a Y-shaped flat.

Getting within shooting range of antelope often requires some tactical maneuvering, especially when the quarry has already been spooked, as had these three bucks. Our plan was simple, though not without obvious flaws and plenty of ways to go wrong—depending on what the antelope had in mind.

We decided that Steve would go back to the nearest draw, where he would be hidden from the antelope by the low ridge where we'd last seen the bucks. From there, he would sneak up on the ridge high enough to see the animals and hand-signal Brad and me as to their general whereabouts and which way they were headed.

Meanwhile, Brad and I would head toward the flat where the two draws converged and be ready to pull off an old-fashioned, outlaw style bushwhack. If—and the "if factor" loomed large—the antelope turned the way we hoped they would.

Following Steve's hand signals, Brad and I got in position, hoping the three bucks would turn to the east when they came out on the flat. But now, something was wrong.

Steve's signals told us the bucks were now close to our position—only a stone's toss away over the backbone of the ridge—and if they cut to the east sooner than expected, they would be awfully close. Too close!

Time has a way of standing still when you're waiting for an animal to appear in your sights, and as the moments oozed by, my mind raced over a dozen things that could—and probably would—go wrong.

First of all, it was only a guess that the trio would turn to the east when they appeared on the grassy flat. If they ventured west, we'd probably never see them. Or one of the smaller bucks could be in the way and block a shot at the buck I wanted. There would only be a moment or two before they looked back and spotted us, and then they'd be away like rockets. *And what if the bigger buck wasn't as big as we thought?*

The times we'd seen him before he was on the move at a considerable distance, so I never got a really good look. But his horns had looked big to all three of us. With circumstances as they were now, there would be only an instant to shoot before they saw us. The crosshairs were on the spot where I expected them to appear, the rifle's safety off, and the tip of my finger on the trigger.

"They're coming . . . the big one is in front," Brad whispered as he knelt down behind me.

Suddenly they appeared, walking slowly and angling away. Even with his head down, I could clearly see the lead buck was the one I wanted. The shot was automatic, as if the scope's crosshairs had a mind of its own and found a mark slightly aft of the buck's mid-chest line that would angle the bullet into his heart.

An instant later the buck was falling, dead even before he hit the ground, struck by a bolt of Weatherby lightning.

Brad was slapping the top of my head and Steve waved his hat from the crest of the ridge where he'd watched our plan unfold.

"I'm not believing this," Steve said as we paced off the 82 steps from where I'd fired at the buck.

Later that day Brad pulled off a truly spectacular shot on a buck even better (he claimed) than mine, and that night we joined other hunters in a cantina that served the kind of Mexican food that can only be quenched with gulps of *cerveza*. It was Saturday night, and we heard happy tales about trophies collected and sad stories about bullets that missed. From time to time a foaming mug would be raised in my direction and a voice would rise from somewhere in the smoky din.

"Hey Carmichel, here's a toast to the shortest shot of the day."

# Guns & Shooting

*"When I moved into my second story office directly across from the courthouse and laid eyes on all those grinning pigeons lined up on the balcony, I knew fate had caught up with me."*

# Chapter 22

# The Great Jonesboro Pigeon Shoot

The whole thing got started when Bob Jenkins' second oldest daughter was accused of shoplifting a brassiere at Maud and Mable's Discount Variety Store.

Bob, whose full name is Robert E. Lee Jenkins (like most folks who live on the lower end of the county), took his daughter's troubles to Fry (for Friedman L.) Bacon, a lawyer of some local repute.

Fry Bacon is one of the last of that dwindling species of attorneys who were admitted to the Bar after a period of having "read law," but with no other formal training. This shortcoming has been of no noticeable difficulty to Fry Bacon, who describes himself as a "champion of poor people's causes." In return for legal services, he has been known to take in chickens, coon hounds, and enough odd parcels of land to make him the county's biggest property owner.

Not one to let textbook law interfere with a good courtroom battle, Fry Bacon's favorite tactic is to open his Bible to some random page, wave it in the faces of judge and jury, shout that there is no higher law than the Law of God, then have the jury get down on its collective knees while he leads a prayer for his dear misguided client who, he claims, has just recently been washed in the Blood of the Lamb and aims to spend the rest of his life doing kind deeds and "helping out widder wimmin."

Fry Bacon was just the man to represent Robert E. Lee Jenkins' daughter.

In Fry Bacon's opinion, the theft of a brassiere was truly a delicate subject and hardly one to be discussed before a mixed courtroom audience. The word "brassiere" was abhorrent to him under such circumstances, and so was the diminutive form "bra." Thus he substituted the phrase "set of briars," thumping his clinched fists to his chest whenever necessary to indicate their approximate purpose and his own apparent meaning.

The case did not go well for Fry Bacon. His assertion that the poor girl was feeble minded did not produce the desired effect, nor did his pleas that the lass was "with child" by a stranger last seen two years before. Seeing no hope in this line of defense, he turned to attacking the two eyewitnesses as "godless sinners" and "short-skirted harlots" and was just warming to this line of reasoning when it happened.

Six tons of pigeon manure came cascading though the courtroom ceiling. It covered the jury, it covered the godless harlots, it covered His Honor the judge and it covered Fry Bacon. It covered them all with 12,000 pounds of dry, dusty, choking pigeon droppings that had been accumulating in the courthouse attic for decades, straining at the ceiling rafters, and needing only the shock wave of Fry Bacon's rhetoric to set it free.

"Ladies and gentlemen of the jury," Fry Bacon is reputed to have said when the dust cleared, "Behold the wrath of The Lord . . . "

The case was dismissed and the courthouse closed for six weeks because, as one Jonesboro wag put it, "The wheels of justice can't turn in that stuff."

The episode wasn't without some warning. Some 15 years earlier Bill Bowman, a leading Jonesboro humanitarian, had noted that the pigeons had so gummed up the courthouse clockworks that each hour was lasting about 80 minutes. The matter was brought up at the city council meeting where Virgil Meeks noted that the additional time was probably a good thing and that the clock should not be tampered with. The council agreed with his logic and voted 11 to 1 to leave the clock alone. The one dissenting vote came from Pearlie Goode, the church organist, who complained that the clock's once silvery chimes were sounding like a pig sloshing through a mud hole. But now with the collapse of the courtroom ceiling, something clearly had to be done.

The first order of business was how to clear out the existing mess and that in itself brought about a political scandal, which almost brought down the county government. The lowest bid to haul away the pigeon manure ran into thousands of dollars, enough to cause a countywide financial crisis. At the last minute Mort Screeb, who owns a tomato farm down by the Chucky River, stepped in and said the stuff was great fertilizer and that he would haul it off for nothing. His one condition, however, was that he be allowed to take it as he needed it, which, further questioning disclosed, might cover a period of three or four years.

In the end, a cleanup crew was hired to cart it off, but the ensuing political fight, with Screeb screaming "kickback," produced a shakeup in Washington County politics that continues even to this day.

The area newspapers called it the Pigeon Krap Kickback Kaper with courthouse insiders becoming known as the Kounty Krap Klan. The local chapter of the KKK objected to this and threatened to burn a cross on a reporter's lawn until they discovered he lived in an apartment owned by the regional Grand Wizard.

Despite all the uproar, a few cool heads noted that nothing was being done about the pigeons. They were as happy as ever, perching high on the belfry railing, roosting in the clockworks, building more nests, hatching babies, and contributing hourly to another avalanche.

The first step in correcting the pigeon problem was to hire professional exterminators. They rigged a cannon-like affair that made a burping noise—guaranteed to frighten pigeons and starlings and other such winged creatures. The Jonesboro pigeons loved it. It would burp and they would coo, and in winter they warmed their feet on its outstretched muzzle. Obviously, stronger measures were called for.

That's when I arrived on the scene.

Living in Jonesboro is unlike living anywhere else on earth. It's a beautiful little town nestled in the wooded valleys of East Tennessee. It was home to a scrappy young lawyer by the name of Andy Jackson and now, after 200 years of existence, is one of the best-preserved towns of its kind to be found anywhere. No power lines ensnarl its streets, no parking meters clutter its curbs, and old-fashioned street lamps cast a warm glow on brick-paved sidewalks.

On the town square is the county courthouse where dwell Jonesboro's pigeons. Even though completed in 1912, it's still called the "new" courthouse by most of Jonesboro's citizens who well remember the "old" courthouse, and probably even the one before that.

Two Jonesboro dowagers have not spoken to each other for over 30 years because each believes that she is the original Scarlett O'Hara and the other an imposter. Another lady is convinced she is Alice in Wonderland and at any given time can produce at least 20 corroborating witnesses to that effect.

Stray dogs, camels, and pack mules eventually find their way home, and it's no different with wandering Jonesboroites. After several years living in the West and exploring lands far beyond, I returned to Jonesboro to spend my declining years near the poor dirt farm where I grew up.

Jonesboro citizens seldom leave town except in a state of acute disgrace, so it was naturally assumed when I left town years before that there must have been a substantial stigma attached to my departure. So of course I was eyed

with some suspicion when I reappeared on the village green. But whatever crimes or indiscretions that vivid imaginations may have reckoned for my departure were apparently forgotten when I opened up a downtown office as bold as brass, looked up old girlfriends, and settled back in place as easily as a puppy taking a nap. Even old Aunt Bessie, who used to slip up behind me and hit me with her cane, now smiled sweetly and said if I would bring her a pumpkin, she'd make me a pie. (Not for a million bucks would I eat one of the mean old woman's pies.)

It was a comfortable reunion but, alas, too good to last. When I moved into my second story office directly across from the courthouse and laid eyes on all those grinning pigeons lined up on the balcony, I knew fate had caught up with me.

No one could argue that the courthouse needed to be rid of the pigeons, and it was equally clear that the only way to solve the problem was to shoot them. Their clock tower fortress was apparently impregnable to all other forms of attack. But until my arrival, no one had possessed both the will and the means of dealing with them, and my second-story office window provided the perfect sniper's roost. Destiny had surely planned the whole thing.

As discretely as enthusiasm permitted, I passed the word that I wouldn't mind taking a few potshots at the pests "just to keep my shooting eye in practice." And just as discretely the word came back that it was my "bound civic duty to rid Jonesboro of the damnable beasts." Even the sheriff, H. H. Hackmore, who is also in charge of courthouse maintenance, stopped by to bestow his blessing on the project.

Second only to the speed of light is the blazing speed of Jonesboro gossip. In no time at all everyone knew that a big game hunter had come to do in the courthouse pigeons. Elvis couldn't have caused a bigger stir.

The distance, as measured to the peak of the clock tower, was 41 yards, and the choice of weapon was my old pump-up pellet rifle. I figured this was the only safe equipment for the job, even though it might handicap me a bit. I didn't know how much of a handicap this would be until I tried adjusting the peep-sight for a 41-yard, dead-on point of impact. The pellets hit everywhere except dead-on, with the group sizes ranging upward of 10 to 12 inches.

I'd made the mistake of announcing that I would begin knocking off the pigeons the following Monday morning. I say mistake because when I arrived at work, pellet rifle in hand, a crowd of onlookers had already gathered in the street. It was going to be a memorable day in Jonesboro history and they wanted to see it happen. There was a smattering of applause when I entered the ancient building, and I think I heard Harry Weems, who runs Harry's Men's shop downstairs, offering to cover all bets.

Filling the rifle's air reserve with ten full strokes of the pump handle, I fed a pellet into the chamber, took a rest on the window sill and leveled the sights on a particularly plump pigeon. The crowd below held its breath. *Pluff* went the air rifle. *Splat* went the wayward pellet on an ornate piece of concrete scroll work. *Coo* went the pigeon. I'd missed clean. A chuckle rippled through the throng.

Feverishly I pumped the rifle and fed another pellet. *Pluff, splat, coo.* The chuckle became a collective guffaw. *Pluff, splat, coo,* as again and again I tried. No results.

"Hey Carmichel," someone shouted from below, "If them was lions, they'd be pickin' their teeth about now."

*Pluff, splat, coo.* Even the pigeons joined in the fun, waddling to the roof's edge for a better view of the sorry spectacle.

By then my audience was drifting off by twos and threes, telling each other it was the biggest disappointment since Jack Hicks' hanging was called off in the spring of 1904. Harry Weems paid off his losses and my disgrace was complete.

That day I called Robert Beeman, the country's leading importer of high-quality air rifles, and ordered his German-made Feinwerkbau Model 124 and a supply of pointed pellets. With a velocity of better than 800 feet-per-second—close on to a .22 Rimfire Short—the FWB-124 was about the hottest thing going in hunting-type air rifles and accurate enough to hit a dime—or a pigeon's head—at 41 yards.

"Send it airmail," I told Bob. "I've got to salvage my reputation."

Revenge would be mine, I told everyone, describing the fancy new air rifle I'd ordered. But sometimes the airmails fly slowly and weeks passed before the M-124 arrived, and by then the whole town was laughing about the "wonderful pigeon gun that existed only in my imagination."

But it did arrive, and my first few test shots with the deadly, pointed pellets showed it to be even more accurate than Beeman had promised. Topped off with a ten-power scope and zeroed at 41 yards, it cut a neat little group about the size of a shirt button.

The next morning a small crowd of onlookers gathered to watch the next chapter in Carmichel's disgrace. Even the pigeons seemed to be interested and about 20 lined up on the courthouse balcony railing to see what was happening. I started on the right end of the row and worked my way to the left.

The first bird toppled off with scarcely a flutter. His neighbor noted his demise only with idle curiosity, but no particular concern. When the next two or three went over the edge, the other pigeons began to get somewhat more curious and cooed at the stricken forms with some amazement. In fact, as more pigeons fell, the remaining birds reacted with increasing perplexity—those on the far left end having to lean way out from their perch, wings aflutter, in order to watch the peculiar behavior of their brethren.

The first run was 14 straight kills, with Harry collecting bets like mad.

The pigeons still hadn't figured out what was going on, but apparently they thought it best to temporarily go somewhere else and give it some thought. That day's tally was 27 pigeons and a few stray starlings. The next day would be even better.

But the following morning, disaster arrived in a totally unexpected form. I was brewing a pot of tea and had just knocked off the first pigeon of the day when "Shorty" Howze, Jonesboro's seven-foot policeman, charged into my office and presented me with an official complaint lodged by one of the townspeople. According to the unnamed plaintiff, I was "molesting Jonesboro's beloved pigeons."

"Com'on Shorty, "I protested, "you've got to be kidding. Everybody wants to get rid of those pigeons—you told me yourself. And besides, I have the sheriff's okay."

"I know," Shorty replied. "The courthouse is county property and you can shoot over there all you want to. But the chief says when you shoot across the street, you're violating Jonesboro air space. So the complaint stands."

"Who complained?" I asked

"I'm not allowed to say."

"I know but tell me anyway . . . is it that crazy-acting woman that just moved into the old Crookshanks' place and has all the cats and makes her husband walk the dog at two in the morning?"

"That's the one."

"Thanks for telling me."

"By the way," he said, stopping at the door and glancing at the air rifle standing by the window, "that's one hell of a pigeon gun."

After that, except for an occasional guarded shot, the rifle stood unused. The pigeons flourished and grew fatter, and life in Jonesboro trudged through an uneventful winter. By spring I'd all but forgotten the ill-fated affair. Then a really splashing event occurred that brought the pigeon problem back into brilliant focus.

The leading character was not me this time but none other than one Judge Hiram Walpole Justice. It seems that Judge Justice, all decked out in his new tailor-made blue suit, had just handed down an important decision and was on the courthouse lawn discussing it with some reporters when a pigeon swooped down and scored a bulls-eye on Judge Justice's jacket. It was seen on TV by thousands.

The judge turned on his heel and stalked back into the courthouse, muttering something about the futility of "holding court in a damned chicken house." That afternoon Judge Justice was in my office learning the finer points of shooting courthouse pigeons with a FWB-124.

Every morning thereafter the judge would declare a recess at about ten o'clock and rush over to my office to blast a few pigeons, giggling fiendishly every time one plopped on the pavement. His Honor became a fine marksman.

This had been going on for about two weeks when one morning Shorty, backed up by the mayor and two constables, crashed into my office and waved a warrant at the backside of the judge.

"Ah ha," yelled the mayor, "we know what you've been up to Carmichel. This time we've got you dead to rights."

With his judicially robed backside to the door, the judge was kneeling on the floor, taking aim with the rifle rested on the windowsill. So intent was his purpose that he didn't even look up, but continued aiming.

"That ain't me," I said, stepping out of the washroom. "That's Judge Justice. And if I was you, I wouldn't bother him right now."

All worthy projects must end, and by late summer the judge had pretty well wiped out the pigeon population, firing something near fifteen-hundred pellets in the process. In all probability, the whole thing would have come to a happy conclusion had it not been for one of those freak August cloudbursts.

The creek behind the courthouse overflowed its banks, poured into the streets of Jonesboro, and for the first time in history, flooded the courthouse basement where 200 years of moldy Jonesboro records were kept. The devastation to the voting records, in particular, was total. Wiped out.

An official inquiry was quickly launched in order to discover the causes of the unprecedented flooding and the final ruling was that: *"One Jim Carmichel, a citizen of Jonesboro, is known to have shot pigeons on the courthouse roof and thereby stopped up the underground drainpipes and thus contributed to the flooding."*

There's a new crop of pigeons living in the clock tower now. I can see them grinning this way.

*"Everyone who shoulders a shotgun has opinions about which targets are tough and which aren't."*

# Chapter 23

# The Toughest Targets That Fly

*So what flying targets are the hardest to hit?*

Everyone who shoulders a shotgun has opinions about which targets are tough and which aren't. Even old time market hunters never tired of arguing over which ducks were most challenging, but I've heard it said that the top guns mostly agreed that a pair of canvasbacks doing a wary fly-by over the outer edge of a decoy spread would definitely separate real gunners from the flock-shooters.

A modern waterfowler, going home sans limit after a day of blasting away at 60-yard Canadas surfing on 40 mile-an-hour tailwinds, will testify with his final breath that the noble goose is invulnerable. Or a twice-a-year dove hunter, who considers himself a pretty fair country wingshot if he can maintain a one-in-four, hit-to-miss ratio, will tell you that basically the dove is an impossible target.

Invulnerable? Impossible? Are they really?

I've spent the better part of a misguided lifetime throwing shot at all sorts of targets on many of this planet's gardens and pastures, and I've formed some semi-firm notions not only about which targets are toughest, but, more to the point, what is it that makes each of them so damnably hard to hit.

There are four ways to classify the difficulty of hitting a winging target with a shotgun. The first and most fundamental of these is simply a matter of distance. A Canada goose flying over a pit blind at 30 yards will probably land on some hunter's table. But double the altitude, putting the target on the outer fringe of shotshell performance, and it's an unlucky goose indeed that gets scratched. Thus the innocent skybuster, who proclaims the invincibility of geese is really only telling us that (a) he is a poor or foolish shot, (b) his gun and ammo are unequal to the task or (c) a goose is smart enough to stay out of his reach.

A second factor in making targets tough, or at least seem tough, are flaws in our individual shooting styles. Everyone has them. They're like weeds in our spiritual rose gardens; as soon as one is pulled, another variety sprouts. For example, we've all observed otherwise fine wingshooters, not to mention ourselves, who repeatedly missed targets flying at a particular angle. The situation is all the more frustrating when other gunners, even less skilled than ourselves, hit targets at the same angle with ease.

Virtually all trap, skeet, and sporting clays shooters experience situations in which a certain target gives them trouble. Sometimes this is only psychological, but usually it's caused by a subtle, almost undetectable, corrosion of technique (remember this phrase, it can be useful) that manifests itself only under certain conditions. Thus a skeet shooter who becomes convinced that the number four station high house is a "tough target" is only telling us that he has developed a shooting problem. After all, thousands of other wingshooters can smoke the four standing on one foot, so it clearly isn't a very tough target. Certainly not the kind of tough targets we're talking about here.

A third and more serious classification of tough targets are those that may or may not be innately hard to hit but manage to put the gunner at a disadvantage. The chukar partridge, for example, though a respectable challenge to any gun, probably won't make the final cut on anyone's toughest targets list unless they throw in a wild card that shifts the odds in their favor, as I've learned while hunting them in a half-dozen western states and in exotic places on far sides of the globe.

The name of their game is exploit the terrain, as they do in such places as the steep, pebble-strewn canyons of western Idaho, where the birds flourish. Of the times I've hunted them there, the problem was simply trying to stand up in order to get off a shot, because on nearly every flush I'd lose my footing and find myself sliding or falling before I could shoulder my shotgun. After one exhausting day of chasing the fiendish birds, a companion asked if I thought chukar were tough targets.

"I'll let you know if I ever get a fair shot," I responded.

Such induced difficulty, be it natural or artificial, is not necessarily a fair gauge as to how hard it is to hit a given target. For instance, we sometimes willingly impose handicaps that make otherwise easy targets become difficult.

This is the essence of the long yardage handicap system in trap shooting and certainly one of the damnably irresistible charms of sporting clays. There is nothing whatever difficult about smashing a crossing target at 25 yards, but hide it behind a barrier of trees or brush so that it's visible only for the briefest of moments and it indeed becomes a tough target. It really isn't the target that's so tough, only the circumstances.

In my book, the really tough targets are those that give you every advantage and then flip you the bird. When you're comfortably situated on open ground, with your choice of shotgun and ammo, and the quarry is in range – and still you miss because it does more tricks than a monkey with a kite – then you're up against a tough target. And when you go after such a critter on its own terms, then you've found yourself a sho'nuff, big-time tough target.

That's why my vote for the Number One toughest target that flies goes to a delicate snipe found on the fabled floating gardens of Kashmir. Most hunters have never heard of it. Little has been said or written, because those who have tested themselves against the dainty bird generally prefer to forget the experience; as if like a bad dream, it never really happened. To understand this gamebird you must know more about the land where it's hunted.

Northernmost of India's provinces, Kashmir is perpetually bathed by cool, saffron-scented air sweeping down from the Himalayas. During the days of the Raj, British bureaucrats stationed in Calcutta or Bombay escaped the scorching summers of those unhealthy places by immigrating to Kashmir, where a curious law regarding foreign ownership of property was neatly bypassed by living in elaborately carved houseboats, permanently moored along the shores of Lake Dal.

Summering in these floating palaces was considered quite fashionable by those who idled away the evenings nibbling spicy hors d'oeuvres, toasting their collective highnesses back in dreary London, and thanking their lucky stars for being born Englishmen and having been posted to this exotic paradise.

Then, as now, existence was largely aquatic, with trade and transportation provided by graceful, high-sterned watercraft poled along Lake Dal's languid surface by the handsome people of India's northern race. In mornings and evenings merchants floated by, selling sweetmeats and melons, tiger skins and pomegranates. Honey-colored women with seductive veils and eyes like frightened gazelles sold garlands of flowers while overhead, chattering birds of rare description and nameless colors dipped and wheeled.

In addition to Kashmir's sweet air and languid lifestyle, the British discovered another of India's treasures: gamebirds of unbelievable variety and uncountable numbers.

The outpouring of Siberia's waterfowl hatchery funneling into Kashmir through Himalayan passes sometimes hide the winter sun with dense clouds of ducks and geese. Partridge dart and chatter through the valleys, and upon the floating gardens a curious and delicate snipe builds its nest. Like similar birds of its race, it might be a reasonably sensible target were it not for its unique habitat.

Many areas of Kashmir have been diked and covered with vast acres of shallow water, and upon these waters generations of farmers have cultivated floating masses of intertwined vegetation dense enough to support crops such as melons and cucumbers. These floating fields are crisscrossed by canals through which the farmers transport themselves and their produce on narrow,

wickedly unstable boats. Since the water is only a few feet deep, the farmers use long poles to propel their boats and as a matter of local pride, every passenger stands, defying both gravity and logic, making every journey a balancing act.

Although the mat of floating vegetation looks firm enough to walk on, it really isn't, which is why laborers who tend these aquatic fields wear what I called "swamp walkers"—wooden hoops that work like snowshoes. Even so, one occasionally sinks through, in which case they merely climb back up the pole they always carry.

There is only one workable way to hunt the snipe of Kashmir, and that itself is part of the challenge. The guns are posted in skinny little boats with their prows pulled up on the edge of the field, making them semi-secure. From the other side of the field, a few hundred yards distant, a line of beaters advance on their swamp walkers, shouting and whopping the quaking mass with their poles. It's the damndest thing you ever saw, especially when one of the beaters sinks out of sight and then quickly reappears, climbing up his pole.

At first there is no action as the snipe run ahead of the beaters on their highly adapted, long-toed feet. Then, pressed between beaters and guns, they take flight like turpentined bats and the show begins. Frankly, I think the Kashmirian snipe is incapable of straight and level flight. Like butterflies, their wings are too big for their bodies and they have no sense of direction. So they constantly jerk and feint side to side faster than a shotgun can follow. Just when you catch up, establish some sort of lead and pull the trigger, the silly thing is headed in the opposite direction. It's ridiculous.

About that time the boatman, who is supposed to stay still and out of the way, gets excited and starts rocking the boat, screaming whatever his words are for "Shoot! Shoot!"

I may be something of an expert hunter on these snipe, having hunted them twice, whereas most hunters do it only once, then forever try to forget the debacle. There is no such thing as the right gun for Kashmirian snipe, but a good choice is something light with 20-inch barrels and no choke whatever, firing fast loads of Number 10 shot—which of course is impossible to find in India.

Roasted over braziers until they sizzle and pop open, scorched snipe are considered great delicacies by the locals who eat them whole, crunching the bones and rolling their eyes heavenward in wonder at the goodness of the tiny finger food. Which may partially explain why Englishmen who come out to India developed a taste for gin and bitters.

In my experience the second toughest target is the red-legged partridge of Spain. This may come as something of a surprise, because after all, Spanish partridge are bagged by the thousands every season. But one reason this is true is because the Spaniards are the world's best wingshots. (Never bet against a Spaniard with a shotgun unless you can afford to lose.) And one reason they get so good is by shooting partridge, the ultimate teacher.

The Spanish partridge, which is a bit larger than a quail and similar in color and markings to its cousin the chukar, isn't all that tough a target when walked up and shot on the flush. But when driven to the guns, the way they do it on Spain's great *estancias,* their flight takes on some evil characteristics.

The usual image of a driven bird shoot is of a moss-backed Englishman, done up in a tweed shooting outfit, politely potting grouse with a pair of side-by-sides handed to him by his loader. In Spain the shooters are no less elegant, but their pursuit of the sport has an air of intense passion that would make any Englishman blush. Nice sets of doubles are seen on every shoot, but the really hot-blooded Spaniards are liable to show up with a brace of five-shot semi-autos, which their loaders, or *secretarios*, stuff with high brass ammo. Thus equipped, they're capable of maintaining magnificent barrages that seemingly transport them into a state of ecstasy. This condition is further elevated by their breathtakingly beautiful wives and mistresses brought along to cheer every downed bird, which they do with unrestrained abandon.

What makes these driven red-legs so tough to hit is not just their extremely fast, darting flight, but the fact that they tend to fly *at* you rather than over. Typically, a flight of partridge will approach your blind only a few feet off the ground contour with alternate wing-beating and gliding. Then, as they are nearly in range, they pour on the coal and you expect them to gain altitude like any sensible bird, passing overhead so you'll have a sporting chance. Instead, they sucker you into holding fire until the last instant, then the flight splits and rockets by on either side of your blind.

American shooters are taught from infancy to avoid taking low shots, which is why the shooting computer between my ears goes haywire and shuts down whenever a target is at muzzle elevation. Presumably, this explains why these low-flying birds are also difficult for many other Americans.

Spanish hunters suffer no such inhibitions and swing on any target with relentless determination— a practice that over the years has added assorted dogs, *secretarios*, wives, foreign diplomats, and fellow grandees to the overflowing bag. And it's the reason why today's participants at any well-run partridge hunt are protected by metal plates on both sides of the blinds.

The red-legged partridge is so fast that they zip by before many shooters can get their guns in gear, which is why so many are shot at going away rather than incoming. Even so, it's possible that they really aren't as tough as I think. It's just that every time I go after a low target, an unseen hand seems to reach out and stop my swing.

My vote for the third toughest target that flies goes to the common wood pigeon. Common, I mean by their everyday presence in virtually all parts of the British Isles, but there's nothing common about the way they fly. Cross a teal with a mourning dove, give it the eyes and I.Q. of a wild turkey and send it to Top Gun school and you've got a wood pigeon.

Not to be confused with city park pigeons, the wood pigeon is a true wild bird, easily identified by their coloration and a distinctive white band on their wings. They nest and roost in wooded areas, often in groups of hundreds, and largely feed on farm crops. Which is their undoing because they are widely

regarded as pests rather than classic gamebirds. This status is changing, however, as more and more gunners become addicted to hunting them.

An English friend of mine became so obsessed by their corkscrewing flight that he quit a high-paying corporate job in London and moved his family to a cottage in wood pigeon country so he could indulge his passion on a daily basis. Now he runs a school on pigeon hunting that draws enthusiastic students from all over Great Britain.

This fanaticism for shooting wood pigeons is difficult to explain unless you've tried it, and then you're hooked for good. A solitary pigeon settling into the decoys can be ridiculously easy to hit, but it's that deception that keeps you off balance. When they light up their after-burners, they are among the world's fastest birds and have an unmatched ability to accelerate in a climbing turn. Which means that if you don't connect with the first shot, your second round will probably be only a farewell salute.

Unlike other hard-to-hit gamebirds that have only one or two elusive tactics in their bag of tricks, wood pigeons can pull off any maneuver except

flying backward, and they can do them all at a velocity that would make a mourning dove turn green with envy. Added to this are dense feathers and heavy musculature, which make them notoriously shot-resistant.

In a land where great wingshots are revered in prose and verse, no great champion hunter of wood pigeons has yet emerged. Indeed, it is the pigeon that's hailed as the conqueror of egos, with the most oft-told story being of a well-known chief instructor of a famous London shooting school who was invited to a pigeon shoot in the Scottish borderlands.

Good wingshooting, he had long expounded, is only an application of proper technique, and indeed his elegant style had earned him a reputation as one of England's best on driven grouse and pheasants. He'd never shot pigeons before, considering them unworthy targets, but had grown weary of hearing about how tough they were to hit. It was time, he reckoned, to show the locals what real gun-handling was all about. Indeed, as I was told by a witness, the locals actually were impressed with the instructor's average— almost one bird for every three shots, taking them as they came, the best shooting they'd seen. At dinner he received a standing ovation when he raised his glass to the wood pigeon and proclaimed, "I've met me match."

*"A box was opened and two gleaming cartridges produced—too big to be real—more like phallic artifacts than ammunition."*

# CHAPTER 24

# THE DAY I SHOT THE .700 EXPRESS

I once read a book about a famous matador who met his death in the bullring. The last hours of his life were described in vivid detail, especially the dressing ritual in which select attendants helped him don his suit of lights and the way his solemn-faced friends and fans touched his hand and offered their blessings. Had they come to see the man practice his craft? Or were they more drawn by the specter of a man willingly and deliberately putting himself in harm's way?

And so it was on a chilly British March afternoon at the Holland & Holland shooting grounds outside London. There were more introductions than I could remember, plus a crowd of spectators, all there for a common purpose: to see a middle-aged gunwriter lift to his shoulder the most awesome sporting rifle of modern times and fire a cartridge that delivers more than four and a half tons of energy! In doing so I would absorb more than 130 pounds of recoil.

For comparison, a .30/06 with a 180-grain bullet delivers about 20 foot-pounds of recoil and the fearsome .375 H&H kicks twice as hard as the .30/06.

The rifle I had come to London to shoot would hit me with a force greater than the combined recoil of three .375s placed against the shoulder and fired simultaneously! The .460 Weatherby Magnum, which until the advent of the .700 Nitro, was billed as the world's most powerful sporting rifle. It was infamous for devastating shoulders and wrecking scopes and mounts with its 80 pounds of recoil.

The rifle I was about to shoot kicks half-again as hard. It is a double-barrel created by the august firm of Holland & Holland in the best of London tradition. There are no muzzle brakes, and the recoil pad, if it can be called that, is only solid rubber covered by a thin layer of leather.

"Oh yeah," you say, "but that rifle is big and heavy. The weight absorbs most of the recoil." The rifle is big, weighing about 19 pounds. But the recoil comparisons I've listed take its weight into account. If it weighed the same as your eight-pound .270, the recoil would be a shattering 325 foot-pounds!

Recoil is the stuff of shooting legend, with many hunting cannons of the past being remembered more for the ferocity of their kick than the efficiency of their projectiles. Probably the most famous fancier of giant caliber rifles was none other than the 19th century hunter-explorer Sir Samuel Baker.

Baker had a penchant for oversize guns and had some impressive artillery built by J. Beattie, a London gunmaker of the time. Baker's rifles were, in fact, of such gigantic bore size and such tremendous recoil that they have caused later-day writers to speculate that he himself was of similar proportion, truly a giant of a man. In fact, though of muscular physique, Baker was of only medium height, which makes his preference for huge rifles all the more impressive.

In one of his books, Baker describes his sporting battery as consisting of four Number 10 double-barreled rifles, a 2-ounce rifle, and a single-barreled 4-ounce rifle weighing 21 pounds. By "four ounces" he meant the rifles was 4-gauge, about .90 caliber, firing a 4-ounce (1750 grains) ball.

In his journals Baker tells of an incident where he fired his four-ounce rifle at an Asian buffalo at a distance of about 600 yards. To steady his aim, he rested the rifle over a native's shoulder, and his bullet, after a flight of "three seconds" duration, passed completely through the animal. Almost as an afterthought, Baker added that the recoiling rifle split the ear of the man's shoulder. The powder charge alone weighed "sixteen drachmas," which is a full ounce or 437 grains.

On another occasion Baker describes hitting a buffalo in the chest with his big rifle and discovering that the 4-ounce ball had passed through the animal lengthwise, exiting through a hindquarter.

Frederick Selous, perhaps the most famous African hunter of all, recounted in his book, *A Hunters Wanderings In Africa,* an incident where he was almost completely disabled by the recoil of his rifle. He was hunting elephant with his 4-gauge muzzleloader and had gotten himself into a tense situation with a charging bull. His rifle had "snapped the cap," but had not fired so he handed it to his gunbearer for a fresh cap. In the confusion, his bearer hastily threw another handful of powder into the barrel and rammed another 4-ounce ball on top of the original charge. In Selous' words, here's what happened:

"I was lifted clean from the ground, and turning round in the air, fell with my face in the sand, whilst the gun was carried yards away over my shoulder. At first I was almost stunned with the shock, and I soon found that I could not lift my right arm. Besides this, I was covered with blood, which spurted from a deep wound under the right cheekbone, caused by the stock of the gun as it flew upwards from the violence of the recoil. The stock itself—though it had been bound round, as are all elephant guns, with the inside skin of an elephant's ear put on green, which when dry holds it as firmly as iron—was shattered to pieces."

Selous' mention of wrapping the stock of his gun with leather is interesting because he apparently had more than usual problems with broken stocks. Eventually he resorted to reinforcing the grips of his stocks with sheets of fitted and contoured metal (usually copper), which have come to be known as Selous Sideplates. By my calculations the recoil of Selous' double-charged 4-bore was somewhere in the neighborhood of 900 foot-pounds.

The era of giant rifles was a brief one, beginning when white hunters first explored the African bush and ending with the advent of smaller caliber, high-velocity "Nitro" cartridges. Altogether a period of not more than 70 years, with its heyday spanning perhaps three decades. It was, however, a period of hunting at its best, a time so rich with adventure and romance that my imagination would not rest until I had personally retraced Selous' African route and hunted the way he had—with a giant muzzleloading rifle. The time was 100 years after Selous first set foot in Africa and one of my companions was Turner Kirkland, the king of black powder.

Turner had an original 4-bore double rifle made by Rawbone of Capetown. Like other adventuresome gunsmiths of the last century, Rawbone had set up shop close to the South African ivory trade and supplied sport hunters with heavy-caliber muzzleloaders. The Rawbone rifle weighed 20 pounds and had a sharp-edged steel buttplate that did nothing whatever to ease recoil. The first time I fired it, at a target pegged on a tough mopane tree, the ball ripped the tree in half like a bolt of lightning. A crowd of curious natives, who had come to see the "magic" of the antique gun, stood in stunned silence, their gaping mouths unable to utter a sound. I shot the 4-bore three or four more times that day but soon got out of the mood.

Kirkland had also brought along a Belgian made 6-bore double rifle. It was a pretty thing, with fancy engraving and gold inlays, that went unused until the last day of our safari. Determined that it should not go home unbloodied, I stalked a small herd of wildebeest and got to within shooting distance behind a gigantic termite mound. The grass was too high for a clear shot so I shinnied up the eight-foot termite mountain for a better view. While holding onto the mound with one hand, I fired the rifle while gripping it in my other hand.

Which was a mistake.

When the smoke—and my head—had cleared somewhat, I found myself sprawled at the bottom of the mound with the rifle lying several feet away. The wildebeest looked like it had been hit by a train, and my tracker, rolling his eyes and moaning, was apparently overcome by the spectacle.

Of late, long-range shooting with rifles chambered for the .50 caliber machine gun cartridge has become the rage, with .50 caliber clubs putting on demonstrations and tournaments. When in the army, I tested a bolt-action .50 caliber sniper rifle. It was fired from a bipod spiked into the ground, which took up a lot of the recoil. Back in those days I figured that getting pounded by a gun was just another way of having fun.

Another time, while attending an open house for a few gun writers, a carload of gunsmithing students showed up with a .50 caliber rifle they had built as a shop project. They had driven all night so their rifle would be christened by their hero, a writer with a well-known proclivity for king-size rifles and cartridges. The writer really didn't seem all that eager to have a one-on-one encounter with the big .50, but there was no way out, so *en masse* they repaired to the local trash dump where some local big game, such as a rat, could be bagged.

At the moment of truth, the famous writer took a rest over the hood of a truck, sighted at something or other, and had at it. The rifle flew up, his cowboy hat came crashing down over his eyes, and he bit the end off his cigar. Further offers to fire the rifle were declined. The recoil of a 20-pound .50 cal. BMG rifle is about 100 foot-pounds, which explains why muzzlebrakes are so popular.

Until Roy Weatherby introduced his .460 Magnum, the most powerful sporting cartridge was the .600 Nitro, which launched a 900-grain bullet at muzzle velocity of 1950 feet-per-second for an energy level of 7,600 foot-pounds. Recoil of the .600 Nitro is 95 foot-pounds.

The .600 Nitro dates back to 1903 and is of purely British origin. One would assume that the new .700 is out of the same English family tree, but truth is, it was born in America, the joint enterprise of a California millionaire and Jim Bell, who specializes in manufacturing new editions of otherwise obsolete or hard-to-find ammunition. Bell has manufactured other heavy-caliber cartridges, such as the .577 Nitro Express and the early Sharps rounds.

With a source of ammunition assured, Holland & Holland agreed to make a .700 Nitro, and in 1988 work was commenced. So far as building the rifle was concerned, very little in the way of new development was required. The venerable London firm has been making Best-quality double rifles for generations and building a .700 Nitro was mainly a matter of enlarging everything about their existing Royal Ejector model. The resulting rifle weighs about six pounds more than those built for lesser cartridges, but the scale is perfect.

Although I admire the craft and artistry involved in building a double rifle, the rifle's balance is all wrong for me, because the weight of the barrels tends to make them sluggish. In England, however, they are icons, and so when the .700 arrived at the shooting grounds, it was escorted by a three-car entourage. Apparently a number of the factory staff turned out to see the results of what they had wrought—or to make sure it came to no harm at the hands of an American gunwriter.

Actually, when I fired the rifle it had already been delivered to its American owner. He had used it on an African safari and I was told that it had accounted for an elephant in the Sudan. Now it was back in London for some minor repair, including replacement of an engraved nameplate that had been dislodged by recoil. Although I already knew the owner's name, the staff at H&H refused to reveal it, (the names of all of their elite clientele are guarded like the numbers of Swiss bank accounts).

After a prelude of fussing about and setting up targets, a large case was opened and, with reverent care, the rifle was presented to me. I noted that before the attendant released his grip on the rifle, he made damn sure it was securely in my grasp. I flipped the thumb lever to open the breech and there staring at me like the eyes of a great horned owl were the two biggest chamber openings I've ever seen in a modern-day rifle. A man's thumb would chamber quite easily.

Targets had been set up in front of a bunker-like concrete backstop thick enough to stop an artillery shell. It would have been fun to shoot the .700 through a row of railroad ties, but the backstop medium was several tons of sand. The people at H&H were keen on investigating the performance of the new cartridge and the sand trap made it possible to recover fired bullets, even those as powerful as the .700 Nitro.

The targets were five-inch black squares and the firing distance was 50 yards, seemingly an easy target, but the H&H personnel were careful to cover the target board with a five-foot strip of white paper. Apparently they didn't have much faith in my marksmanship and wanted to see how far I would miss the target. That's when I resolved to squeeze the trigger gently and aim as carefully as if I were shooting a .22. Recoil be damned, I wanted to show the Brits that an American could shoot their rifle and shoot it well.

The 50-yard shooting station had a padded T-rest that could be used for a steadier aim but I elected to go it offhand. A padded shooting jacket or some extra padding at the shoulder would have been a smart idea when shooting the .700, but I wore only a light coat. After all, I came to see what it was really like to shoot the world's most powerful sporting rifle, so my only protections were ear muffs and shooting glasses.

The time had come and I squared myself at the target. Cameras clicked in all directions. My wife Linda looked solemn and our American friends were clearly concerned. Other onlookers wore expressions that said, "I'm glad it's you chum and not me."

A box was opened and two gleaming cartridges produced—too big to be real—more like phallic artifacts than ammunition. I had anticipated firing the rifle only once but here were two rounds. *Was I twice blessed?* At a cost of more than $100 each for the .700 cartridges, my friends at H&H were being more than generous. *Or was it worth it to see an American get kicked on his pants?*

For a moment I rested the sights on the target, then opened the breech. One of the Holland staff dropped a round into the right barrel, then stepped well back. Clicking the safety to off, I raised the rifle and settled the plump bead in the wide notch of the express sight. For a few seconds my aim was steady and I gradually increased trigger pressure. But it wouldn't fire. After what felt like ten pounds of pull, I gave up, dropped the muzzles to the T-rest and took another breath. The trigger pull was too heavy and more than the usual finger pressure would be needed to release the sear. So again I raised the rifle, braced myself and hauled back on the trigger.

The effect was not like being kicked on the shoulder, but instead like running into a brick wall in the dark. The recoil of heavy-caliber rifles has been described by some writers as a "push." With a .700 Nitro, such a silly description doesn't apply unless having a 130-pound sandbag dropped on you can be called a push. There was also a momentary impression that my nose and jaw were no longer in alignment.

Eventually my eyes refocused on the target and the .700 caliber hole was easy to see, but not in the black square where I had aimed.

"Put another one in," I ordered, opening the breech so the attendant could load the left barrel. This time my finger was on the rear trigger, a somewhat better position, and

I determined to squeeze it as carefully as possible.

The next recoil seemed more violent than the first.

The muzzles reared to a nearly vertical angle, causing the butt to slip off my shoulder. For an instant I fought to hold onto the rifle but then regained my grip. The second hole missed the center of the square by only an inch. There was applause and more applause, and a kiss from my wife.

I had fired the mighty .700 Nitro.

*"During my first year on the job I received marriage proposals from no fewer than three different women of apparently unrestrained libido."*

# Chapter 25

# It's In the Mail

ou wouldn't believe some of the letters that came in during my nearly four decades at *Outdoor Life.* Most were about guns and hunting, but there were others ranging from death threats from terrorists to intimate confessions that would make a sex counselor blush.

During my first year on the job I received marriage proposals from no fewer than three different women of apparently unrestrained libido. All three seemed quite sincere, and I gave a lot of thought to each before replying because there is no telling what a scorned woman is liable to do. Fortunately, after a year on the job my picture had appeared often enough for female readers to have some idea what I looked like, so there were no further proposals. But there were plenty of other letters; indeed, hundreds of pounds of them.

One of the reasons I got so much mail was because *Outdoor Life* had a long-standing policy of replying to just about every letter that came our way. Bill Rae, the imperious chief editor who hired me, was a great believer in reader correspondence and made it clear that an important part of my job was keeping up with my mail and contributing to the magazine's monthly "Questions & Answers" department.

Those were the days of real mail, when letters came in envelops with stamps on them. The writers of such letters had put some thought and expense into their compositions and expected their efforts to be rewarded with similarly thoughtful replies.

The situation reached tsunami proportions following WWII when returning GIs discovered the magazine's editorials, and hunting and fishing writers seemed ready and willing to personally field any and every question that came their way. Naturally, the bulk of their letters were about guns and hunting, so much so that then Shooting Editor Jack O'Connor had to farm out some of his letter answering to a gunsmith and technical expert by the name of Roy Dunlap.

The more technically minded Dunlap fielded questions about ballistics and other such shooting esoterica while O'Connor devoted his time and expertise to questions about hunting and sporting firearms and places to pursue big game. Their combined efforts made *Outdoor Life* the go-to place for questions about shooting and hunting and no doubt accounted for the volumes of mail I was to inherit when I came on board.

Dunlap was to become a well-known author in his own right, especially for his books and articles on gunsmithing, plus a line of target rifles of his own design. (One of which I still own.) I met Dunlap in the '70s when he and I were collaborating on a book about gun care. He told me the magazine paid him all of four bits per letter back when he was helping O'Connor, which probably averaged out to about a buck and a half an hour if he typed fast, which may have been pretty good pay back in the late 1940s.

By the time I arrived at *Outdoor Life*, the avalanches of post-war mail had subsided enough that I could pretty well handle it myself with the aid of a dictating machine and part-time typist. Most of it came through our New York City office, from whence it was forwarded to my Arizona hideout in weekly bundles. Upon opening, I'd give the letters a quick scan and separate them into three stacks. The first stack included those I could answer with a quickly dictated reply; the second were those needing further research or fact checking; and the remaining letters were put on hold until my secretary-typist could help me decipher the authors' handwriting and/or figure out exactly what he or she wanted to know.

On a typical day of my three-day office week I would have a pile of letters dictated by the time my secretary arrived. That kept her busy until later in the day when she switched to the more daunting task of decoding my own handwritten manuscripts.

I saved all of those many years of letters until about a week after I had retired and began sorting out my office storage room. Among other accumulati stacked against the walls were seven full-length pasteboard file boxes stuffed with all that reader mail, each with a copy of my reply attached. Those big file boxes weighed about 85 pounds each, which when added together, amounted to more than a quarter-ton of mail. The postage alone had totaled in the thousands of dollars, and the hours of reading and answering them are uncountable.

All in all, I considered my time well spent because some of the mail from readers tipped me off to coming trends in the shooting-hunting world as well as provided valuable insights as to what our readers were thinking about. Many other letters provided ideas for my columns and articles.

Generally, my reader correspondence fell into three categories. The most common category included requests ranging from the best places to hunt elephants to the value of an old gun found in Granddaddy's attic. This latter question, by the way, posed a rather touchy situation because old guns were almost invariably assumed to be rare and of immense value. Which put me in the rather uncomfortable position, more often than not, of gently letting my correspondent know that hoards of gun collectors probably wouldn't be kicking down the doors with buckets of cash for Granddad's rusty old smokepole.

I could count on at least three or four of these inquiries in every week's mail. One reason behind this influx was that for about a 40-year period beginning in the 1880s, a flurry of imported and domestically made private brand guns had invaded the American market. Private Brand meaning they were hand stamped with whatever name or logo the customer—usually distributors or large dealers—wanted.

Many of these guns are still around and the variety of unfamiliar names causes much confusion among owners. Firearms stamped with quasi-familiar sounding names such as "Sam Holt" or "W. Richards" or "C. Parker" were, in fact, semi-fraudulent names intended to capitalize on the names and reputations of well-known, high-quality gunmakers. All too often these deliberate deceptions caused innocent and otherwise unsuspecting gun owners to believe they possessed a gold mine. Once, after I had written an article about the incomparable gunmaker Joseph Manton, I received a half-dozen letters from readers claiming to have shotguns made by the British master. As it turned out, each of the supposed rare Mantons were deceptively marked J. Manton & Co. and had actually been made by an American company specializing in shoddy, private brand shotguns. Even after I had cautiously explained the deception, a couple of disappointed owners took their ire out on me, claiming I was trying to swindle them out of their valuable Mantons.

I don't recall getting more than a couple dozen letters asking about a gun that turned out to be truly rare and valuable. There have been two or three of these I would have dearly loved to own; one was a Model 1886 Winchester and perhaps a couple of high-grade shotguns, but my policy was to direct them to a few dealers and collectors who I knew would provide them fair evaluations and offers.

More often there were letters from readers who had retired from hunting and only wanted to know what their used guns were worth and how to dispose of them. In each case I would politely explain there was no way that I, or anyone else, could appraise a gun sight unseen and that their safest course would be consult a reliable guide to gun values, such as Fjestad's *Blue Book,* or show the guns to a few (more than one) dealers or collectors at gun shows.

Another letter that always hoisted my caution flag began with something like: "Me and the guys at work are having an argument we want you to settle." Right away I knew that only some of the "guys at work" would be happy with my verdict and the rest would be mad at . . . guess who. So I tried to phrase my responses with the caution of a cat gnawing a spinning grindstone.

Usually such questions were of a technical nature such as "do you aim high or low when shooting uphill?" or "does a bullet rise when it leaves the muzzle?" So being the coward that I am, I tried to appease all parties by explaining that shooting lore is filled with inaccuracies and misconceptions that have been handed down by generations of ill-informed writers and misguided experts. But then, as now, I was also well aware that old myths die hard and for every one killed, three more are born, and that's what kept the letters coming.

Some of my most interesting letters came from places where people obviously had plenty of spare time on their hands—prisons. (Come to think of it, I wonder if my three marriage proposals came from incarcerated damsels?) During one especially memorable period, I received a series of letters written in a script so beautiful they were almost works of art. In his first letter the writer described in exact detail his collection of fine shotguns and custom-made rifles in exotic calibers. Similar letters were not all that uncommon but this guy's letters stood out not just because of his penmanship, but because of the scope and excellence of his collection.

After sending a note congratulating him on his fine taste in firearms, I got more letters from him, again beautifully crafted and describing an even grander collection of fine guns. After a few more such letters my curiosity got the best of me, so I researched his address and found it to be none other than that of a notorious federal penitentiary. His collection of fine guns was all fantasy, but I'll say this for him, he knew a lot about good guns, if only in his dreams. I'm still wondering if his exquisite penmanship led to a career in forgery that eventually put him behind bars.

Speaking of prisoners, some of my most entertaining letters came from a gaggle of inmates who entertained themselves by dreaming up unlikely conflicts and asking me to pass judgment on eventual victors. Although they made little effort to hide their penchant for violence, they often showed great imagination, such as snakes and armadillos mud wrestling. My favorite letter sought my opinion on a fight to the death between a Kodiak bear and a Cape buffalo. I answered that it would be an interesting fight and be sure to let me know if they ever saw one. Their letters eventually stopped so I guess they served out their time and went back into politics.

Less entertaining was a letter asking about explosives that could be used for a Black Sunday type of massacre. The tone of the letter was so sincere and apparently authentic that I called the FBI. As it turned out, a couple of FBI agents not only followed up on the letter but wanted to look at similar mail I'd been getting. That was in the 1970s when the country was aflame with campus protests and civil riots, and eco-terrorists had also commenced their dirty tricks.

The FBI really got my attention when they let me know that my name was on a hit list found when they busted a cabal of eco-nuts in California. For a long while after that any suspicious looking mail and packages were x-rayed before being opened.

Another rather common type of letter began with something like "why don't you . . . " Meaning they had a project in mind for me, such as writing about a particular gun, gauge or caliber, scope or whatever. Sometimes I'd be able to do what they requested, if in fact the subject appealed to a large enough segment of our readers. But just as often the "why don't you" letters were a request for me to take their side in a quarrel with a gunmaker or manufacturer of shooting equipment. Typically, they were having accuracy problems with a rifle and wanted me to lean on the manufacturer to get it fixed or replaced. To which I was obliged to explain that any influence I might have was largely imaginary, and tried to diplomatically point out that a major component of "accuracy" is personal marksmanship. A rifle that shot one-inch groups in carefully controlled tests may have shot no better than three inches when fired by someone who flinched and jerked the trigger. But suggesting to a dedicated reader that he might just be a lousy shot was about as risky as telling him his wife is fat and ugly. Possibly even riskier.

For a time I was getting letters from readers complaining about the performance of one particular make and model of big game rifle. All of the letters described the same problem, so I tipped off the rifle's maker that they ought to check it out. As it turned out, there was indeed a problem with the way their barrels were prepped, so the maker solved the problem and the complaints stopped.

Among my favorite letters were those about problems that could be easily fixed. Like the one from a pitiful sounding guy who said he was so recoil shy that even a .243 caused him to flinch. Could I recommend any way to keep his guns from kicking so hard? I told him to get a good set of ear plugs or muffs. A few weeks later I got another letter that was almost tearful in gratitude. He'd never realized the pain of recoil was actually a reaction to the sound of the muzzle blast and his "recoil" problem was solved.

My favorite letters of all were those from young readers who spelled out their dreams of a first gun, a first hunt, or the hunting they hoped to do when they grew up. A 10-year old lad once wrote a poem for me and others sent hand-made Christmas cards. Those were the writers who received my longest and best replies, because I once had dreams just like theirs.

*"If you own a shotgun, and if you are liable to shoot it in the company of two or more other shotgunners, you're going to need to acquire some skill in defensive snobbery."*

# Chapter 26

# How to be A Shotgun Snob - A Primer -

ave you heard about defensive snobbery? It's not a new art exactly, having been practiced in certain elite circles for centuries. Snobs are found in every corner of society of course, but shotgun snobbery is a fairly recent phenomenon, at least here in the States, and having taken root in the fertile soil of certain gun clubs and elite shooting venues, it's fast becoming a major social force wherever shotgunners gather.

If you own a shotgun, and if you are liable to shoot it in the company of two or more other shotgunners, you're going to need to acquire some skill in defensive snobbery. Mostly, it's a learned skill, like learning how to lead a target, but a privileged few seem to have a natural talent for it. My wife is one of this gifted class.

Until recently there was little need for defensive snobbery because there weren't all that many shotgun snobs. Of course, there are and always have been a few snobs lurking around gun clubs, but in the main these are natural snobs who are snobbish about everything they do. In the main they have been given some slack for being snobbish about their shotguns because it is only an extension of their natural snobbery.

But now it has come to pass that we have a new race of shotgun snobs: otherwise pleasant souls who never before raised a sneer or curled a lip at anyone or anything. Not, that is, until they got their hands on a shotgun and fell under the influence of practicing shotgun snobs. But these, like a gentle dog gone mad, can be the most vicious of all. Which explains why you need to develop some defensive snobbery even if you have been brought up to regard snobbery as naturally repugnant. If it makes you feel better, just look on defensive snobbery as a psychological flak jacket. Like a martial art, you can develop your defensive snobbery as far as you want to take it; all the way to a black belt, or just enough so that you'll feel safe at the gun club and more at ease in shops that peddle pretty guns.

The main reason for the recent outbreak in shotgun snobbery is the game of sporting clays, which like several other forms of advanced snobbery, originated in England. Though the importers of the game did so with the very best of intentions, we must never forget that other exotic imports, such as kudzu and starlings, were similarly well intended.

Of course, we have been playing shotgun games here in America for generations, and in case you are wondering why a strong strain of snobbery didn't develop before, the reason is easy to explain: the peculiar genetic aberration that makes people want to shoot trap simply has not as yet mutated a snob chromosome. And too, trap shooters tend to be obsessed with more elemental goals, such as winning enough money to get home.

As one sage trap shooter once pointed out, "It's hard to be a snob when you're carrying a lunch bucket."

Skeet shooters have long had the potential for outlandish snobbery, but the tendency is held in check because in skeet circles, the right to be a snob must be earned. If, for example, you score a perfect 100 straight with a .410, you are granted the right to practice snobbery on a temporary basis. Which explains why there are relatively few skeet snobs.

Sporting clays, on the other hand, is the only shotgunning game in which a snob can miss every target on the course and emerge from the experience with his snobbery absolutely undiminished. Obviously, that sort of hard core snobbishness is hard to stamp out, which is all the more reason you'll have to learn some defensive snobbery if you hope to survive as a wingshooter in the 21st century.

If you've been hanging out at some upscale shotgun clubs, you have already discovered that snobbery comes in several distinct forms, not necessarily related to each other. You've probably also noticed that snobbery begins at the parking lot, continuing into the clubhouse, on to the gun racks, and at every shooting station. That's why it has been found necessary to categorize the various guises of shotgun snobbery and develop effective means for dealing with each.

The various classifications of snobbery that you will encounter at a gun club include:

- *Gun Snobs*
- *Shooting Snobs*
- *Dress Snobs*
- *Vehicle Snobs*
- *Dog Snobs*
- *General Snobs or, if you will, Snobs At Large*

There are, of course, various refinements and subcategories of these classifications, but dealing with the more sophisticated and bizarre forms of snobbery requires advanced studies and more highly refined techniques. So consider the following only as a primer, with the understanding that confronting perpetrators of the various forms of snobbery requires the application of certain basic methods and techniques. With time and experience you will develop an individual technique that best suits your temperament, and will, in fact, become an extension of your personality. Since your first encounter with gun club snobbery can occur the instant you drive into the parking lot, let's begin with vehicle snobs.

They are easy to spot because the first thing a vehicle snob does upon emerging from his own vehicle is size up every other car in the lot. This indicates where he ranks among other vehicle snobs and can have a profound effect on his behavior during the remainder of the day. That's why the first and most inflexible rule of defensive vehicle snobbery is to never drive your family sedan to the gun club. Nothing makes a worse impression. Vehicle snobs will think it is the only car you own, and no matter how new or expensive your sedan may be, the impression is a bad one with lingering side effects. Station wagons and vans do not make nearly so poor an impression, but they are risky because they place you in a somewhat vulnerable position.

Sports cars and pickup trucks were acceptable a few years ago, but nowadays they condemn you as surely as wearing a narrow tie or new boots. The only vehicle you can be seen in at a proper gun club is a four-wheel drive SUV. It doesn't matter if every inch of road from your driveway to the club is paved and dry, or if you have no need or intention of ever shifting all four wheels into drive mode, the 4x4 SUV is *de rigueur* at the club. Don't arrive in anything else.

If you frequent one of the particularly snobbish Eastern clubs, I must further warn you that not just any SUV will do. You have, in fact, only two choices. The first option is that it be very expensive and very new. But even this seemingly simple option has its pitfalls. Never, for example, show yourself in a sparkling clean SUV. It should be well covered with mud from bumper to bumper. This gives the impression that you are *(A)* a go-to-hell sort of fellow or that *(B)* you have just returned from shooting a television commercial. Any romantics at the club will take it from there. (And there are always a few.) In the event that there are no means available for having it properly muddied, you might make arrangements with your car dealer to have it periodically re-muddied. Remember, fresh mud impresses best, but old dried mud is perfectly acceptable.

The second option in vehicle snobbery guaranteed to stop a snob in his tracks is a battered 4x4 at least 20 years old. A 1970 Jeep Waggoneer, for example, implies that you drove SUVs long before it was fashionable to do so and identifies you as a trendsetter to be reckoned with. All the better if rust is ample, and a cracked windshield goes a long way toward informing the world that you are a traveler of adventuresome trails. No shiny new vehicle can make such a powerful statement or is so effective at putting vehicle snobs in their place.

Be careful that you don't overstate your position, but there are a few accessories that will put your vintage vehicle in a class by itself. My favorites include crumpled, half-empty boxes of shotshells (the older the better) along with a can or two of gun oil scattered across the top of the dashboard where they can been seen by anyone looking your way. Never a domestic brand of gun oil, mind you, but something exotic such as Holland & Holland's Rangoon. (Be sure the label is visible, as vehicle snobs habitually peek into cars.)

If you anticipate trouble with dog snobs, you might further decorate the cluttered dash of your rusty 4x4 with a box of hypodermic syringes and a veterinarian-size bottle of canine vaccine (both half-empty). This gives the impression that you own or train so many dogs that you do your own vaccinating. No dog snob will dare tangle with such authority.

When leaving the club always raise the hood of your vehicle and check the oil. Make sure someone is looking your way or the effect is wasted. As they glance your way, shrug your shoulders and say: "It's an old habit from my racing days." This gives the impression that you and Jackie Stewart are old pals and probably shoot together. Blandly wiping the dipstick with your fingers and then your pants, the way race drivers do, adds a particularly convincing touch and has a riveting effect on dress snobs.

Speaking of which, there are two very effective ways of defending yourself against dress snobs. But just as important, it is absolutely essential that you not succumb to any of the other pitfalls that will fatally label you as a *poseur.* In other words, the last thing you want to do is to look like the snobs you are defending yourself against.

Your first option in defensive dress is traveling to London and having yourself outfitted by a Savile Row tailor. The last time I priced a bespoke (made-to-measure) shooting jacket with matching accessories, the tally came to just short of $4,500. (Be sure to go when the dollar/pound exchange rate is favorable.) And of course you'll need at least two complete outfits, so what with air tickets, a decent London hotel and afternoon tea, you can round off the total tab at about ten grand. A bit steep? Not when you consider it will keep the dress snobs at bay for at least a year.

Your second option is reverse snobbery. It is my favorite gambit and can be deadly effective, but you need a certain *je ne sais quoi* to pull it off. The trick is dressing like the club snobs but with your own special affectations. For example, never wear a new waxed cotton jacket to the club. To do so makes you look like just another bush league snob, and nothing—I mean *nothing*—is more passé than a new waxed cotton jacket. The impression you want to convey is that you were wearing waxed cotton before it was the thing to do. So your waxed cotton must be worn, torn, and smelly. (Where is the clever entrepreneur who will market pre-distressed jackets?)

The best way to break in a new jacket and pants is to crawl through a barbed wire fence about 50 times. This will make you look like you've been hunting pheasants in South Dakota for many years and every hunt snob at the club will itch with envy. For all-around perfection, however, a new jacket should be used for kennel bedding at least six months. Filling the pockets with sand or bird-shot aids in capturing the much sought-after baggy effect as well as improving your shooting if you tend to over-lead the target.

Shooting gloves are *de rigueur*, of course, even on the hottest days, but again, the older-the-better rule applies. Ideally, they should be greasy and blood-stained so as to appear to have handled the hundreds of pheasants, quail, and grouse you've bagged. This can be quickly and easily accomplished by simply wearing new gloves while making hamburger patties. If you find this technique somewhat off-putting, have your wife do it.

Footwear is a simple matter of *always*—summer and winter, wet or dry—appearing at the club wearing old rubber-bottomed, leather-top boots. Never, under any circumstances, however, lace them to the top. Ideally, the leather tops should flap open, and one trouser leg tucked in adds a dramatic touch. This is a powerful statement of your personal dash and flair for fashion and will cause the club's dress snobs to go into a complete swoon. Tying new boots to the bumper of a New York taxi for a couple of weeks does wonders in achieving the "right" look, as does four or five vulcanized patches. (Make an appointment with your tire dealer, he'll know just what you need.)

Dog snobs are friendly enough, but they can be a nuisance if you let them. The worst sort of are those who are convinced that everyone loves their dog(s) as much as they do and share their delight when the unleashed beasts careen across the club grounds like predatory wolves while they themselves alternately shout and blow their whistles until their faces flame like radishes. Such performances are not especially enjoyable when you are shooting and trying to concentrate on the Bounding Rabbit or Flushing Woodcock stations. Even if you aren't shooting, an untethered dog can send cold chills up your spine, given that peculiar canine blindness that renders them utterly unable to differentiate between a fireplug and a standing rack of fine shotguns.

The first line of defensive dog snobbery is to project the image of a dog handler of unmatched experience. This means you always wear a whistle whether you own a dog or not. This whistle and its lanyard (need I say?) must be well battered, signifying age and use. A dozen or so duck bands strung on the lanyard straps like prayer beads lend a powerful note of authority and simultaneously proclaim your waterfowl-hunting prowess. The obvious way to make your whistle necklace look properly battered is to wear it all the time; to work, mowing the lawn, in the shower, and of course, while in bed.

Your attitude towards dogs and their owners should be modeled after a judge at the Westminster Kennel Show, meaning that you regard them only with wordless contempt, hands clutched behind your back, as if guarding against a slobbering kiss. If an owner persists in positioning his dog where it can't be avoided, gaze balefully at the animal, then at the owner, then back to the dog, as if they are a pair of illegal aliens and you are deciding the most appropriate punishment. Most dog owners wilt under such scrutiny and slink away. If, however, they persist in demanding your attention, you might inquire if the poor beast is still on medication.

"What medication?" To which you respond, eyebrows raised in astonishment, "You mean this poor desperate creature isn't being treated?"

That will almost always do the trick, though from time to time you might also consider dropping the names of fashionable veterinarians they should consult. Be sure to offer such advice only as a whispered confidence, as just you and he are aware of the poor animal's suffering.

The greatest challenges of all are the gun snobs. Not only are they the most obnoxious, but there are more of them. They are arguably the most fun to deal with, but by the same token a hard-core gun snob can be a tough nut to crack, often requiring advanced defensive measures.

Before launching your anti-snob attack, you must first look to your own defenses. It is an absolute certainty that your shotgun(s) will be closely scrutinized by every snob at the club. The impressions derived from such scrutiny will form their opinions and judgments on everything from how your potty training was conducted to your current love life. Which means that you've got to be mighty careful about what sort of guns to take to the club. Especially on your first visit.

There are two schools of thought on how to approach this problem.

The first, and obviously the easiest course of action is simply to show up with a Fabbri embellished with a Galeazzi engraving of your parents on one side of the receiver, and on the reverse side a gold inlaid engraving of your family tree, going back to King Arthur. There was an easier time when you could pass muster with a pair of Purdeys, a Boss or two, or a set of Holland & Holland Royal self-openers, but now that simply everyone shoots them, you'd be just another face in the crowd. However, a 1930s era Woodward or Boss over/under is still a safe bet.

The danger of taking an expensive gun to the club is what do you do for an encore? You need to be aware that shooting a run-of-the-mill Purdey is as dismally gauche as driving last year's Bentley, and once the gun snobs detect such a weakness in your defense, they'll be on you like a pack of hyenas. That's why the smart movement in defensive gun snobbery is toward the other end of the price scale. That's right—the cheapest, roughest shotgun that will fire safely and allow you to hit the occasional target.

It takes a lot of nerve but standing your ground is an essential part of the anti-snob defensive posture. Sooner or later someone is bound to ask why you own such paltry shooting ware and this is where you dig into your defensive position: "Oh, this isn't mine (be casually matter of fact), it belongs to (name the manufacturer), and they sent it to me to try because they're always wanting my opinion." This drives gun snobs bonkers because it categorizes you as a recognized expert on guns and shooting. Very few gun snobs dare joust with so powerful a presence, and at the same time forever frees you to take whatever gun to the club that pleases you. The assumption will always be that you are "checking out" a gun for the manufacturer.

Still, there are the formidable problems of dealing with snobs who insist that you be impressed by *their* guns. Happily, I can suggest a few phrases and tricks to provide some relief. For example, when a snob appears overly proud of a particularly nice shotgun, stick your hands in your pocket (Your body English will imply you wouldn't want to touch such a thing) and state simply, "Oh yes, they're rather nice. I owned six or eight of them when I was at (name an exclusive prep school) but got rid of them when I upgraded my collection."

(Note: Always use the terms "got rid of" or "disposed," because to say you "sold" or "traded" it relegates you to the merchant class.)

Also, referring to all shotguns, yours and others, as "sticks" has a nice ring and gun snobs will be jealous of your fluent familiarity. And as a further hint, only newcomers to the game call it sporting clays. The British only say sporting, or just clays, and true old-timers call it hard bird, so peppering your conversations with these terms will mark you as an old school regular.

If a gun snob persists in eliciting your admiration for his stick, your next defensive volley is to remove any rings, then put on your shooting gloves. The ring gambit shows that you know and respect guns, and that you don't want to risk marring any gun, even his, with finger jewelry. This demonstration has a decisively humbling effect and thereafter he'll probably remove his rings too, in obedient imitation of your example. Donning your shooting gloves with all the hamburger grease and blood will likewise make an unforgettable impression. Especially if the gun snob is also a closet dress snob.

When handling the proffered shotgun, it is vital that you register no interest whatever in the beauty of the wood, the quality of the engraving, or any of the other features normally admired about a fine shotgun. This gives the impression that you own, or have seen so many great guns that you could care less about looking at another. Instead, you peer intently under the barrels. "Nothing there," you remark casually, returning the gun. "Nothing what?" he'll inquire, galvanized by your comment.

"Oh nothing much really," you say with a shrug, "it's just that I am personally acquainted with most of the craftsmen who make this particular model and happen to be one of the few people who know that when they turn out a particularly good specimen, they mark it with a secret bench code. Nothing on your gun though . . . must have been made for the walk-in trade."

Be aware, however, that some gun snobs are already onto this gambit and may, in fact, attempt to use it to put *you* in your place, which calls for powerful counter-counter measures. The best defense in the case of someone who proclaims mechanical expertise and attempts to lecture you about the fine points of a gun is to simply look down your nose, sniff and state. "Oh really,

I wasn't aware. Are you a repairman or iron-monger? I'll have my gardener contact you when next our mowers need sharpening."

And finally, dealing with the shooting snob who just ran a straight at a difficult station. The only defense I know is the tried-and-true appearance of not having noticed. Simply appear to be gazing off in absent-minded boredom when he approaches for the congratulations he feels his due.

"Oh, I'm so sorry . . . I wasn't watching. *Did you hit any?"*

*"Yep, that's right, bird dogs didn't just happen you know.*

*They were invented."*

# Chapter 27

# Marvelous Creations

ne evening when I was clicking my TV remote, I happened across a so-called educational program that had a panel of assorted know-it-alls discussing mankind's greatest achievements. I am normally suspicious of people who declare themselves experts on all subjects, but after watching for a while, I found myself agreeing with much of what they had to say.

I went along with their ranking the ancient Roman aqueducts with the great bridges of modern day, and had no quarrel with them equating the cave paintings of prehistoric man with Michelangelo's Sistine Chapel. Especially since those cave guys created some great art without indulgent patrons or handouts from the NEA (National Endowment for the Arts). The panel didn't seem off base in praising the literary labors of the likes of Homer and Cervantes. But to my acute annoyance, the program ended without their once mentioning what I consider one of mankind's most exquisite achievements—the bird dog.

Yep, that's right, bird dogs didn't just happen you know.

They were *invented.*

We can suppose, with reasonable certainty, that at some instant in unrecorded time a hunter realized that his wolf-like companion was "seeing" game that was invisible to his own eyes. And from that moment of brilliant cognition, man began refining that unique gift and perfecting it to his own needs.

Nowhere does the genius of man glitter more brilliantly than when he recognizes the genius of another species and harnesses it for the betterment of both himself and that species. And to my mind, the invention of the bird dog is all the grander because it is the result of many generations of humanity sharing a dream no less inspiring than those of the greatest artists, writers, and bridge builders.

Even as we marvel at ourselves for piercing the heavens, spanning great waters, and creating worldwide communications, what other invention can we lay claim to that finds a quail with breathtaking precision, brings it to our hand, faithfully trusts and tolerates us in spite of what we are, asking only in return the pleasure of our company, a scratch on its ear, and a murmured "well done old boy."

Which is why I'd rather spend my days with marvelous creations called bird dogs than with artists, bridge builders, and writers.

*"Whoever said,*
*'beware the man with one gun,'*
*must have had Pete in mind."*

# Chapter 28

# One-Gun Pete

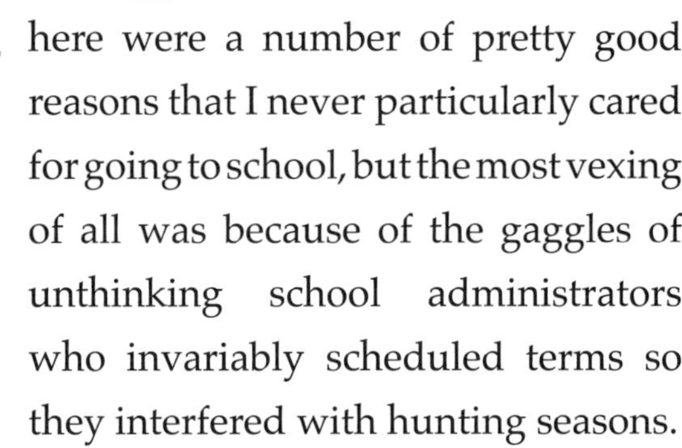

There were a number of pretty good reasons that I never particularly cared for going to school, but the most vexing of all was because of the gaggles of unthinking school administrators who invariably scheduled terms so they interfered with hunting seasons.

Which caused me, on more than a few days when attending classes didn't seem a sensible thing to do, to seek the company of a local ne'er-do-well whose sole purpose in life, so far as I could discover, was hunting and fishing. In addition to this virtue, he had the good grace to let me hide my hunting clothes in a rickety tool shed behind his rickety house. He could roll a cigarette or tie on a fly with one hand and wore high-top work shoes in the summer and fall (not that he recognized either of these seasons as a fit time to be working). The rest of the year he went around with patched boots flopping about his knees. I never saw him without a faded red leather cap with fuzzy earflaps that he would flop down when the windchill hit minus 20F.

His name was Pete and he had a sour-tempered wife who had a regular job in town. What I probably remember best about Pete was the long-barreled

12-gauge Model 12 Winchester pump that for six months of the year was an extension of his person and personality.

Whoever said, "beware the man with one gun," must have had Pete in mind, because he was probably the most consistently deadly wingshot I've ever hunted with. Doves, quail, rabbits, or ducks, he hunted them all with the full choked M-12, but he was particularly awesome when shooting from the hardscrabble duck blinds we'd make from cedar brush and driftwood.

That was before steel shot, of course, when high brass 4s were Pete's choice and 50 yards overhead was "about right." But I saw him take 'em a lot higher and kill them so dead they tumbled in a long trajectory from where they'd been hit.

He'd shuck a sweet-smelling paper case out of the old shotgun, give me a wink and say, "Boy, run get that there duck."

I ran and got lots of ducks for Pete, and every time I see a Model 12 that has been worn to glassy slickness, I think of ducks falling out of winter skies.

Those days were classic, and so were Pete and his Model 12.

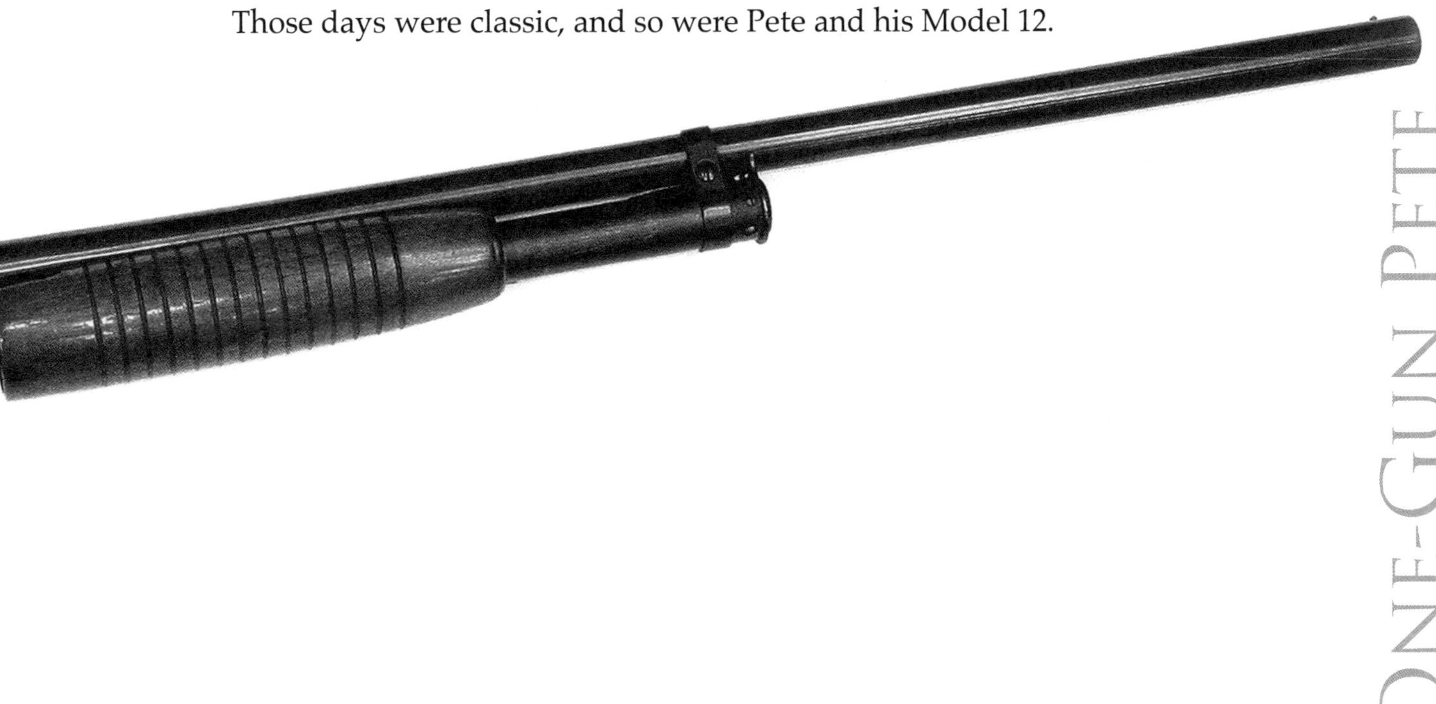

*"Bench shooters are notoriously persnickety about what they stick in their barrels and would rather kiss a frog than use an ordinary cleaning rod."*

# Chapter 29

# How Benchrest Shooters Improve Your Hunting Rifle

There are only a few thousand of them at most. When they get together, a crowd of only 60 to 80 is considered a major happening, and their biggest event of the year will be attended by only a few hundred. They call themselves Benchrest Shooters, and the object of their game is simple: firing five, sometimes ten, shots into a single round hole that is no larger than the diameter of the bullet. This may seem like a pointless enterprise, especially since after decades of trying no one has managed to do it, but along the way, they have changed the face of today's riflery. The rifle you hunt with, the ammo you use, the scope you sight with, even the way you clean your rifle barrel—all have been greatly influenced by this small, but intensely dedicated, band of riflemen.

Benchrest shooting gets its name from the way rifles are fired from solid benches, usually concrete, with the rifles rested on sandbags (some of these "sandbags" by the way, eat up most of a thousand-dollar bill). The purpose is to eliminate, as much as possible, errors in holding and aiming. But don't let anyone tell you bench shooters aren't keen marksmen. Many are long-time target shooters who have simply graduated to a higher degree of accuracy.

Call it a blending of fine marksmanhip, technology, and extreme accuracy, with a big dose of competitiveness tossed in to keep the kettle simmering.

An accomplished benchrest shooter will judge within a tenth of an inch the effect crosswinds will have on his bullet's flight at 100 yards, and aim accordingly. And he or she (never bet against a female bench shooter) will do it dozens of times during the course of a tournament. No other target-shooting game cuts it anywhere near this fine.

The common image of benchrest shooters and the game they play is a bunch of wild-eyed accuracy geeks with Rube Goldberg contraptions that look more like

*Star Wars* laser guns than ordinary rifles. This conception—or misconception—is reinforced from time to time by pictures of these iron monster rifles in various shooting magazines. Usually these rifles are pictured only as curiosities without explaining that they represent a relatively small and steadily diminishing segment of organized benchrest competition, and no longer represent the razor edge of rifle development.

That's because several years ago some of the wiser heads in the benchrest game realized that despite their ingenuity and fascination, the monster rifles were taking them down a one-way street. Searching for the Holy Grail of pure accuracy was largely a fool's errand and if benchrest shooting was to have any lasting purpose, beyond the swapping of ingenious ideas, their rifles would have to be more like—well—like rifles ought to be.

Which is why if you visited a benchrest competition today, say a major competition like the Firearms Industry Super Shoot, you would see scores of rifles that, other than looking like they had been painted by a graffiti artist on a manic high, are not all that different in shape and weight from, say, your Remington or Savage heavy-barreled varmint rifle. Surprise!

This by no means is to imply that we should expect our factory-made hunting rifles to be as accurate as Bench rifles, because a winning performance in the Varmint Classes of benchrest rifles will be five, five-shot groups probably averaging about two-tenths of an inch or less!

When I set a new world record for the Light Varmint Class, no rifle and scope could weigh more than 10½ pounds. The average size of my five-shot groups was .1441-inch, which is about ⅛-inch. That was in 2012 and as of this writing my record has already been broken twice, which gives you some perspective of what fine accuracy is all about.

In contrast, of the hundreds of factory and non-benchrest custom rifles I've tested over the years, only a skimpy handful have delivered even one group that small, and quite by accident at that. Never mind website chatterboxes who proclaim themselves possessors of hunting rifles that will print half-inch groups "all day long." Apparently, such claimants have been putting beans in their noses.

The "gold standard" for a really accurate hunting rifle is one that will deliver 100-yard, five-shot groups that measure about one inch on a more or less regular basis. Even among heavy-barreled varmint rifles a true half-incher is a jewel. In either case, extremely good ammo is necessary for fine accuracy, which complicates matters considerably.

The point here, however, is not to compare the rifles we take deer hunting with expensive custom-made benchrest rifles, but to make clear the definitions of accuracy and how rifles you now buy off a dealer's rack, and the ammo on his shelf, have benefited greatly from rifle developments and improvements first tried and proven by benchrest shooters.

Take for example the effect benchresters have had on scopes. I've yet to meet a benchrest shooter who was entirely satisfied with his scope (or anything else for that matter), and they are constantly barraging the scope manufacturers with complaints and suggestions. Scope-makers tend to pay close attention to benchrest shooters, which is why there has been a constant stream of newer and improved target and varmint-type scopes over the past several years, with more and more optics companies getting into the act. New developments and improvements in scopes, proven at the benchrest, filter down to hunting-type scopes, which is readily apparent when you compare the quality of hunting scopes made today with the best of those made a generation ago.

If you're like thousands of other new rifle-buyers, you practice breaking in a new barrel, an accuracy-enhancing trick originated by benchrest shooters several years ago that has become very much in vogue even among non-benchresters. But by the time such advances have become common practice in the general world of shooting, they may have been rendered obsolete in the esoteric world of benchrest by newer and even better discoveries.

A case in point being the accuracy-improving technique known as pillar-bedding. Benchresters were doing this years ago, but by the time it was adopted by everyday gunsmiths and gunmakers, it had already been abandoned by bench shooters in favor of the even more accurate method of actually epoxy gluing the rifle's action into the stock. (Don't try this with your hunting rifle.)

Though it would be unfair to say that benchresters taught bullet-makers how to make accurate bullets, there's no denying that they picked up on the benchrest concept. Not only liberally applying the term "benchrest" to their most accurate bullets, but borrowing the hollow-point profile of handmade bullets cranked out one at a time by benchrest shooters.

Nowadays, there are a dozen or so makers of custom bullets who cater to the benchrest market, and while their jewel-like bullets are suitable only for punching holes in paper or varmints, they set the standard for accuracy that other bullets are measured by. By continuously raising the bar on accuracy, these custom-made benchrest bullets have forced ammo-makers to produce increasingly accurate cartridges, to the benefit of all shooters and hunters.

The best-known fallout from benchrest is, of course, fiberglass stocks. They were developed by bench shooters who wanted a combination of strength, light weight, and stability.

Chet Brown was one of the first makers of fiberglass stocks. Back in the early 1970s, Chet loaned me one of the very first fiberglass stocks to appear in benchrest competition. Painted a bright yellow, it caused quite a sensation, but nearly everyone loved wood back then and most allowed they would rather date the bearded lady at the County Fair than be seen with a fiberglass stock like I was shooting.

This opinion was also shared by hunters when synthetic stocks began appearing on their rifles—but their resistance didn't last long. Nowadays, synthetic stocks of one material or another are about as common as camo T-shirts.

Meanwhile, benchrest shooters have continued to improve on fiberglass with even lighter and stronger materials such as carbon fiber.

Paradoxically, wood stocks have now returned to the bench game. Creative stock-makers like Terry Leonard have united wood with carbon fiber to produce stocks that are amazingly strong, light, and even rather pretty. I expect this benchrest development will eventually make the leap to hunting rifles, and they will certainly be better looking than today's "Tupperware" stocks. But don't expect them to be cheap.

Cruise the gun care departments of a shop or thumb through a shooting gear catalog and you'll see plenty of products that were incubated in the benchrest hothouse. Popular bore-cleaning chemicals such as Wipe-Out, Montana, Extreme, and Butch's Bore Shine first showed up on the bench range, with their commercial success coming about only after the critical trials and final acceptance of the benchrest clan.

Bench shooters are notoriously persnickety about what they stick in their barrels and would rather kiss a frog than use an ordinary cleaning rod. Several years ago benchrest shooter John Dewey got fed up with existing rods that he suspected were hurting—even ruining—fine barrels and introduced the line of super-slick Dewey rods widely used by all types of shooters. Other, even more improved rods made of carbon fiber and the polished stainless steel rods I personally favor, were hatched in the benchrest game.

Despite this constantly growing list of rifle improvements we've inherited from the benchrest world, if I had to name the most lasting contribution, it would be the revolution in our understanding of accuracy and in the attitudes of makers of guns and ammo.

Benchrest shooters and their rifles established reasonable benchmarks of accuracy and thereby served notice to the gun industry what their customers should expect in the way of accuracy. There was a time, not too long ago, when gunmakers didn't want to talk much about accuracy, as if it were some sort of immoral subject best kept hidden from inquiring minds. Sure, their advertisements unfailingly described their rifles as being "accurate" but only in nebulous terms.

A good example of this attitude was an expensive rifle purchased by a friend who could afford such things. Made by a big name manufacturer, it turned out to be dismally inaccurate. Tinkering with it as we might, our 100-yard groups were seldom better than three inches and usually even worse. So my pal packed it up and returned it to the manufacturer with a sampling of the target groups.

Naturally, he expected the maker to do whatever necessary to improve the rifle, but they simply sent it back with a form letter stating that his rifle fell "within their accuracy specifications." They never explained, however, what those "specifications" were, and remained smug and untouchable, just as they had for generations past. But that gunmaker couldn't get away with it these days.

That's because two organizations—the National Bench Rest Shooting Association. (NBRSA) and International Benchrest Shooters (IBS)—sanction tournaments and regularly publish new records plus the performance winners and also-rans of bench matches. (Check out **Benchrest.com** and you'll see what I mean.) This has put real numbers before the shooting public and flushed gunmakers out of hiding from behind their mysterious "within our specifications" wall. Previously unknown terms such as "sub-minute-of-angle" have become part of our everyday shooting lingo, and now when gunmakers claim to make "accurate" rifles, they had better be ready to back it up. And some of them actually do, thanks to those funny talking guys with their peculiar-looking rifles.

*"The thrill of the chase is part of the charm of hunting gun treasures."*

# Chapter 30

# Guns As Investments

ow many investments can you name that virtually guarantee a sizeable return on your money and also offer the added bonus of pride of ownership? Sure, there are a few; buying antique automobiles may be one, and collecting fine art is certainly another, but unless you named gun collecting, you missed one of the surest bets around.

But first, what is a gun collector? According to the rad-lib media, a gun collector is some weird misanthrope who stockpiles guns and ammo in anticipation of invasion from the IRS or government agents in black helicopters. Which is about the same as calling a collector of Islamic art a terrorist.

More to the point, the guy who owns a rifle for a once-a-year deer hunt is simply a gun owner. Whereas someone—you, for example—who buys guns because he admires their beauty, workmanship, function, and value can rightly call himself a collector.

All collections, guns or art, begin with the acquisition of a single piece. And as with the art collector who began with a painting or sculpture for a few dollars and grew his passion into a collection worth millions, the collector of guns needs an "eye" for beauty, style, and talent, plus the shrewd investor's sense of what will be in demand years hence. Unlike the art collector who also depends on a certain amount of luck, capricious critics, and the whimsy of fashion, gun collectors play by safer and more predictable rules.

There are several categories of gun collecting. Of these, perhaps the most exciting is "treasure hunting," in which the collector prowls gun shows, pawn shops, yard sales, and even obituaries. *("Sorry to hear about your husband, ma'am, wish I had known him. By the way, did he leave any old guns?")* But to be a successful treasure hunter you need to have a broad-based knowledge of guns and their value, plus plenty of spare time and the dedication of a bloodhound.

The thrill of the chase is part of the charm of hunting gun treasures, and is occasionally spurred on by reports of collectors finding such things as Walker Colt revolvers in junk shops for a few dollars and reselling for a quarter-mil. But the likelihood of such finds is about the same as discovering a doubloon-laden Spanish galleon in your swimming pool.

Another type of gun collecting is the "specialized category" in which the collector sets out to accumulate specimens of only one brand or even a single model within a brand. Examples of this are collectors who search only for, say, Parker or Fox shotguns, Colt pistols, or Winchester rifles. This is a fairly secure and disciplined form of gun collecting. It has a broad appeal because it offers pride of ownership (and the envy of other collectors) with an almost guaranteed solid return on your investment, provided that you've bought prudently.

The downside of most specialized collecting is that owners would rather have a hip replacement without anesthetic than endure the stress of taking one of their guns afield and actually shooting it.

These and other types of gun collecting have their own special attractions, but one thing you don't want to lose sight of is that those old and rare Parkers and Winchesters were once new and bought to be used. Which is why I advise any fledgling collector to take a careful look at the guns being built today and decide which of them will be a rare jewel tomorrow. Perhaps surprisingly, there are solid rules to follow that will virtually assure a sound investment.

*Rule Number One.* It's simple: buy a gun you like. In other words trust your sense of style and good taste. If it turns out later that your choice wasn't such a smart investment after all, at least you will have a gun that you enjoy looking at and using.

The best example of tasteful gun-buying occurred just a few months after Linda and I were married. We were at a firearms trade show, her first ever, and while I went about my business, she wandered off to learn what sort of peculiar world she had married into. A couple hours later she caught up with me and made a startling announcement: "I've bought a gun."

This bit of news, I admit, was met with apprehension. After all, she knew little about guns, had never bought one in her life, and being, well, a woman, there was no telling what sort of chrome-plated claptrap might have tickled her fancy. So, keeping a stiff upper lip, I allowed her to lead me to the manufacturer's exhibit where she had purchased her first gun.

Astonishment does not nearly describe my reaction as she proudly pointed to a 28-gauge Parker Reproduction side-by-side, complete with gorgeous wood, skeleton buttplate, and fitted leather case. Of the hundreds of guns on display, she had picked out the most beautiful and stylish.

Later that day, over olive-bearing refreshments, I confessed my amazement. "Why did you buy that particular gun?" I had to know.

"Because," she replied, "it looks like what I think a gun ought to look like."

I've read scores of gun books, and hundreds of articles on the subject, not counting the hundreds I've written myself, but never have I seen so much gun wisdom expressed in so few words. So remember, when investing in a gun—does it look like a gun ought to? And trust your good taste.

*Rule Number Two.* Buy types of guns that have a history of increasing in value. The bluest of "blue chip" shotgun investments have long been side-by-side doubles, with certain over/unders also being highly desirable. Smaller-gauge guns almost always appreciate faster than larger bores, typically because there are fewer of them.

A clean Parker Bros double in 12-gauge DH Grade will now sell for upwards of eight grand, whereas you can expect the same grade in 28 gauge to fetch about four times that; if a .410, you can double even that.

Another good indicator of the increasing demand for good doubles exists in Model 21 Winchesters. Nowadays, you're lucky to find a good used 12 gauge for less than seven thousand. If you had bought the same gun new 20 or even a dozen years ago, you would have made a solid 10 percent per annum on your investment, plus owning and using a shotgun that says a lot about who you are.

*Rule Number Three.* Buy the best you can afford—and then some. I have frequent urges to kick myself, most usually when I look at a gun I bought with great pride and now wish I had bit the bullet harder and stressed my finances a bit further. Higher-grade guns appreciate at a faster rater because there are fewer of them. Research the value index of Belgian-made Browning Superposed shotguns in the various grades and you'll get an eye-popping example of the return on top-quality guns.

Likewise, when investing in used guns, buy only the most pristine examples. This insures that when you choose to sell the gun, the buyer won't have anything to complain about except your price.

Some years ago, when I was a member of a panel discussion on gun collecting, someone in the audience asked me if I ever regretted selling any of my guns.

"Sure," I confessed, "every one of them."

And therein lies the fallacy of collecting guns as an investment: a fine gun can become a lifetime friend, providing practical use and enjoyment, while requiring only simple care in return. Friends like that are hard to find and harder to part with, so go back and read Rule Number One again.